RECOVERED

BOOK ONE

Absolute Victory Over Alcoholism

RECOVERED

BOOK ONE

Absolute Victory
Over Alcoholism

Recovered alcoholics from around the United States share their experiences with God and the recovery process in the hope that others might also achieve absolute victory over alcoholism.

Edited by

Amy Crozier and Dr. John

Ursa Publishing Company

ISBN: 1-893808-00-9
Library of Congress Catalog Card Number: 99-75781
Book design and production by Tabby House

Disclaimer

The publication of this work does not imply, nor does it suggest any affiliation with, nor approval of or endorsement from Alcoholics Anonymous World Services. All quotations from the first one hundred and sixty-four pages of *Alcoholics Anonymous* can be found in the first and second editions of that book, said pages lying in the public domain.

Each contributor to this volume warrants that he or she is expressing his or her own views in respect to all parts of his or her share of the production of this collaborative work. Out of deference to the A.A. tradition of anonymity, the writers are using only their first names and last initials. Their towns of residence are listed only to show the diversity of geography in which one will find the recovered alcoholic. Those persons who may be identified further have given their express written consent. Quotations from the book *Alcoholics Anonymous,* contained in most pieces, are credited within the text, and originate in the editions of that book that lie in the public domain. The sole exception to this rule is the piece by Dr. John, which supplies its own endnotes.

 URSA PUBLISHING COMPANY, INC.
P.O. Box 864
Palm Harbor, FL 34682
Worldwide E-mail: Ursa 2000@aol.com

*This book is dedicated to
the first one hundred and all who have,
and will surely, follow.*

*"This man and over one hundred others
appear to have recovered."*
—Alcoholics Anonymous
(From "The Doctor's Opinion" p. xxiii)

Contents

Section Two: Coincidence

Section Three: Alcoholics and Their Ideas of God

Preface

A score of recovered alcoholics set out to produce a work written solely by those who have no doubt of their complete recovery from alcoholism. None of the writers of this work are "in recovery," none suffer from alcoholism, and none believe in malingering convalescence or dependence on Twelve Step meetings for sobriety.

Each of the writers worked the Twelve Steps to complete recovery in a matter of days or weeks, not years.

None of the persons in this book have needed to look any further than the Twelve Steps as originally written in the book *Alcoholics Anonymous* for an answer to the alcoholic dilemma which faced them. Each had passed down to them the original message of the Twelve Steps and has found that path to be their salvation from a life of alcoholic hell—as well as their launching point into a new life, free from the mental and emotional bondage, and the spiritual lack, which marked their lives while drinking.

All have moved on beyond the first nine Steps, living daily the last three Steps, which they believe contain the answer to all their problems, their pasts having faded as their new lives grew exponentially. There are none among them who consider themselves "recovering," that process having been fulfilled along the path of the Twelve Steps.

It is the collective hope of these persons that the alcoholic who still suffers will find something from this book on which to base his own recovery and return to wellness. It is in the sharing of their experience and their respective ideas about God that they feel they can best serve humanity.

If you have been told there is no such thing as complete recovery from alcoholism, the writers ask that you continue reading this book, putting aside all prejudice you have previously fostered, and take an in-depth look at each of their lives. They have laid bare their journey through the restorative Twelve Steps and their ideas of the nature of God are here for all to examine.

It is their sincere hope that by the sharing of their own true-life experience that a spark will be lit in the mind of the person who suffers from alcoholism.

These alcoholics have one common bond: They have found a Power that has healed them of their malady and has taken them to a state of Grace where they had never been before.

Recovered.

"Recovered—What does it All Mean?"

What exactly do we mean when we use the word "recovered" ?

We, the writers of this book have all reached the ultimate aim of the Twelve Steps: Spiritual Awakening. And, during the course of our two hundred-plus years of combined, continuous sobriety, surely we have learned something worth knowing: Alcoholism is a deadly foe, but also a foe that can be defeated. In its simplest form, and in the context in which we've used it here, it simply means that we have gained back our own personal well-being and mental health, have regained or built a spiritual foundation, and have healed from all harmful facets of the malady known as alcoholism. How did we do this, despite the fact that many of us were told that we *never recover*? We certainly didn't come to A.A. to stay sick and suffering, terminally insane, or dependent on group therapy-type meetings for happiness. We were doing quite a job of staying that way on our own human power. How were we able to accomplish the seemingly impossible in the face of those who told us we would be *in recovery for life*?

We became simple. We quit debating semantics with those around us who stayed sober on fear and fellowship. We got beyond the naysayings of those people who were dependent on meetings for their sobriety, and we went back to the original message—as we understood it—as it is simply and plainly written in the suggested path called the Twelve Steps, contained in the original manuscript of the book later titled *Alcoholics Anonymous*. This book is about our own personal experiences with those Twelve Steps and the amazing results we achieved following them to their intended purpose without quitting or falling-short due to fear or laziness.

During the course of our recovery processes, we all encountered those who simply skimmed through the basic text of A.A., acting as though they understood its miraculous content, but who lived in daily fear of drinking.

We chose to get beyond that, to move on toward the ever-expanding horizon that lay beyond the rebuilding of our lives through adherence to the principles contained within those Steps. We did not desire a life built on dependency on meetings, nor did we wish to entertain the thought of a life lived in fear of the next drink. After all, if we wanted to stay sick and suffering, we could have done that on our own; in fact that's precisely what we were doing. We no longer wanted the cop-out we often heard, "Well, I can just blame my insanity on my disease!" Once we got beyond the need to have a scapegoat for our human condition, we saw that there was a limitless scope of new life and happiness beyond "living in the disease." We wanted more.

During the course of our personal examination of those steps, persons who still believed in the original message of the founding fellowship came to our aid. Those persons showed us the simplicity of the recovery program as it had originally been taught and learned since the inception of the Twelve Steps into the recovery phenomena. In our collective attendance of meetings, we see those "around the tables" who consider themselves sponsors, but who live lives of trepidation at the very mention of being around alcohol. And, it is these same people who pass on a message that is contrary to that of A.A.'s founders. Why do they do this? Possibly because they know no better.

None of the writers of this book are uncomfortable around drinkers or drinking, and none have ever had another drink. The years of sobriety of the writers run from one and one half to thirty-odd years, and yet not one has ever picked up another drink after having worked the Twelve Steps, nor does any consider him or herself "recovering." Why?

We believe it has to do with the thoroughness of our foundation work, those countless hours we spent looking at the true principles behind the Twelve Steps. When we first began to attend meetings, some of us were daunted by the apparently overwhelming scope of change necessary to bring about the healing that was rumored to be contained within those Steps. We saw the banners on the walls, listing and quoting the Steps, and at times thought, "Wow! All that?" On closer, and simpler examination, we found the Steps to be among the simplest of tasks, and when broken down to their elemental parts, we found them very logical and sensible. The Steps follow a very concise and definite plan, and as has been our own experience a very definite end to alcoholic thinking and living. What amazed us more was the life that lay beyond. Freedom from alcohol was only a beginning for us, and we found that once we learned and inculcated those principles into our lives that all sorts of wondrous events lay ahead.

We do not debate words these days; that has become old hat in many circles. We don't pretend to be perfect, nor do we disdain any other path of recovery from alcoholism. We simply seek to show evidence in our own lives that the original message and the original intent of the Twelve Steps still lives on in us. It is through the sharing of our own experience, and the sharing of our diverse understanding of God, that we hope to give credence to the program of recovery founded by early A.A. members. Our stories run the gamut of alcoholic experience and our geographic locations are as varied as our personalities and backgrounds. We are not an A.A. group, and do not attend meetings together. We are spread out across the country with no apparent pattern with regard to our locations. We simply came together to write our stories and to share them with you, asking that you take what you want, leave what you don't. The one thing we share above all else is that we know beyond doubt that our alcohol problems have been removed, and that we are no longer plagued by that which once nearly took our lives. There is no doubt of our recovery; else we wouldn't feel we had anything worthwhile to share with you.

Among the other common ground among us is the fact that we do not pass on the diluted version of the Steps we hear commonly spoken by the unknowing in meeting rooms across the country. We adhere strictly to the Big Book—as it was originally written—when teaching and leading another along the path of recovery. Our own ideas, at best, were mostly worthless. But those ideas contained in the original text of A.A. solved our problems when nothing else would.

All of us attribute our wellness to having made contact with a Power that is beyond anything human. We don't claim to have found the only path to that Power, but we are solidly agreed that a path to that Power does exist, and that the Power itself is indisputable, considering the tremendous effect it has had on our own lives.

This book is divided into three sections, the first being the accounts of our individual life experience with regard to our drinking and our recovery from it. In each of our stories we tell our own experiences, truthfully and accurately as they actually occurred, leaving you to decide for yourself what we have found. The language in some of the stories is quite stark, and it was agreed at the onset of production of this book that the editors would allow the writers to tell their stories in their own words. Many of the writers have mentioned or quoted parts of the book, *Alcoholics Anonymous*. They share from their own experience with that text, and none doubts the validity of their words since no one but they themselves are qualified to tell exactly what happened to them along the path of the Steps.

The second section is a piece which seeks to provoke thought as to how this Divine Power might have had its advent into our lives from the onset of the founding of the path called the Twelve Steps. This section on "coincidence" may perhaps intrigue you, make you wonder at the mystery of it all. None of us doubts the hand of something bigger having had a part in our life-changing experiences. We no longer doubt the existence of something of great magnitude that has the Power to heal those who earnestly seek to touch it.

In the third section, the writers share their concepts of God, the "no-no" word for some, but in our newfound way of thinking, the single most indispensable revelation ever to come into our lives. You'll notice how varied our concepts are, and how diverse our childhood ideas themselves were, and how they changed over time. We believe that the development of our concepts was vital to our complete recovery, and we openly admit that they are still changing and evolving with regard to the growing wonder we encounter by contact with this Power, as we grow daily into more fruitful and productive persons.

You'll find a way to contact us at the back of this book should you have questions or comments. We have a mailbox and an E-mail address.

Are we *cured* of alcoholism? Can we drink safely? No. None of us thinks that is possible. What's more important than the debating of degrees of removal of our alcoholic problem is the inner knowledge we all possess, the surety that our problem has been removed by following a simple path of spiritual enlightenment. We all feel a great debt and thankfulness toward those early members of A.A. who founded the path which led us back to peaceful sanity, right-thinking attitudes, mental calm and serenity, and above all else, spiritual fulfillment. We feel indebted for having had our lives restored to us through miraculous means, and we are thankful that our pasts no longer hold any power whatsoever over us. Being free, happy, and healthy, to us, is what it truly means to have recovered. Gone from our lives is the fear, the uncertainty of our state of wellness. Today we all live in the knowledge that a Power, which makes us whole, is now a working part of our daily lives, and our eternal futures.

We encourage you to seek out from each story that which fits your own life, and to draw from it what will best aid you to overcome, once and for all, the deadly, but surmountable, malady known as alcoholism.

Section One

The True Life Stories
of Recovered Alcoholics
from across the Country

In this section, alcoholics from across the United States tell their own experiences with working the Twelve Steps. All of them have become well by using the same path to a Power that healed them. Please read on and see for yourself what their lives were like while they were drinking, and how they have changed during the recovery process.

Bill G.'s Story

Bill G.—Southern Oregon

Not long ago someone asked me: "You still go to meetings?"

And, my answer was, "Of course."

He knew of my longtime sobriety, and wondered if I still needed to go to meetings. I explained, "I like what I have today; the alternative sucks." And the comment was made: "Wow, you must have been through a lot in that time."

"Mmm, yeah, I have," and that started some old tapes running: How did I get where I am today from where I was?

I started drinking fairly early, maybe age ten or eleven, not too sure when, but, I do remember how I felt. It gagged me at first but the warmth and feeling of well-being that seemed to flow through me was wonderful, and gave me the feeling that I could do anything. Never had that exact same feeling again, though I tried hard and long to recapture it. I was no longer the kid who didn't fit, now I became the kid who would do anything for attention. The brat that mothers warned their kids to stay away from. "No! You can't go with Billy . . . he's too wild."

Drinking allowed me to fit in, to be a part of the crowd, not apart from it. In grammar school I had been promoted a couple of grades ahead so, right off, I didn't fit. I was either too young to do that, or too old. "Billy, act your age!" I got my driver's license two months before graduation from high school. Want to guess how my social life was? Somewhere along the line someone had done an I.Q. test on me. I think they were trying to prove I was certifiable, and when the teachers found out, I was "potentialed" to death, like: "Mrs. G, Billy's not living up to his potential." Hell no, I wasn't, I was bored to death.

In school, I found others like me, and we hung around together. Cutting class to go to the park and drink, long lunches, early out in the afternoon. All based around drinking as a sport, avocation, and need. It got so bad that some of these friends got to the point of avoiding me.

Several of them tried to get me to cut down on my drinking. In high school, yet!

I played ball, and lettered both years. The other team members liked having me in the games, but would have nothing to do with me either before or after practice or games. I had found a point of release for anger, and boy, did I let it out. Played pretty much sixty-minute ball; our quarterback loved having me on the front line, and opposing Q.B.s got kinda antsy when I was facing them. But I still didn't fit. I wasn't invited to parties or get-togethers—in fact I felt avoided. So my answer was to try harder, that meant more drinking . . . right? And that I could do.

After graduation in 1956, I started with the National Forest Service as a "pickup" firefighter. I had found a home! These guys drank like I did! (Not like that anymore though, the service has changed since.) Went to smoke-jump school in northern part of my state and really found a home.

These guys really knew how to drink. We would go out most of the nights, and then run five to seven miles every morning. You could tell where folks got sick—along the trail the grass was greener on the right side for fifty or sixty feet. And that was fun! Now, can you imagine what it was like to do jumps over mountains in high winds and with huge hangovers? That was fun! Oh yeah. You know, those jump suits don't wash easy, and boy, did they stink.

Along in here somehow I got through college and did a four and one-half year course in three years. Hell, we all can do that, never mind some instructors who challenged me. Finally ended up with two degrees, one in forestry, and the other in civil engineering.

Got one of those infamous "Greetings from the Government" letters, and being the bright smart young man I was, I thought, "Bill, which service has good bunks, hot food, and not too much chance of getting in trouble for drinking?" You see how important drinking was to me; I based my service decision on the various services' reputed tolerance for drinking. And we all know how sailors drink; that decision was easy.

I assumed I'd do my service as an enlisted man, so I did boot camp, learned how to drink Aqua Velva, made recruit master at arms, now had extra privileges, like smoking times and unstructured time. And, you know I found ways to drink. I met an old master chief bos'n mate who drank like I did. He taught me how to get and make what I needed. At "B" and "C" schools there was a way of getting "white lightning" by tying a five-dollar bill in a rag on the back fence of the training compound. Wow!

That stuff could burn like a flame in your gizzard. It came in gallon milk containers; lasted maybe a week. Now folks, you know I was getting into some crazy things, like putting a gallon of that in the juice dispenser for morning chow . . . almost got court-martialed—would've if I'd been caught. We planned our liberties so we could drink later. Our base was across the river from a state whose shut-off time for buying liquor was an hour later than ours. You know we took advantage of that! Got picked up once for being drunk in public—across the river by shore patrol—hauled in before the chief of the watch. While the shore patrolmen were telling him how bad we were, several more guys were brought in passed out. Well, he could see we could still stand and let us go—before the S.P.s could tell him about the Buick in the reflecting pool in front of the city hall.

Things like that happened to me many times. My father was a captain with the sheriff's department, and many of the deputies had a perception that busting the captain's kid wasn't good for their careers. So I was released many times when I shouldn't have been. Hell, I was on first-name basis with the jailer. Got E-5 when I graduated from "C" school, and was sent to a squadron. Found lots of drinkers there, too, (amazing how we seem to find each other, huh?). My C.O. told me he couldn't order me to take the tests for officer school, but he could give me every opportunity to take 'em. That he did.

Went to Pensacola for flight training. Now, that was tougher than boot camp. My drinking had progressed to a "need" point. Like, almost constantly. Because of my college degree I was commissioned twelve months later, instead of eighteen months like many in my class. Now I had access to the "O" club, and let me tell you, there is a world of difference when training as an officer instead of as a cadet. Now when I got busted, I was called "sir." As in, "Sir, will you please put your hands behind you?"

Unlike the Army, the Navy does try to fit folks to a compatible position. I guess because of my personality—being a loner—I was assigned to some special training. While there I did things with aircraft that folks said couldn't be done. Well, weren't supposed to be done.

Like diving under bridges, buzzing the training command captain's lawn party at five hundred knots, fifty feet off the deck. Boy, were they pissed! The craziness of alkies, huh? No idea why I wasn't thrown out of the Navy for that; maybe they needed some hot-shit pilot for some things. I wasn't smart enough to be scared.

'Nam was just starting to be in the news. Somehow I graduated number two in my class and that gave me options. Being the good alkie I was, I thought I'd skate by picking low-level attack. Yeah, sure. Right! I think my personality had something to do with being assigned to a Dark Moon Squadron. That meant flying missions solo; no more hitting my wingman's O_2 supply to cure my hangovers. That meant I got to fly by myself. No one around to rat on me for herding cattle with a million-dollar machine.

Did the 'Nam thing from '60–'64.

Did we drink? You know it! Lots of it! When I came back to the States I didn't fit in any better than before, but still was seeking something.

Approval, maybe? I remember once when several pilots were sitting around Pineapple's Bar in Long Beach, playing first liar doesn't stand a chance, and I got called. Someone had said they had looped the bridge in San Pedro. I believe I said something like, "Hell, any damned fool can do that in daytime. It takes real balls to do it at night." At least it was so reported by a somewhat reliable guy, (that means he was less drunk than the rest of us).

Yep, you got it, I have seen a 16mm film of a Bull Stearman looping the Vincent Thomas Bridge at night with ships passing in the channel . . . twice. I think I remember being disoriented and not being sure of whether I had completed the loop or not. So, just to be sure, I did it again. Now you gotta know how crazy that was. The bottom of the causeway is one hundred and thirty-nine feet from the water at high tide, I'm told. I think the FAA is still looking for that plane. Is that alkie behavior?

My last drink was on my fourth wedding anniversary. I had blacked out (again), only this time I was in real trouble. When I came out of the blackout I was "restrained" about a foot off the ground by some really big guys, and there were several blue and tan uniforms lying on the grass. Had several felony charges against me, and the jailer I knew, (Remember him?) asked me "Bill, did it ever occur to you, you get in trouble every time you drink? I don't think I can help you on this one."

Well, now that he mentioned it, I thought he was right and had no idea what to do. I was released on own recognition somehow, maybe because of my father. This with eight felony counts.

Oh yeah, I think I forgot to mention I had gotten to the point of being unemployable as a pilot, and was working in a gas station as a mechanic.

Drinking all the time, stealing from my employer, customers, whoever. . . . My need for alcohol was so strong.

I had worked on a woman's car whose credit card was from the local council on alcoholism, and for some reason I had to have her home phone number on the work order. She was very reluctant to give it to me, telling me that she was rarely home at night and wouldn't her office number be sufficient? (Later I found out why she wasn't home, she was at A.A. meetings!) I didn't think I had a problem, but the guy I worked with was a real alkie, missing for days at times, sloppy workmanship, dropping tools, etc. Like me, he was ex-Navy. We drank together lots. Remember I had said I used to go for long lunches in high school? Well, that was nothing compared to what he and I did together. I knew he had a problem; not me of course, and I was getting this woman's phone number for him, thinking I was gonna help him with his drinking, so when I got her number I put it in my wallet. You all know how we are self-centered about our supply? We don't tolerate folks screwing with our stash, right? Well, we can be selfish about it too. I recall once when my wife was pregnant and needed a new bra and they were on sale for only ten dollars. (She was, after all, big-busted, why else would I have married her?) I had the ten dollars but no way would I let her have it. That was for my weekend supply. I made many promises to her, meant 'em too, when I made 'em. Like, "I won't drink 'til Labor Day" or "I'll only drink beer." Hell, you all probably made the same promises.

Anyway I lost that lady's number—'til I really needed it. Maybe my Higher Power was watching out for me even then. No, I never used it for my partner; he disappeared completely. After I got out of jail I quit drinking. I poured out several bottles, trying to convince my wife to return. You know how hard it is to balance whiskey bottles on their necks, so that they look like they were just set there casually? But she never saw my efforts. Damn! Likely wouldn't have worked anyway.

I was trying to show her I had quit drinking. She left anyway. It was one of many promises she made, but this is one of the few she kept: If I ever got locked up again for drinking, she was gone. And, she was.

Well at least my son never saw me drunk, but he's heard all the stories. It was ten days of hell before I got to my first meeting; I toughed it out.

To my knowledge, I had never believed there was really an A.A.— never thought to look in phone book for what I thought of as a bar joke. One Sunday evening I watched a movie, maybe it was *Lost Weekend* or *Days of Wine and Roses*. Whatever it was, it really got to me. I figured I had no hope left.

The book speaks to this as "pitiful and incomprehensible demoralization," not a term I was familiar with then. I only knew it as feeling very hopeless, morally bankrupt, with no idea which way to turn. I, like many of us, had "prayed" but with a bargain hunter's objective. Like, "Get me out of this one, God, and I'll never drink again."

That night I sat on the couch with a .357 pistol in my hand, pulled the trigger twice—NOTHING! Hell, I couldn't even do that right. Checked to see if it was really loaded. I gave up and just sobbed for help, from who or what I had no idea. I just needed help. I recall a feeling of calmness, and something or someone said, "Go get that phone number." I looked; there was no one there. Well, I knew it was lost, but thought I'd try again any way.

Ahh! I found it immediately, and not paying too close attention to the time of night, I called it. Got the lady on the phone. Told her who I was.

She said, "Who?" She knew me by my nickname. For the next two or three hours this woman gave up her sleep to talk to me, and I cried. No one had ever understood me until then, but she did. She asked me if I could go until about 0930 without a drink. I said I had gone a whole week so far without one, but didn't know if I could do it another week. She said, "One minute at a time if you need to."

I called her office at the appointed time, and she asked if I could last until 1500 without a drink. I thought I could. She said, "Come in then and we'll talk." We did talk. She had many resources to refer me to, but chose A.A., and recommended that I attend. Gave me a meeting list. When I told her I couldn't make the meetings for next several nights, she didn't let it go. She said, "OK, I'll be talking to you," Hell, she told everybody that I was apparently in earnest about quitting drinking. Anyway, on the Wednesday evening following our Monday chat, I showed up at her place in a coat and tie as she suggested. (I guessed she thought I'd be less likely to start some shit dressed up. Today, I know why she had me dress that way). We went to a meeting held in a women's club and, walking in I noticed several cars I had worked on, and wondered what they would think, seeing me at an A.A. meeting. It never occurred to me why they might be there. I wanted what I saw there that night, badly enough to do whatever they said to do. If someone said they'd stood on their head in the corner at high noon drinking Pepsi, I would've done it. Whatever it was they had, I wanted it. The women all had great smiles, and straight makeup; the guys had on clean shirts and their neckties didn't have spaghetti stains on them. But, the realness of all the folks who welcomed me got to me.

Hell, I'm now ten days from my last drink, and still jumping through my asshole (sorry, no other way to put it). The folks gave me half-cups of coffee. I sounded like a drum roll just sitting in the chair, I was shakin' so bad. Remember the voice I told you about? Well, it also said there was a way to live without drinking if I wanted it. I had seen a partial glimpse of how it could be done.

I heard some statements like: "Ninety meetings in ninety days." "Keep it simple." "Get a Big Book." "Get a sponsor." "Get phone numbers."

Hell, none made sense to me. One I did hear really made some sense, "Put the plug in the jug"—that, I felt, I could do. And I was very fearful I'd have my sobriety revoked if I couldn't get to ninety meetings in ninety days as I worked two nights a week.

Little by little I did those things. This woman acted as my sponsor pro tem, but she kept saying things like, "You need a man sponsor." Oh really?

Hell, she was good lookin', ex-model type, so why? Well, by now you know I had designs on her, right? Never happened. Which is a good thing, for it would have ruined a very strong friendship. She said to look for someone who has long-term comfortable sobriety. I found such a guy, thought he was a wimp, didn't agree with his politics, didn't like the way he dressed, but he had something I wanted badly: comfortable long-term sobriety. He was a no-nonsense shitstomper, and he had a big foot, too, which he routinely planted in my ass. He put my butt into the Big Book right off and he said, "No wasting time on feeling sorry for yourself. You can sit on the pity pot fifteen minutes each week, all at once or piecemeal it out to last all week, but when your fifteen minutes are up, no more." And he meant it, too. Then he had me making coffee at meetings, then Big Surprise: "OK, you've had it easy for three weeks. Now it's time to get busy. You've had the first three Steps. Now, DO YOUR FOURTH! Just like the book says."

Well, you know, I learned to love that man. He died with some forty-two years sobriety. Today I sometimes think I have it rough, then I remember how it was for him. The things he had happen in his life were terrible, and yet he didn't drink over them. Hell I can do this standing on my head! He later told me why he let me slide for those weeks; he felt I couldn't put two straight thoughts together long enough to write anything coherent.

Back when I quit drinking, cigarettes were $3.50 a carton and damned few folks would've loaned me the price; today I have unlimited lines of credit from my vendors. Today I have the respect of many folks; when I was drinking, my dog didn't even respect me. Today I have real friends, folks who I have let know me, and they still like me. Back when I was drinking, my only friends were those who saw I still had some in the bottle to share with them.

I have had close family deaths, bankruptcies, marriages and divorces (Yeah, plural, that qualifies me as alkie, right?), all without having to drink. It might have been nice sometimes, but it wasn't necessary, and I have found a Higher Power I am comfortable with.

How did I become comfortable with my sobriety? That's a question I've been asked several times . . . even asked myself that, too. In *Alcoholics Anonymous* on page fifty-eight, there are twelve suggested "Steps to Recovery." There it says, " . . . rarely have we seen a person fail, who has thoroughly followed our path . . . ." I read all the Steps for myself again, and thought well these aren't too hard, but why are they read at every A.A. meeting? That I'm still unable to answer. I had done the first three Steps with the lady from the council on alcoholism. She asked me questions straight from the first three Steps . . . like "Are you powerless over alcohol?" "Is your life unmanageable?" Then we talked about my answers . . . she talked, I listened, is more like how it really was because she already knew what I'd gone through. She asked me about my belief in God, and when I'd said I had grown up in a religious family, she said, "THAT'S NOT WHAT I ASKED YOU." I had to say I didn't really believe in God. Then she asked if I could believe she believed? Yeah, I could. She next asked if I believed there might be a Power greater than myself? I tried to evade that one, but she was like a pit bull, she never let go. Finally I had to admit there just might be a power greater than myself.

Then she asked me if I thought I was crazy and with the help of that "something" greater than me, whether it would be possible that I could get sane again.

That was one of my biggest fears, that I was losing my mind, and when she put it like that . . . I knew whether I believed or not, I needed something somewhere that could help me regain my sanity.

Next she asked if I was capable of making a decision for my own good. I thought I could . . . and walked right in to her trap. She said, "Well your way got you here, now will you try it our way?" She had me read the Third Step prayer on page sixty-three several times aloud, then asked me again if I could turn my life over to a concept of a higher power I didn't understand? Hell, I had nowhere else to go and told her what I'd thought she wanted to hear. She just smiled and said "OK, act as if. . . ." That I could do, I was an accomplished actor/liar as most alkies are.

So for sometime the group was my Higher Power, they were doing what I could not by myself . . . staying sober. And that was as far into the Steps as she would take me. When I asked the fellow who would be my sponsor and friend for the next several years, if he would sponsor me, he just looked at me and asked, "Are you worth my time and effort?" I had no answer for that. Must have looked pretty stupid to him then. Remember I'd said I would do anything to have what I'd seen in A.A. so far. He finally grinned and said he'd try if I would. NOT JUST YES, BUT HELL YES! I would. Well he'd gotten sober from a gutter literally, and had come from the very dregs of society. But right then he seemed like a prince to me. "OK," he says, "here's the way it is . . . my way or the highway."

"Now you have a Big Book?" I had to say I didn't because my financial condition was just about drowning in debt. "No excuses," he said, "GET ONE! Hell, steal one if you have to!" Someone gave me a B.B. that night.

"Now," says he, "get started on the Fourth! TONIGHT!" He yelled a lot, too, must've thought I was deaf as well as stupid. "You can read, can't you? Do it just like the Book says. I'll call you tomorrow." His definition of tomorrow meant 0500—on my day off yet. I had gotten the paper lined like it is suggested in the B.B. "Not good enough, I'll call tomorrow." And he hung up.

Well, being crafty and somewhat lazy, I thought I'd skate by on this by writing down all the thoughts I had on match book covers, little slips of paper, then put 'em all together on my list. Told him what I was doing . . . major mistake! Got his size twelve in my ass right off. *We are not going to get along too well*, I thought. Hell, I couldn't con him like I had every one else. He told me, "It's either drink or write." So I tried to do exactly like the book said. He did have me look up the word "listed" in the dictionary. I made a list of resentments, folks I was angry with, my grudge list . . . all the patterns of low self-esteem, financial conditions, relationships, sex . . . everything that scared me.

Now he'd told me not to sit on my Fourth after I had completed it, but to move on to my Fifth ASAFP. This was on a Wednesday and we had made an appointment to do it on Saturday. Well he was a project engineer for a major defense contractor and was called out of town that Saturday. So I called a good friend of his and asked if he would do the Fifth with me.

Coincidentally, this man was also an old hard-ass A.A. type, and a close friend of my sponsor. He laughed and said, "Well hell it's about time! Yeah, sure I'll come over . . . NOW!" Click! Whoa, not now, I have to. . . . He showed up about fifteen minutes later. We drank pots of coffee, cried together, laughed together and after I had done it all he said now it's time for the next Steps. WAIT. WAIT. DON'T I GET A BREAK HERE? No way. So he guided me through the next three Steps, being willing to have all these defects removed (I still hadn't found a Higher Power I was comfortable with) by a Higher Power. Step Six, ergo! And I humbly (he made me look that one up also) asked Him to remove my shortcomings. There, Step Seven was done!

And as I already had a list, he showed me where to start making amends to the persons I had harmed, beginning with the hardest one on my list; no slacking off with this guy. Hell, he's even tougher than my sponsor is. Step Eight and Nine were done! Not that hard!

Now I do the last three Steps daily, continue a personal inventory, and seek to improve my conscious contact with my H.P. Yes, today I have one, and He has one helluva a sense of humor. He watches me bang my head against a wall trying to do things my way, 'til I get tired and back off saying, "God, I can't do this by myself." Then He says, "Step three feet over to your left. That's why I put that door there." And finally I have found a great peace in myself with these Steps and now try to share my recovery with all those who seek it.

Yes, I still go to meetings, and I like the way it is today, and I'll do whatever I have to do to protect my sobriety. My wish for you is that you find the happiness here that I have found.

No Longer a Rock

Laurie S.—New Hampshire

"Mom? Mommmmmmm! I'm going to Colleen's house to swim. I'll be back by dinnertime."

"Just be careful riding your bike and don't get lost this time," she laughed.

Age seven. Things seemed so simple then. I was raised in a white-collar neighborhood in small-town New England. Bad things did not happen there. The worst of my town's crimes were all in good fun. The headline of a top news story in the local paper might read, "Three Teens Caught Throwing Eggs at Trick-or-Treaters." So simple.

Then, something inside me changed, and it changed drastically. I went from being a happy, energetic, and friendly extrovert to a deeply saddened and introverted alcoholic who struggled with recovery. I can look back through my life and see some of the changes as they were happening.

By the time I reached age fourteen, the change toward self-destruction was already transpiring, though I did not know it at the time. I recall sitting in study hall with my best friend and passing notes back and forth about how much life sucked. My philosophy at the time was, "It's not so much that I want the presence of death, but just the absence of life."

Outwardly, things looked fantastic to most people. My family and I spent summers at Cape Cod and took week-long ski trips in the winter. I was well-dressed, earning decent grades, and wanting for nothing material. On the inside, however, I was turning lifeless.

Since both of my parents were working, I would return from school to an empty house and isolate myself in my bedroom. I did not want to be around people. Eventually, I was permitted to eat my meals in my room away from my family. I would sit there for hours and write out the lyrics to depressing songs. One of my favorites was "I am a Rock" by Simon and Garfunkel. "I have no need of friendship. Friendship causes pain. It's laughter and it's loving I disdain," or better yet, "I am shielded in my armor. Hiding in my room, safe within my womb. I touch no one and no one touches me. I am a rock. I am an island." I lived by this song for over a decade; the lyrics became my religion, my personal anthem, my credo.

I built huge walls to protect myself—ones I could not tear down. I was unable. I was losing control. As the years went by, the walls became stronger and higher, and I existed in a comfort-zone behind them. I was never going to allow anyone in. Of course, there were slight fissures in these mighty walls, and some people could look in and see a small part of my world—but only the part I allowed them to see.

I learned at a young age that if you give out trust, it will be broken, and it will hurt. A lot. A damned lot. From this I learned fear—fear of other people, fear of myself, fear of being vulnerable. I was a rock.

This pattern of isolation continued through my senior year in high school. By that time, I had few friends and rarely smiled or laughed. I spoke only to lash out at those who ridiculed me for being overweight. It made me feel superior and powerful. Living in this solitary state seemed to cause less pain than having to deal with other people. It was at this point that I gave up my two passions: fishing and softball. Instead, I drank.

While walking to school in the mornings, I would stop in the woods long enough to smoke a few cigarettes and get a buzz from whatever alcohol I had scraped up for that day. On a lucky day, I would score a joint to smoke. The drinking I did then seems like a distant dream at this point. It was a mere prelude to my later bout with the bottle.

Ironically, I was taking groups of teens on weekend religious retreats. I was a complete phony. I would tell them how to gain a personal closeness with God, yet I had lost all contact with Him myself. I was full of anger, resentment, fear, dishonesty, and selfishness. My fears bred more fears. My selfishness caused me to become more selfish. I was scared and alone. Very alone. Alone and lonely. Me and my self-will. I was an island.

And spiritually sick.

In April of my senior year in high school, my parents sent me to a treatment center for alcohol and drug abuse. In hindsight, I probably was more in need of a psychiatric hospital, since it was during this time that I was slicing my arms and hands with dull knives and paper clips and allowing my cat to claw me until I bled. I was spiritually void and in such mental pain that causing self-inflicted physical pain somehow seemed to ease the mental anguish and craziness in my head. My mind seemed to spin with a very painful and indescribable emptiness.

The physical scars from my self-inflicted wounds are still visible today. They are daily reminders of how sick I was during those years and how much I need my Higher Power. Insanity was definitely not a comfortable way of life.

After seven weeks of alcohol rehabilitation, I returned home to graduate from high school. Summer passed, and I moved to New Hampshire to begin my freshman year in college. I thought I had a new life, new wings. I thought I was OK. Hell, I was sober. I was full of false pride and believed that I could conquer anything.

But I couldn't. I was an island.

A month or two passed, and I returned to my old hermit lifestyle—only without alcohol and drugs this time. I carried my meals from the cafeteria and ate alone in my dorm room. I was afraid of other people, and I had few friends. Classmates would knock on my door, but I continuously made excuses not to go out with them. I sabotaged the friendships I did have. It was the one thing I was really good at doing. "I have no need of friendship. Friendship causes pain."

I remained alcohol- and drug-free for my first three years of college. I was very active in A.A. I was even involved in an on-campus Peer Support Team; I spoke to other students personally and conducted presentations about alcoholism and what I thought was recovery. I really thought I had this thing licked.

Then, I hit a milestone. I turned twenty-one. Big trouble. Since I never really had recovered spiritually, all of my old problems with self came flying back at me. It was as if I had never stopped drinking.

My entire senior year was one long drunken binge. I became a daily drinker and cocaine user. I even stooped to using crack—something I never thought I would do. I was a drunk, and I could not tolerate myself. Instead of stopping, I drank and drugged more to fill the void that was within my soul. My drinking and drug usage brought me to places that a small-town girl never thought she would see: crack houses, dingy bars, and city street corners to name a few. While this lifestyle once seemed glamorous and exciting, it was actually quite terrifying.

After graduation from college, I sobered up a bit, only to drink again and again. Now my binges were set six months apart and only lasted a day or two, but the feelings of worthlessness and the insanity continued to be daily battles and reminders of how sick I truly was.

Where was that little girl I once knew? Had I lost her forever? Buried far beneath my self-created rubble? I yearned for her. I wanted what others had: happiness, serenity, peace of mind, and the one thing I had fought against for years, a conscious contact with a Higher Power. I was sick of lying and pretending to be sober. I just did not know how to acquire any of these things, and I realized I never really had any of it. Not once. Not even close.

Those who had truly recovered from alcoholism appeared to possess a certain peace of mind and serenity. There really was a God because I could see Him in their eyes, hear Him in their words, and feel Him in their actions. I had seen God before in my life—at times when my soul seemed so lost—even though I rejected Him for many years.

During my teenage years, I spent many August nights lying on a seawall on Cape Cod, staring up at the galaxy, counting the shooting stars, and gazing into the vast expanse of the universe. I knew there had to be something bigger and more powerful out there than any human being. The night sky mesmerized me. Little did I know I was being entranced by Him.

I would lay there for hours, praying for some inner peace and some sort of change within myself that would help me to feel more sane. I knew I could not do it on my own. My past lingered and haunted me. All the selfishness, fear, dishonesty, and resentments were killing my spirit. I had not begun to let go of any of these things, so becoming well was out of the question. I was stuck in my lifeless shell of a physical body. I was one with nothing. I was an island.

I thought I was bad, useless, and a social reject. How could a person who could not hang on to a simple friendship; who had purposely smashed another person's car in a fit of anger; who gave nothing of herself to her family; who stole money from everyone she had ever met; who had been given up for adoption and seemingly rejected by her birth mother, be anything but bad? I expected and feared that others would reject me, and I learned to reject and hate myself. It became a vicious circle of madness, sadness, and loneliness.

When I was twenty-four, I met two alcoholics, a couple, in an Internet chat room. Little did I know they would bring me through the

Twelve Steps nearly two and a half years later. They would show me that I was spiritually sick, not a bad and evil person.

One summer day, I made plans to visit. They lived together, but the man was away for the month. I was looking forward to having some fun, having "girl talk," and perhaps even diving into the Big Book a bit. I had no idea what actually was in store for me those five days.

The day I arrived, we took a boat ride and got to know each other a bit. I felt completely at ease, very much at home. I could see God in this woman's eyes, and I wanted Him to be seen in mine. I no longer was a rock.

On the second day, she suggested we sunbathe on the lawn, read and discuss some of the Big Book, sip juices, and smoke cigarettes. This was the beginning of the quest for my Higher Power and the beginning of the unraveling of the old me. This was the moment when I began to feel my Higher Power and His will took over. We read the first few chapters of the Big Book and then discussed the first three Steps.

Admitting alcohol had kicked my ass was easy. This was very clear. I was at the point where I could no longer find happiness from myself, others, or the bottle. My one last hope of finding some meaning for my life was working the Steps. I was defeated by alcohol, drugs, and my self. I was woeful both drunk and sober. More than just being powerless over alcohol, I was powerless over myself. My miserable life was unmanageable because I could not fix it. Step One was complete. On to Step Two.

Was I willing to believe that a Higher Power could take away my craziness and bring some peace and sanity to my life? Yes. I had to believe this because trying to recover on my own had gotten me nowhere. I struggled for more than nine years, and I was still at square one. In that second, I was willing to turn my will over and live out God's will, letting Him work for me. Steps Two and Three were done.

After getting through Step Three, seemingly with ease, we stopped for the day. That night I started to write out my Fourth Step which I thought would be a disaster. It seems to me that some people are confused about how to do this Step. I was shown that the Big Book actually tells us how to do it. Could this already be one of the Promises coming true? I was no longer baffled by Step Four.

I wrote for quite a few hours that night, racking my brain for instances of selfishness, fear, dishonesty and resentment. As I was going to sleep, I was startled by a knock at the door. The man had driven twenty hours to come back home. I did not yet know what a blessing his presence would be in the next few days.

Day three was spent at a river where we played like kids, God's children. There were three generations of people all playing harmoniously on this river, respecting each other and all of the surroundings. Everything was becoming beautiful to my eyes. I could see God and sense His presence in my life and in these people. Still, the experience is beyond words.

That night the three of us sat at the kitchen table reading and discussing Step Four. It had to be fearless and thorough if I wanted this to work. I had tried other easier ways, all of which failed. This time I was doing the Steps exactly the way they were laid out in the Big Book. It was happening. I was finally recovering.

That night I completed my Fourth Step. It was done honestly and to the best of my ability. I recall lying in bed that night, praying for the courage to go through with Step Five. I had always been a private person, so I knew telling someone else what I had written would be a difficult task. The old thoughts of rejection were lingering around my mind as well. I did not want these people to reject me, and I immensely feared the possibility. I asked for the fears to be removed and they were—almost immediately. I knew at that moment that I had truly established a conscious contact with my Higher Power. It was a staggering feeling.

On the fourth day of this journey, the three of us went through my Fifth Step. Not only did I list the people who had seemingly harmed me at some point in my life, but we also discussed the possible reasons for their behaviors. Had I just said, "I hold a resentment against Julie P. for spitting at me in first grade and calling me a loser," I probably would not have been able to forgive her. Being able to see that some of these people were spiritually sick, just as I was, lent me the ability to forgive them for their misdeeds. I felt forgiveness in my heart, a place where before this moment I had not felt much of anything. Perhaps this Julie P. from the first grade was from an abusive home and was only doing to me what had been done to her so many times before. I could forgive her for that, and so I did with my other resentments.

After discussing resentments for hours, it was time to take a look at my own spiritual sickness. We tackled my written pages on selfishness, dishonesty, and fear. Before going through these sections, I prayed for strength and honesty. I knew that if I did not, I would surely skip a few of the more embarrassing parts of my story. I did not want to leave anything out, for to do so would cause me to remain sick. I was recovering, and I did not want to interfere with this process. I put it in the hands of my Higher Power, and we trudged onward.

After a nearly ten-hour process with a break for dinner, I was finished. My Fifth Step was nearly complete. I was sent to my bedroom for an hour to think, pray, and ensure that I had not left anything out of my Fourth and Fifth Steps. The Big Book suggests taking this time. I think many people skip or miss this important element. I returned nearly an hour later with two more fears on my list. I admitted them, and they were discussed. On to Steps Six and Seven.

Was I ready to have my Higher Power remove all the selfishness, resentment, fear, and dishonesty we had discussed? These were the things that had kept me so sick for longer than I could remember. Yes, I wanted them removed. Step Six was complete.

Then, we said a prayer together, and I later said one alone, asking my Higher Power to remove these defects of character. Step Seven was finished. I could not believe that I was at Step Eight.

Making a list of people I had harmed was a cinch; they were already listed in my Fourth Step. Basically, I reviewed my Fourth Step and made a list of people to whom I would have to make amends. After my list was complete, the question was posed, "Laurie, are you willing to go to any lengths to make amends to these people, no matter how hard it will be?" Yes, I was. I did not come this far just to give up. Those to whom I could not make amends—because it would injure them or others and perhaps hurt their spirit—I crossed off the list. I would have to make my amends to them in an indirect way. Step Eight was finished.

I would make my amends when I returned home. It was the middle of the night and not the appropriate time to call people. At this point, Steps Ten through Twelve were explained to me. They are the maintenance Steps of the program and must be completed on a daily basis. After discussing my program of maintenance for nearly two more hours, I was quite tired. Retiring for the day was the most logical step.

The next day, I drove the six hours back home in a trancelike state, partly because I was still exhausted but more so because of the freedom I had received. I was almost completely free. All I had to do was to make my amends, and I could rid myself of the past. It was like being reborn. I had a new self, and I could start over.

Making amends was so easy to do once I became truly humble. The next few days were filled with long-distance phone calls to old friends and roommates and visits to family members, both alive and deceased. I even sent twenty dollars to my friend's mother because I had once taken a twenty-dollar bill from her bureau to buy some beer.

There was one person on my list whom I could not contact. Nobody knew where she lived. I did my best to track her down but was unsuccessful. I had to make a pact with my Higher Power that if I ever cross her path in the future, I will make my amends. I was finally free.

If we practice Steps Ten through Twelve daily, we will remain spiritually well and will never again have to repeat Steps One through Nine—only if One through Nine have been done honestly and thoroughly. For this alcoholic, they were.

Every day when I awaken, I talk to my Higher Power, asking for His will for the day. I meditate until I feel His presence within me. Then, I know I am ready to face the world. During the day, I sometimes take back my will and become selfish, dishonest, fearful, or harbor resentments. When I catch myself doing so, I immediately ask for a return of His will and for the guidance to stay on track. If I have harmed someone, I will immediately make amends. Living this way has become second nature.

Today, as I sit here in my home in New Hampshire, I can see why true recovery eluded me for so long. While attending meetings from ages seventeen to twenty-one, I was poorly guided by others in the Fellowship who thought that they "had it," but who were still spiritually sick. I did what I was told to do because I did not know any better. Since I was so lost and sick, I was unable to recognize who was actually spiritually well. I attended meetings, stayed active in my home group, and found myself a sponsor. I took all of the basic suggestions of these well-intentioned people, yet nobody ever really showed me how to do the Twelve Steps. Nobody ever brought me through them.

I hated it. I hated all of it. I was forced to be sober because it was the will of other people. I was doing it for them, not for me. I was thoroughly confused when a speaker would point to the poster of the Twelve Steps and firmly declare, "The answer is found in these." People in the Fellowship would tell me to work the Steps, but I had no idea where to begin. I had no idea what "working them" really meant.

Speakers at the meetings would perpetually use catch phrases and clichés such as, "Don't drink. Don't think. Go to meetings." The human mind is never at rest. It is an impossibility for me to have my mind void of any thoughts. It is unfeasible for this human being to not think.

Another cliché that I heard numerous times was, "Take the cotton out of your ears and stick it in your mouth." To me, this was a nice way of people telling me to shut up and listen. Being quiet and listening to what others have to say is indeed beneficial, but for an alcoholic, especially a newcomer, there is much they need to say and process at times. Telling a newcomer not to talk is harmful in my opinion.

I even know a member who claims over twenty years sobriety who, when speaking from the podium, brags, "I don't get resentments, I give them." This same person seems to take great pleasure in inflicting malicious comments on newcomers just to see them squirm. It is this type occurrence in meetings today that causes me to wonder where the original message has gone, and it saddens me to see these trends taking the Fellowship away from the true message of Alcoholics Anonymous: the message of love and acceptance, of helping and caring, and the nurturing of newcomers as was practiced by Bill W. and the founding members.

It is now my purpose to pass this message on as it says to do in Step Twelve. At times, I actively seek out opportunities to help another human being, to show them the Steps the Big Book way. I do not walk around the planet trying to find people I can help recover from alcoholism. That is not my purpose at all, but if there is someone who asks for my help, I give it. If the phone rings in the middle of the night, I answer it. If someone knocks at my door in the middle of dinner, I open it. I treat others how I would like to be treated. There is much to be said for the Golden Rule. Yes, at times I may falter, but that is when Step Ten kicks in and I realize that I am wrong, using my will and not God's, and I make an amends when necessary.

Life is beautiful today. I have very clear-cut goals for myself, and I have no fear that those goals will not come to fruition as long as I stay on the same path as my Higher Power. I am now twenty-seven and just beginning my life. Fear, resentment, dishonesty, and selfishness no longer dictate my actions. Instead, my actions are dictated by the will of my Higher Power. I know that as time goes on, my will and His will, will be one in the same. I will forever remain grateful for the Twelve Steps, my Higher Power, and the two people who showed me the Truth.

Gail's Story

Gail L.—Minnesota

Most alcoholics believe they are unique, and I was no exception. For a long time, I wouldn't consider being one. After all, I had a nice home, nice clothes, and money in the bank. I'd never even been arrested. Sure, I had a tendency to be obnoxious when I consumed too much, but I believed everyone did. Therefore, my behavior was "normal."

When I was a child, my mother bragged about how cute I was when I drank. She often gave me sips of beer because "it wasn't going to hurt anything." She said it was better to drink in front of her than behind her back. So I did, and I loved the freedom. By the time I was a teenager, my mother and I became drinking buddies. I drank openly with her, but that wasn't as exciting as being with my friends. So I started sneaking booze out of the house and stealing from liquor cabinets when I baby-sat.

At seventeen, I often stood outside the liquor store with money in hand, asking passersby to buy my drinks. Also, I kept a flask of vodka in my locker at school to have during the lunch hour. Vodka was a smart choice since it didn't make my breath smell.

This spilled over into my college years. What an adventure that was! I still believed my behavior was normal. Most people let loose at college, I thought. I convinced myself I was happy, carefree, and liberated. Except for the hangovers, I felt immune to the world. I felt indestructible.

By the time I was married with children, that feeling of immunity vanished. Something happened: I didn't drink for thrills anymore. I drank to escape and to simply get drunk. Each morning, I would literally lie in bed organizing my thoughts and plans for the day, deciding when and how I could have my first drink. I often dodged the days' activities for my convenience. Getting that first drink had become the number one priority in my life, and after getting it, I didn't stop until my head hit the pillow that evening.

My drinking and my life became totally out of control. I felt totally useless and was filled with constant guilt and self-pity. So I delighted in the sensations alcohol produced. It gave me false courage and pride. With alcohol in my system, I was Superwoman. Because of my dependence on booze, I lost the respect of my family and friends. I even lost the desire to live and eventually ended up in the hospital after a suicide attempt. Alcohol was more powerful than I was.

I never envisioned myself being completely dependent upon alcohol or it being my best friend until I was forced to quit. I was substituting alcohol for my loneliness, anxiety, stress, and disappointments of everyday life. I blamed everyone else for my unhappiness, and without knowing it, I was anesthetizing these feelings by literally saturating my void with alcohol. I had the desperation to quit; yet the obsession overpowered me.

I decided to quit cold turkey and thought it would be a cinch. That lasted only one night. Prior to this, I had experimented in several different ways to cut back on my consumption: switching brands and types of alcohol; mixing weaker cocktails; drinking at a slower pace; and limiting the number of drinks I'd take within a certain time period. But I had no luck. All my tricks failed. I was surrounded by fear and realized I could not do this on my own. It was then that I admitted I was powerless over alcohol and my life was unmanageable. I didn't know where to turn or who to talk to until someone suggested that I call A.A.

There, I heard other recovering alcoholics talk of warmth, happiness, freedom, and spirituality. I wanted what they had, but I sat speechless. Every night, I would lie in bed and mouth the words "Help me." Abstaining from alcohol for up to two weeks at a time was a major accomplishment, but a longer period of time seemed impossible. Was I really mentally, physically, and spiritually sick?

As fate would have had it, along came an angel: a recovered alcoholic whom I met on the Internet. She appeared at a time when I was desperate to receive help. This encounter began my fearless journey. I flew over 1,000 miles to this stranger's house and was greeted with an open heart and home. She showed me I was not a bad person but a very sick person. We discussed the disease of alcoholism, exchanged stories, studied the Big Book, and spoke of God. She was encouraging and patient and gave of herself freely. After discussing God with her, I became willing to believe in a Power greater than myself and to turn my thinking over to that Power, believing He would restore me.

Next came the inventory. I spent many hours preparing for this. I uncovered every dark corner just as I was told to do. I understood it was the only way I would begin to recover. I was prepared and determined to sit with this angel and admit to it all. When I did, we completed Step Five. Afterwards, I retreated for some quiet time. I felt inner peace as I rested, prayed, and thanked God. After taking a good look at myself, I was more than ready to have God remove my defects, and I prayed He would take them all.

That same night, we reviewed my inventory and discussed which amends needed to be made. I plunged right in that evening, making them without hesitation. I resolved to finish the remaining ones when I returned home, and I was overcome with relief after doing so. I could see how God was changing my life.

To keep this inner peace, the last three Steps (as outlined in the Big Book) must be done on a daily basis. I must continue to connect with God by continuing to inventory my behavior, pray and meditate, and help other alcoholics. Because I do so, I no longer trudge through life. Instead, I look forward to each day and the opportunity it brings. I am a different person now; I am recovered.

Being recovered from alcoholism is the end of the insanity I once possessed and the elimination of the preoccupation with having a drink in hand. It means having a certain calmness and relief; it means inner peace and peace of mind. I have overcome many obstacles along the way, including fear, self-loathing, jealousy, and self-pity.

Being recovered means handling life's misfortunes with much less anxiety. I can handle uncomfortable situations with less fear, knowing in my heart that all will turn out as it is intended to. It is knowing that whatever circumstances cross my path, I will be all right. My attitude toward life is good. But I did not rebuild or reconstruct my thinking alone. I had help from a Power greater than myself who has taught me kindness and love for Him, others, and myself around me. I know He is present everywhere, guiding and protecting me. I wholly attribute this fresh new life—the state of being recovered—to Grace of God.

The Difference between Telling and Showing

Michael B.—Philadelphia

God, if you're really up there, I thought as I reached for my gun, *I'll see you in ten minutes.*

I had been dry for nearly one year, yet I constantly thought of drinking. It was an ongoing battle I had never won. I could not get alcohol out of my mind. A.A.s told me to concentrate on working the First Step, and I did. After all, I made a meeting a day like the rehab counselors instructed; I took coffee commitments and chaired meetings; I called a guy my sponsor; I fellowshipped with other A.A.s. I knew I was powerless, but I didn't know what to do about it. I didn't know how to stop feeling this way. But no more, I thought, as I wrapped my fingers around the imitation wood handle of the pistol.

I was reminded of how other A.A.s shared their suicidal thoughts in meetings and how I would pull them aside to explain that it wasn't worth it. I couldn't make that explanation to myself. I was overcome with the battle, and when I shared about it, I got the standard responses: "Keep coming back" and "Just don't drink." If I just didn't drink, I wouldn't need to keep coming back. I pulled the steel closer to my temple, and the telephone rang.

Who would be calling me now? And what would I say? I tried to ignore it. I buzzed. Hmmmmmm . . . but the more I ignored it, the louder it sounded. My fingers were loosening, and I began to question myself. I began to question God. Maybe He was trying to tell me something. Maybe it was a just wrong number. I had to find out, so I shoved the gun into the drawer beside my bed and picked up the phone.

"Yo, Mike," Steve said. He was a tall and sometimes erratic guy from A.A. Before I could respond, he said he was on his way to my house to show me something. I knew he had been reading the A.A. book. In the last week or so, he started to carry it with him everywhere and refer to it often. If that's what he had in mind, I figured I would OK him until he got tired of talking.

He arrived in less than five minutes with a Big Book in his hand and a bag of highlighters. "I met a guy who's taking me through the Steps," he said.

"Isn't it too soon to be worrying about the Steps?" I said, repeating what I heard many times in the rooms. I was told I was still in a fog, a mental detox, which probably wouldn't fade for another year or eighteen months.

"What! Do a Step a year?" he asked with a smart-ass grin. "Or just work that First Step?" He shook his head.

Steve was different since we last spoke. He was poised and confident. He opened his book and pointed out the word "recovered" on the first page. "Do you want to recover like these men did or do you want to stay sick?" he asked.

"I thought we never recover?" I didn't understand. His statement contradicted almost everything I had learned in the meetings. He opened his book, and I knew a sermon was forthcoming.

"I did too, but this guy showed me different." His face was so fixed, so calm, so different.

After telling me to get a dictionary, we sat at my dining room table, and he pushed a purple highlighter toward me. As we read the preface and the forewords, Steve pointed out some vital information: the Big Book is a text; the first one hundred and sixty-four pages have remained untouched since the first printing; the Big Book will show any alcoholic "precisely" (meaning exactly) how to recover; work with others was "vital to permanent recovery"; A.A. had a success rate of 75 percent; and the program (meaning the Steps) would lead to freedom. My highlighter moved fast and frequently.

"That's as far as I can take you," he said, as we finished the third foreword. "But I know someone who can take you further, if you want."

I did want more. I wanted more of the hope in Steve's eyes. I wanted his confidence, his enthusiasm, and his composure. I wanted a way out. He said if I was willing, honest, and open-minded the battle would end.

Later that night, Steve took me to a meeting and introduced me to a tall, lanky guy named Bob who agreed to share his experience, strength, and hope with the group. He came backed by a handful of A.A. supporters which he called his posse; they had a glow to them, a genuine look of happiness. He said something very curious: "I no longer have a drinking problem. I have a Bob problem."

"How's that?" I asked after the end of the meeting. I was told alcoholism was permanent. I had alcohol*is*m, not alcohol*was*m, I repeated to myself.

"I'll show you." We exchanged phone numbers. No one had ever offered to show me before. Bob proved the difference between telling and showing.

He and I began to read the Big Book together, and I was enthralled by every word—the mental obsession, the physical craving, and the spiritual malady. I could relate! Alcohol was my master. I had tried drinking on weekends, drinking beer only, and replacing alcohol with marijuana. But I always ended up on a spree—most of which had to be recounted for me by one of my friends. I calmed my shaking hands every morning with a quick drink or smoke. I stole, lied, destroyed private property, missed work frequently, and became violent. Once I started drinking, I could not stop. So when Bob asked me the First Step question, it didn't take me long to answer. I conceded to my innermost self that I was alcoholic. We read on.

In the next chapter, we paused once again and he asked, "Do you now believe or are you willing to believe in a power greater than yourself?" I was powerless and needed power. Did I really believe in God? I thought of myself sitting in a dark room with a gun to my head, of Steve's timely phone call, of his unexpected visit which paralleled Ebby's visit to Bill. I thought of the many times I should have died and didn't. Maybe there was a point to life; maybe I just wasn't privy to it. I concluded there had to be something out there, some kind of Higher Being. I was willing to investigate and willing to believe that this Power could restore my sanity if I rightly related myself to Him.

"Yes, yes, I do!" Step Two was complete.

"That's all for now. We'll meet up tomorrow."

The next day, he picked me up and introduced me to a beautiful girl named Amy, whose voice I was sure to remember when I went to bed. Bob had taken her through the Steps also and was showing her how to work with others. At his house, the three of us went through the Third Step, where I learned that selfishness was the root of my troubles and that I must be rid of it. I made a decision to move on and complete the remaining Steps. The next thing I knew, we were on our knees, and I gave myself to God without hesitation or reservation. I asked God to take my will and my life and to direct my thoughts and actions. We remained silent for a few minutes while the lusty feelings I had for Amy dissolved. The room was filled with a new Presence, and the three of us sought comfort from it.

"Great, huh?" Bob said. "But won't have much effect unless you take a searching and fearless moral inventory." He showed me that the Big Book does give instructions on when to do this Step. It says "at once."

He explained I would "swallow some big chunks of truth about myself," and I would list my resentments, fears, and harms done. I discovered I was selfish, dishonest, self-seeking, and frightened, and I realized these defects had been blocking me from God. I assured him I would begin at once.

I wrote one time for about an hour. Bob would call me now and then to check on my progress, instructing me to call him if I had trouble. I never called. I felt good, so good in fact that I didn't see the need to reveal myself. What good would it do, I thought, to dredge up my past? After all, I had already made a decision to change my life and behavior. But Bob was right: the decision didn't carry me as far as I thought it would. The feeling of freedom which resulted from my Third Step began to wither. My prayers slowed down, almost coming to a complete halt. I began yelling at everybody and everything, and I didn't understand why. Finally, I called Bob.

"Mike, you obviously haven't been writing, have you?" he said.

That weekend, we went on a spiritual retreat, a trip on which I would lose the obsession to drink once and for all. On this trip, I finished writing my inventory and shared everything from my past with Bob and God. I shared my resentments, fears, and harms done to others and revealed my character defects. I saw myself for what I was—a sinner. I was relieved, strange to say, because I knew that change could start from here.

The next morning, after considering the first five Steps, Bob and I opened our books to page seventy-six. He stressed the importance of willingness in the Sixth and Seventh Steps. I had to be willing to have God remove those things which blocked me. Was I? I considered my inventory—the hundreds of resentments, fears, and harms done. I saw the part I played, the stage I constantly tried to create. I was willing, and I asked God to take every defect from me; I asked for the strength to make amends and to set things right. We went back over my inventory and circled the people to whom I owed amends. I had completed five Steps in less than two days.

Bob explained I was not to put any of the blame on others. I was to express my faults and ask for forgiveness. Sorry wasn't enough.

"I thought I just had to apologize, " I said.

"How many times in the past have you simply said you were sorry?"

"All the time." I smiled.

"Right, and how many times did you do it again?"

I shook my head in agreement. I asked him if staying sober was considered amends. After all, my sobriety would benefit the peace of mind and wallets of others. Many old-timers agreed. Bob, however, turned to page eighty-two and exuberantly read, "We feel a man is unthinking when he says sobriety is enough." In other words, no. My recovery demanded action. I was nervous about the responses I would get, so I asked God to remove my fear. I agreed to test the waters.

When I returned home, I wrote my stepfather a lengthy letter to explain my actions and ask for forgiveness. I included a check for one hundred dollars to cover the cost of something I had stolen. There was no verbal reaction to this amends. Instead, he began to talk with me and show a general concern for my progress and well-being. He hadn't done this for as long as I can remember. He had given me a fresh start, and I was thankful.

I started to feel free, happy, and faithful. I could feel God moving through me, in me, with me like a river. I continued to make amends in pool halls and diners—wherever I saw people whom I had harmed (and boy, did I see them often). My spirit had been asleep for so long, and now, it was awakened. I felt reborn.

In order to keep this awesome feeling, I had to persist. I had cleaned up the wreckage of my past. Those Steps that once frightened me were now complete. I felt at ease and wanted to keep this feeling. I learned we maintain our sobriety and sanity by practicing the last three Steps on a daily basis. The strength and willingness to do so is contingent upon my daily prayer and meditation.

I first thought meditation involved sitting with my legs crossed while chanting loud noises. Soon after studying the Ten and Eleventh Steps with Bob, I discovered it simply meant listening to God. I have since learned an effective way of meditating which allows me to sit on my butt and merely write whatever pops into my head. Then, I test my thoughts to see if they are self-centered or God-centered. Selfishness, dishonesty, fear, and self-seeking are the watchwords. When these crop up (and they often do), I ask God to remove them, make amends if necessary, and seek a better course of action for the future. Still, more work was necessary.

"You know what I did with you?" Bobby asked.

"Yeah."

"Well, you actually helped me more than I helped you."

"Yeah right, "I said. "How?"

He pointed me to the chapter entitled "Working with Others." The first sentence reads, "Practical experience shows that nothing will so much ensure immunity from drinking as intensive work with other alcoholics." I had to follow Bob's lead; I had to help others—those alcoholics, in and out of the rooms, who have not yet heard the message of Alcoholics Anonymous. There is a solution. I have since traveled to many forlorn houses, listened to many horror stories, grieved a few deaths, been rebuked by other A.A.s, and witnessed several successes. It is my job and my privilege. "Keep on the firing line of life with these motives," the Big Book says, "and God will keep you unharmed."

While writing this piece, I remembered something that Steve said to me the day he introduced me to the Big Book. He said, "All that I thought was the truth is turning out to be false, and all that I thought was false is turning out to be the truth." I thank God (and those alcoholics who worked so diligently with me) for that Truth. It has saved my life.

A Woman Reborn

Jennifer Page—Upstate New York

According to family legend, my first drink was at age two. My family and I were out for dinner at a favorite restaurant and my mother had ordered a kiddie cocktail for me, while my grandmother ordered a manhattan. The waiter inadvertently mixed up the drink order, and I sipped the manhattan while my grandmother enjoyed my kiddie cocktail. The story goes that I drank the whole thing perched in my highchair, and held up the empty glass for a refill.

I lived among a family where booze was plentiful and life was quite social. I remember saying as a child that I would never drink when I grew up since I did not care for the way others around me acted when they were drinking. My first real drunk occurred when I was fourteen years of age, and my last drink was at age forty.

In the summer of 1969, I wanted to see for myself what it was really like, so I uncorked a bottle of wine from the case of bottles my family kept in our breezeway. As I began to consume the entire bottle, I felt a warm, numbing sensation go through my body. I loved the way booze made me feel; I hated the way booze made me feel. *So this is what being drunk is like,* I thought. *This is what the big deal is about.* After a few hours of getting into the role of being drunk, purposely slurring my words and exaggerated staggering around, I got sick and passed out. Thus began my career of drinking, with occasional episodes of drinking throughout the year.

—Once an alcoholic, always an alcoholic.—

During my high school years I began drinking on weekends, and this trend continued into my college years when blackouts started to occur during my sprees. Changes occurred in my behavior when drinking which were evident in my insane actions while on the weekend drunks. I rationalized that this was college, after all, and students are supposed to participate in this rite of passage.

Throughout my first marriage I was getting drunk about three or four times a month despite the blackouts and regardless of the reports of my actions while drinking, most of which I simply did not recall. That marriage ended in divorce. My drinking continued into my second marriage, with me still getting drunk on the average of four or five times a month, and continuing with the blackouts and insane behavior. Things were getting worse as time went on. I was arrested in March of 1994 for DWI, after a three-hour lunch, which consisted of only one glass of wine—with about fifteen refills. Someone reported to the sheriff's department that a car was driving erratically on the back roads. Of course! Less traffic, more room to swerve. Have they ever tried keeping to the right of the traffic line while talking on the car phone, smoking a cigarette and swilling Listerine? At the time of my arrest, my blood-alcohol level was recorded at .23. After being processed in jail, my car was impounded, and I was released on my own recognizance. I was too embarrassed to call my family to let them know what had happened, so the sheriffs called me a cab. I tried to convince the cab driver to pull over to a bar somewhere. He explained he didn't drink, and that he had been a member of A.A. for several years. "A conspiracy!" I concluded. "They're out to get me! The sheriffs must have asked specifically for this cabbie." I launched into Plan B. " This guy surely must know how badly I want a drink, so I'll impress him with my knowledge of A.A. (from my older brother being a member for ten years) and then he'll pull over and buy me a six-pack of beer." I slurred the Serenity Prayer, something akin to, "God, grant me the wisdom of the courage to accept the serenity of the difference and change things, man." It worked. He got me my beer.

When I got home, I had to face the music. I hid the rest of the six-pack in the garage, and staggered into the house like nothing had happened. This was after telling my family that I was going out for lunch and would be home by three in the afternoon, and it was now eleven at night. By this time, my husband had put up with enough of my insanity and suggested we separate. My son and I moved out, and that marriage eventually ended in another divorce.

—A life run on self-will can hardly be a success.—

While living in my new apartment, I began drinking alone, something I had never done before as I was so accustomed to the social scene and to hanging out in bars. I considered drinking at home to be "safer" since at that time, my driver's license was suspended and I could not take the risk of driving and being arrested again. After all, one DWI was bad enough. My other options included calling friends to take me to the bars, and this I did from time to time. I also tried some of the forms of "self-deception and experimentation" described on page thirty of the Big Book.

When my license was restored, I swore up and down that I would never drink and drive again, yet I placed a dead bumblebee on the console of my car. My reasoning behind this madness was that, just in case I were stopped again by the police while drinking and swerving as I had in the past, I could show the bee to the officer and tell the officer, "Officer (slur), there was a bee flying around in my car (hic)! That's why I was swerving—I was trying to swat it! See? Here is it. I killed it!" My insanity at its finest, the purest in alcoholic thinking.

After one year of "being good" about drinking and driving, on a blizzardy night, March 9, 1995, I was arrested for DWI again. This was after a two-hour dinner with wine, and plenty of it. This time, I rolled the truck I had borrowed from my brother down a ravine, nearly taking out the local fish hatchery. My very first thought was, "Darn! I left my BEE in my other car!" It occurred to me only later, much later, that bees do not fly around during snow storms in upstate New York. And perhaps the evidence of frayed wings, dust and lint and might be a dead giveaway that the insect had long since expired.

There I was in the overturned vehicle, suspended by the shoulder harness, devising my escape plan options. Probably no one heard or saw the crash, since it was one o' clock in the morning. I could climb out of the truck through the smashed out sunroof, turn the vehicle right side up, and drive it up and out of the ravine and go home. Yeah! Or, I could simply flee from the scene, run four miles home, have the truck towed out at a more convenient time, and explain to my brother that his truck was in the shop for a minor "fender bender." Unbeknownst to me, the sheriffs had indeed been alerted and were on their way to the scene. Damn! No escape now! Time to launch plan C: the "accident victim" role, for sympathy. Surely they wouldn't arrest a bloodied woman, trapped in an overturned vehicle, who had escaped death in a treacherous snow storm. However, they would probably insist upon me taking the field test. They did. I complied. I sang the alphabet, and tried my best fox-trot when walking the line, lifting my knee, and touching my nose. My blood-alcohol was once again .23. At least my luck was consistent.

I attempted to persuade the sheriffs that they needn't give me a DWI, since I already had one. No dice. My rights were read to me as I nodded that I was already familiar with that formal jargon in a, "Yes, right, get on with it, let's move along with this so I can get home and have a drink" manner. I was escorted into the squad car and handcuffed to the door. Off to jail, again. A repeat performance of fingerprints and mug shots. It was while handcuffed and sitting on a cold bench in jail, that reality and remorse set in and I began to cry.

After returning home from jail again, I opened the refrigerator and took out a bottle of beer, opened it and drank half of the contents. Next, I set the bottle on the counter and said aloud, "I'm done." I looked back over my life. Every time I had gotten into trouble, it was because of my drinking. Alcohol had kicked my derriere and I was beat (Step One).

I was riddled with shame, guilt and remorse over my actions when drunk. I wanted to die that night; to take my own life so I would not have to wake up the next day and again face reality. I planned my suicide while lying in bed that night—sleeping pills. Surely death would relieve me of all my pain; this hell I was in—the hell I had created by my own self-will and insanity. Then something within me changed. I realized a self-induced exit from life was not the answer—getting on with life was. As I drifted off to sleep, my thoughts turned to facing the next day.

The next day I set forth on a mission to start cleaning up my life. First, I had to find out where my brother's truck had been towed, and view the damage. It was not pretty. I was damn lucky to be alive. Next was calling my brother to let him know what I had done. He had an inkling something was up, because I had phoned him earlier at work— a family business—and asked him to meet me outside of his office. I did not want to see any other family members. I was too ashamed. I told him everything. He said, "It's just a truck. You're my sister." My brother had been aware for many years of the hold that alcohol had on me. He hugged me as I cried and apologized, and I went on my way. After I arrived home, I called the local Alcoholics Anonymous line, to get a meeting schedule. I also called a nearby drug and alcohol clinic, to set up outpatient counseling.

The very next day, my estranged husband came by to take our son from me. He said he thought I was suicidal, and he could not trust me anymore. Now I was truly in hell, and very alone. For several days that followed, I isolated myself in my apartment, riddled with fear.

—*Pitiful and incomprehensible demoralization.*—

One week later, I called a woman friend who I knew was in A.A. I asked her if I could go to a meeting with her that night. "Aren't you scared?" she asked. "No. I'm ready," was my response. We went that night, and I continued to attend meetings, listening to suggestions such as, "Don't think, don't drink, no matter what." Another I heard often was, "Ninety meetings in ninety days." Others included, "Get a sponsor," "Your disease is in the parking lot, doing push-ups." "It's waiting out there to get you. It wants you dead." and other slogans which only confused me more.

I got a sponsor like "they" told me to, but I was under the impression that a sponsor was to be my baby-sitter. Apparently, I was wrong, because four months later, I had a drink. I reasoned that since others at the meetings were slipping, why shouldn't I? I finally realized I hadn't gotten past the First Step, and that I was still powerless over alcohol. How could this be? I thought I was doing the right things "they" were telling me to do. I felt lost for the longest time—clueless. It seemed as though there just had to be more to it than those "just don't drink" clichés I was hearing.

In November of 1995, I checked myself into an aftercare program at Hazelden, "The place to go," thinking I could find more answers there. The programs they offered appeared to help me, however, it was short-lived. Although I had no desire to drink, my life seemed to be at a stand still. I continued on this way for another eighteen months.

—*We feel a man is unthinking when he says*
sobriety alone is enough.—

Almost two years to the day I first started going to A.A., I found out that the real purpose of a sponsor is to take another alcoholic through the Twelve Steps as outlined in the Big Book so the suffering person can get well and recover from alcoholism. I knew of a man who had great knowledge of the program outlined in the Book who always referred to himself as "a recovered alcoholic." These words brought to mind the words of chapter seven, "If he says yes, his attention should be drawn to you as a man who has recovered," on page ninety of my book.

My plan was to ask him for help the next time we talked, and one evening as I was about to ask him, he said to me, "As I recall, you said you were stuck somewhere in the Steps. Would you like some help?" What a relief. I felt as though I was on my way. I got out my book—which up until this time was collecting dust after having been sent to me by my brother almost two years previously—and I dove into that book with a burning hunger. My "guide" pointed out what to read first, oddly enough, the title page: *Alcoholics Anonymous—The Story of How Many Thousands of Men and Women Have Recovered From Alcoholism,* and he had me continue reading all the way through the first one hundred and sixty-four pages and then we commenced working the program exactly as it is outlined there. I had met the requirements for beginning the program of the Steps since I was now honest enough, willing, and open-minded to the point I could listen to what I was being shown and taught. I had to be all of these things; I was tired of living the old ways.

Step Two enabled me to tap into the Power of God, and since I did believe in a Great Spirit already, it was an easy transition. Step Three was simply a decision. Since I was tired of living in the old ways of "self," I concluded that, yes, I would try to live in ways that God would want me to in order for me to get well.

Step Four followed immediately after making that decision, like the Big Book stated in its directions. This inventory involved writing down all my resentments, fears, selfishness, and dishonesty, as far back as I could remember. As I looked back over my life and the events that occurred since I was a little girl, the memories seemed to just pour out of me, and onto the pages of my notebook. Every twisted thing that I ever did, or was done to me was finally cast out of the dark and into the light. In Step five, I told all my deep dark secrets to a trusted person. I was shown where I had wronged others, others had wronged me, and that I was still a good person in spite of all those things that kept me sick for so long. At long last, those secrets held no more power over me. Better still, I was actually able to forgive all those people who had hurt me; I was able to forgive myself. And God forgave me, all along.

Step Six was after an hour of review, some praying, making sure I was on solid ground with God, and that I had left nothing out of my inventory. Yes, I was now ready to have God take away all that stuff. Who in their right mind would want to hold on to it? In Step Seven, I knelt beside my bed. I knew that the original version of this Step was, "Humbly, on our knees, asking Him to remove our shortcomings, holding nothing back." And I sincerely wanted my Creator to know I meant business. I honestly wanted my old ways gone. I asked Him to take away my fears, resentments, selfishness, and dishonesty. Feeling a sense of peace, I rested for the night, and continued on with the housecleaning Steps the next morning.

Step Eight was in two parts, the first of which was already done; "Made a list." I had my list from my Fourth Step. The second part, "became willing," was done too. I had been willing since the night before, only then it was too late in the evening to be calling people and causing more resentments. I spent the day on the telephone making amends to all the people I had harmed. Amazingly enough, some of these people confessed amends to me, and some broken relationships were restored. There were some amends I could not make directly, because those people would be hurt if they knew the real truth. Those amends I gave to God. After the last call was made, I burned my list in the fireplace, and I felt absolutely reborn. My past was now just that, the past. No more shame or guilt. A new woman danced before the fire that day, both childlike and womanish, enraptured to a newfound music of life, confident and with head held high before God and the world, marvelling in the knowledge that the promises on pages eighty-three and eighty-four had indeed come true.

—A new freedom and a new happiness.—

I am whole now. Complete. I have recovered from alcoholism, and I do not doubt that God did for me what I could not do alone. My alcohol problem is long since gone, and my sanity has been restored. I am no longer the selfish center of the universe I once was. The Promises continue to manifest in my life daily. I have a family who loves and respects me today, and I love them all back, the best way I know how. I have a remarkably loving mate with whom I share the common bond of God's Plan. He is also a recovered alcoholic. Together, we have come to know the meaning of True and Absolute Spiritual Love. We have a way of turning our seeming problems into advantages and opportunities for growth in our life together by remaining grounded in God. We work as a team helping others in and outside the realm of A.A. We have made countless lifelong friendships in this fellowship. Our life as partners in Faith is amazing.

How is this all possible? Simple. This Way of Life is maintained by living by spiritual principles to the best of my ability, daily, in the last three Steps. I continue to watch for defects and try to correct them, as directed in Step Ten. I talk to God, I listen to God; Step Eleven. I share my experience of getting well with suffering alcoholics, and try to be of help to any person in need; Step Twelve.

—Practice these principles in all our affairs.—

So simple. And it works. If you are a newcomer to A.A., or just picking up this book in search of answers, my experience tells me that you would do well to find someone who talks of God, of the Big Book, and the Steps. Find someone who lives this way of life and ask them to guide you. You are the lifeblood of A.A., and you deserve to know the Truth. Ask them to show you this Path called the Twelve Steps which leads to the Miracle . . . then, pass it on.

Note: The sentences set apart in italics are from the Big Book.

Lou's Story

Louise L.—Southern Oregon

What I remember to be my first drink was communion wine. I may have had sips here and there before that, but that drink of communion wine changed the course of events where alcohol was concerned. That was the beginning of a long journey in search of a feeling that I was never to find again.

I knelt there, anxious and feeling "on exhibit." The priest worked his way down the row and finally came to me. I reached up and lightly touched the base of the chalice as he guided it to my lips. I got a mouth full of wine. It was warm and sweetly bitter. I swallowed fast.

The warm turned to hot as I felt it go down my throat. From there that heat exploded inside me, radiating from my stomach out my arms, to the tips of my fingers. Down my legs to my knees then on to my toes. I felt a flush come over my face and a warm buzzing sound in my head. My body was glowing, every inch of it. The events around me had become just background noise. What seemed like hours was actually a minute or two and then I had to stand and walk back to the pew. By the time I reached the pew, all I was feeling was my heartbeat in my ears. The glow had vanished.

From that time, 'til I was sixteen, I snuck nips from my mother's wine bottle from time to time, always terrified I would be caught. From age sixteen until I stopped drinking, I drank for effect. I was in search of that glow. I lived away from my family and hung out with a much older crowd. I learned how to drink hard liquor in jazz nightclubs. No one questioned my age. I was accepted, something that I craved. I learned how to drink beer hanging out with my new buddies. I'd never had buddies before. I learned about fine wines in the restaurant I worked at. I wanted to be an informed employee and I was promoted rapidly.

Yet that glow still evaded me. I was introduced to other mind-altering substances. I became an amateur chemist, mixing and trying to match booze and drugs to bring me that glow.

All this time, my thinking was telling me that I would never amount to anything. I was doomed to be a drunk, just like everyone in my father's family. No one I hung out with or worked with saw that part of me. What they saw was the worker who showed up early or at least on time for work. They had a friend who would go out of her way to help them in their time of need. I took a lot of pride in my ability to drink most everyone under the table and still make it to work in the morning. I took pride that I never missed a day of work because of my drinking.

During my drinking career I was a chef and had easy and constant access to alcohol. I took pride in the fact that I never drank before coming to work. Most of the time I was still drunk, having stayed up all night pursuing my "glow." I was a blackout drunk. I always drank to get drunk and would end up passed out. All this pride I exuded got me friends that drank like I drank so I wouldn't stand out. I wanted to fit in and I did. If you didn't drink like me, you weren't in my company.

The men in my life were there to keep the booze flowing. I was living with an alcoholic; I drank with him as a way of keeping an eye on him while he was at the bars. We had a very stormy eight-year relationship. At about year five, his drinking got in the way. I took him to treatment. Within a month, we were right back where we had left off. This happened a couple of times . . . detox, treatment, promises of sobriety. Yet always ending up drunk. I stayed because it was all I knew. He stayed because I had the paycheck. It was a perfect match for a couple of active alcoholics. Yes, I knew I was an alcoholic. I believed with all my heart and soul that I was a hopeless, helpless alcoholic. Doomed to the drinking way of life. I had no other way to deal with the bombardment of feelings and emotions. The booze eased that pain for a long, long time. One day, it stopped working. The pain wouldn't go away, no matter how much I drank.

On January 21, 1982 at about 4:30 in the afternoon, I left the bar. I hadn't even drunk anything, just stopped in after work to get a pack of cigarettes. I lived across the street from the bar. There was a well-beaten path cutting across the street in the middle of the block between my apartment building and the bar. This cold and gray winter afternoon, I walked out of the bar and turned right and started walking to the crosswalk, something I had never done. I was like a zombie.

The pain I was feeling in my soul was so overwhelming; I didn't know where to turn now that the booze wasn't working. I got to the crosswalk and pushed the button and waited for the light to change. The light changed and I stepped out into the street. I got to the other side, stepping up on the curb, and everything around me came to a complete halt. I was frozen in time and space. I couldn't hear the traffic that was filling the streets.

What I did hear was a voice, not my own. That voice was deep and soft, reassuring and firm. "You are going to die if you keep this up. Is that what you want?"

Those were the words I heard. Just as quickly as time and space had frozen; they came back to life and with tears welling up in my eyes and my head reeling, I walked to my building. I got inside my apartment and locked the door and drew the curtains, leaving the lights off. I found myself in the dark corner of my bedroom, sitting and crying. I was sure that not only was I a hopeless and helpless alcoholic but that I was also certifiably crazed. I was hearing voices. I didn't tell anyone about the voice and its question and warning. I couldn't. They would have me locked up. I didn't drink after that either. I knew somewhere deep within me that I really didn't want to die; I just wanted the pain to end. That was all I was willing to see at that time. I knew that what I had to do was to pull myself up by the bootstraps and fix my life. I didn't have a clue what that really meant. I thought that if I knew why everyone around me was so messed up then I would be better. I thought solving *their* problems would solve *mine*.

Along the path of my drinking and drug use there was somewhat of a spiritual quest. A deep desire to find some kind of meaning to my existence. Now I see that the booze got in my way of that quest. It was the barrier I couldn't overcome, not on my own. I heard what other's experiences were. Most of those who had found that place within themselves hadn't found it with drugs and or alcohol. They had experienced some kind of epiphany or as I was to learn to call it, a spiritual awakening. I did a lot of reading and pondering. I could see some of what the authors were talking about but it was still through a fog in my thinking.

I found myself still feeling that emptiness, that void in my soul. I knew that alcohol wasn't the answer; it had stopped working. I also knew that what that voice had told me was the truth. I kept up my outside appearances. I moved on in my career. I continued the isolation from my family. I had no real friends. I couldn't allow anyone close enough to see the real me. The pain was too great and kept growing. My options seemed so limited. I flirted with ending my life a few times, never taking any action.

Now action seemed to be the only way out of the pain I was in. I came up with a plan, one I was sure would work. Before I carried out that plan though, I wanted one last walk on the beach. My visits to the beach were one of the few comforts I had, an ebb in the pain. I felt like one of those grains of sand, a part of something so big, so vast, that no one could grasp the whole thing. I knew I couldn't.

So, it was there on the beach that I heard the voice again. The same voice that I had heard almost ten years prior to that. The voice that I thought meant I was crazy in the head. This time the voice said, "It's OK to be afraid. I will help you." I broke down on the beach that day. I sat sobbing, not understanding what was going on. I wasn't alone yet I felt such a void within me. I was coming to believe that whatever this voice was, it was my way out of the pain I was feeling. I knew I had to "do" something, take some kind of action, yet I didn't have a clue where to begin. Needless to say, I didn't go through with my plan to end my life. I went about my daily routine of work and isolation. At work I met a woman who was sober five years. She just appeared out of nowhere, even though she had worked in the same building as me for the past year. She and I spoke over coffee and agreed I would go with her to an open A.A. speaker meeting the next night.

I was interviewing someone for a job opening in my department. He told me he was a sober alcoholic. We talked about his sobriety, his journey of recovering. I hired him.

These people were messengers from the Voice. In my heart, I knew that. I bravely let myself listen to what they had to say. I still felt different because I didn't need to stop drinking, I needed to find a way to live life without the booze. They assured me that sobriety was threefold, physical, emotional, and spiritual. Having all three was the key to full sobriety. *This* is what I was craving. That emptiness, that void I was feeling was my soul telling me it needed nourishment. The kind of nourishment that can be found by first becoming physically sober, then working a set pattern of things that would heal the emotions and allow my soul to grow and continue to grow. This is what I learned to be the key of Alcoholics Anonymous, the Twelve Steps. I had bought a Big Book at an Al-Anon meeting and it had been there on the shelf, unread, for over a year. I picked up the book after that first meeting. I started reading. The language was different from any book I had read before. Yet it spoke to a part of me that instinctively trusted the words, even though I wasn't completely sure of their meaning. I read phrases like "Nearly all have recovered. They have solved the drink problem." "The tremendous fact for every one of us is that we have discovered a common solution." "We feel that elimination of our drinking problem is but a beginning." ". . . in the face of expert opinion to the contrary, we have recovered from a hopeless condition of mind and body. If you are an alcoholic who wants to get over it, you may already be asking What do I have to do? It is the purpose of this book to answer such questions specifically." Statements like this told me that if I kept reading, I would find out what I had to do to find the solution, and then how to use the solution in my life, how to apply it. Directions. An answer to my problem.

I started going to meetings, raising my hand when they asked for newcomers. I got some strange looks when they heard when my last drink was. But that didn't deter me. I found a meeting in a small white church. It was a Monday night. I sat in a chair next to a wall. I listened to folks share. A woman sitting in front of me at the table shared. There was something about her story that clicked with me. Her life was very different than mine. She had been married twice and had a teenage son. She grew up in a religious family, missionaries. She was eighteen years older than I was; yet there was something so familiar about her, it was almost scary. She put words to feelings that I had no words for. She had been where I was and had walked a path of sobriety to a new way of life. I wanted what she had.

After the meeting, she came up to me and gave me a hug and welcomed me. I thanked her and asked her to be my sponsor. She laughed and said I needed to think about that. And that she wanted me to write out twenty-five reasons that I thought I was an alcoholic. I was to call her the next evening and we would go over my reasons.

I went home that night and wrote out my reasons. That was simple to do. In every aspect of my life, alcohol had some affect. Even during my years of physical sobriety, alcohol still had its death grip on me. I still had that emptiness within me. I was miserable with my life. Almost as much as when I was drinking. The only real difference being I didn't have the blackouts, the hangovers. I still had all the pain and anguish, left unnumbed from alcohol. The doom and gloom hadn't gone away when I stopped drinking. This is what I came to understand was meant when Bill W. said, "Alcohol is but a symptom. . . ." My whole life was in shambles. Maybe not so much on the outside, but my insides were a wasteland.

At work the next day, I got a phone call. It was Judi, the woman I had asked to sponsor me. I had told her where I worked. She just wanted to call and say hello. We agreed to talk later that evening about my list of reasons.

We went over each and every item on my list. I still have it somewhere in a box. There was no doubt in my mind or hers that I was an alcoholic. I felt at home with that. I knew there was something I could do about it. The helplessness and hopelessness was gone. Judi was going out of town for three weeks. I had my instructions while she was gone. I was to go to as many meetings as I could, get to know people in the fellowship. And I was to read the Big Book, cover to cover. We agreed that, as soon as she returned, we would begin going through the Steps as outlined in the Big Book. In my mind, we had done Step One (my list of unmanageability). What I did was find my Higher Power in reading the Big Book. I had not had an agreeable relationship with God from my childhood. I wanted nothing to do with that vengeful God. I knew that there was a power out there that oversaw everything and I wanted a connection with that power. Just knowing it existed wasn't enough; I wanted something tangible, something I could touch. I had isolated myself so far from the world, from people, my surroundings, and me. I had a wall around my physical space that no one could budge. The only place I felt connected with the earth was while at the beach, so, I went for a walk to my favorite spot. I sat down and watched the surf, feeling the sand between my fingers. Letting it sift through my palm. It was there that I found my connection. I found a small stone that had been worn smooth by the surf and sand. It fit perfectly between my thumb and forefinger. This was to represent my relationship to *my* Higher Power. This is what I needed to make the connection. I kept that rock in a pocket of whatever I was wearing. I could reach in there and grab hold and *feel connected* with my Higher Power. When I felt connected, I felt that my sanity could and would be restored. This is how I came to believe.

Judi returned and we got together after a Sunday-night meeting. I had decided this group would be my home group. It was a Step Study group. I felt like this was the purpose of meetings, to gather and talk about how the Steps are worked and how they have worked in our lives. The policy of the group was to only allow sharing about a Step that you had completed. It was May, and we were on Step Five. I had only done Steps One and Two. So I got to listen to a lot of experience, strength and hope. Judi and I talked about what my relationship to my Higher Power was. Having to try and define it, someone really helped me. I wasn't doing it for her approval or to pass some kind of test. She wanted me to vocalize what I had come to believe. The foundation of having a good grip on my concept of my Higher Power would become apparent to me as we worked through the remaining ten Steps. We said the Third Step prayer, not on our knees, but just sitting there. I really did believe that this power greater than myself could relieve me of the bondage of self and take away my difficulties. My part was to be willing to do my Higher Power's will for me and to bear witness (pass the message on to others). That done, Step Four sat there, waiting for me.

Judi loaned me a set of audio tapes by a couple of old-timers named Joe and Charlie. They talked about the Big Book page by page. Explaining a lot of the plain English meaning behind Bill Wilson's fancy 1930s grammar. When they talked about the Fourth Step being a list of truths, this made sense to me. I was not making the list to define the good and the bad (that was my Higher Power's job), but I was making a list of all the truths about me. The framework for this list of truths was to be resentments, them being the "number one offender." I read along in the Big Book, trying to see what they were seeing, I couldn't. Judi gave me a "form" for the columns. It referred back to what page and paragraph in the B.B. to read, then do the column. Read some more; do the next column. This made more sense to me and I used that form. I still have it and now pass it out to women I sponsor. The structure of it is what kept me focused on exactly the task at hand. One task at a time, not jumping around or getting ahead of myself. This kind of discipline has been a learned thing for me, learned in A.A., taught by example from others in A.A. I got to the sex part of my inventory and hit a wall. What it boiled down to was I didn't want to look at my part in it. I thought if I wrote it all down, I was to blame for it all. Once again, sharing with Judi some of my fears about proceeding, I was able to see that no matter what I wrote down, my Higher Power already knew what I had done. I knew what I had done. And she was the only other one that would. Maybe it was a matter of trust. That one last reservation on my part. I got through that part of the inventory and on with my list of people.

Judi and I got together to do my Fifth Step. We met for lunch first, then walked up to her house. Her husband was gone for the day and she took the phone off the hook. We sat down to start. I was terrified and she could see that. She suggested we say a prayer. I let her say it. She asked God to help me be willing to trust and share openly about myself. That God be there with us. That calmed my nerves enough for me to get started. We were there all afternoon, me reading, and her listening and asking some questions. Her sharing some things that were similar with her own inventory. Some crying and hugs. Even some laughing. We got done with it finally.

Lots of people burn what they have written. I wasn't one of those people. First of all, I would later need that list of folks for my Eighth Step. Second, I didn't wish to have that piece of history about myself disappear. Who knows, I may need it some day.

I left Judi to go to my favorite quiet spot, the beach. I sat on the beach with my B.B. and read from the bottom of page seventy-five. The questions we need to ask before we proceed with the next Steps. I could answer them all truthfully and honestly and to my satisfaction. I was ready for Step Six. I was ready for my Higher Power to remove these defects of character I had just faced in my Fourth and Fifth Steps. Being ready, I was now at Step Seven. I said the Seventh Step prayer.

I had heard a lot said about Steps Six and Seven. And when I read them in the B.B. and the Twelve and Twelve, not a lot is really said about them. Being OK with the simplistic nature of those Steps is now OK with me; it wasn't back then. There were no big instructions, no big to-do list. They are two very simple Steps. The asking of self about willingness and then the asking of a Power Greater than Self for assistance. It's this alcoholic mind that wants to complicate the hell out of these Steps. The defects of character just don't evaporate because we have asked for them to be removed. For me, these two Steps are an affirmation of my foundation in my Higher Power. It is up to me to continue on with the remaining Steps to bring those changes about in my life. If my faith isn't there, isn't true and certain, then I won't have the willingness to move onto the remaining Steps. My character defects will continue to make their demands on me, and I alone do not have the ability to say NO to them. This knowledge didn't just "come to me." It came from listening to others share about what their experiences were, reading the B.B., and discussing what it says. And, praying for direction. And listening for that intuitive inspiration.

70

Step Eight for me was basically done. I had heard on those Joe and Charlie B.B. tapes about Step Eight and they had a suggestion to divide the list of people in to three categories. First one was those we were immediately willing without any reservation to make amends to. The second were those we had some reservation about or their whereabouts we needed to research. The third was those that we didn't want to face. Their experiences were that as we worked on the first group, those in the second group began to surface and move up in the list and that those in the third group did the same. So by the time we were done with the original first group, the second group was now the first and the third was now the second. And on through those until we were done. This way of organizing the list helped me to stay focused and directional. There were a lot of people I didn't know where they were, let alone their last name to contact them. I wrote some letters that went unsent that said my part in what I owed them an amends for. I wrote some other letters to those in the third group (the people I was hesitant to face) and those letters helped me be more comfortable about facing them. I must say, there were a lot of people that I couldn't find, couldn't contact. I made efforts to do so, to no avail. Judi talked with me about "living amends." Changing my way of living so in future similar situations, I didn't repeat those past behaviors. I still use that today, especially with my family.

Steps Ten, Eleven and Twelve are those Steps I work on a daily basis. In Step Ten, I continue, daily, to take my own inventory. This is like a mini section of Steps Four to Nine. If I do it daily, then it won't get built up.

Step Eleven is my daily affirmation that there is a God and I am not it. My sobriety is a gift, and my serenity with my sobriety is contingent upon maintaining my conscious contact with my Higher Power. Conscious contact means to me that I need to bring my Higher Power into ALL aspects of my life. When I remember this, I am the most content.

Step Twelve is the reminder to me that I promised in Step Three to bear witness, to pass on what I have experienced. The result of doing the previous eleven Steps is a spiritual wakening. I believe there are many varieties of spiritual awakenings and that I have had many of them.

Spiritual awakening sounds like some kind of burning bush or hearing voices. Sure, I just told you my story and talked about hearing voices. At the time, I didn't know what that experience was. I had no way to describe it other than as a form of insanity. What I have come to believe them to be for me is a new awareness. Awareness of my place in this world. Awareness of the true simplicity of the perfections all around me. I always wanted to feel a part of something. That awareness happens now.

Guided By Spiritual Principles

Dan B.—Pennsylvania

I took my first drink at the age of thirteen. I made a decision; I paid my money; and I drank forty-eight ounces of Iron City Beer—nectar of the gods. Now, I knew that thirteen-year-old kids are not supposed to drink, but it was part of the rite of passage in the inner city Irish neighborhood where I lived. What a wonderful experience it was for about an hour or so. But then, I got so sick that I actually prayed to God, promising that if He would make this bellyache go away I would never drink again.

Being a product of parochial schools, I had the idea there were negative consequences for living contrary to the principles that I was taught, and although I did not perceive drinking beer as a serious violation of those principles, it was still an infraction. I had the mistaken belief that God was inflicting those negative consequences, and He would diminish them if I sincerely promised to mend my ways. This was the start of my life of drinking and bargaining with God. Had I kept my part of the deal, I would not be writing this. But the fact is, I found the effect of alcohol so seductive that I tried it again and again and eventually learned to drink without getting sick. I came to believe that God didn't make me sick; improper drinking did. All I had to do was learn how to drink properly, and I was an eager student.

When my drinking started, I had the same ambitions most kids do. By the time I was seventeen, alcohol had diminished most of those goals. I had little interest in any activity that didn't include drinking. I still get a tingle when I think about standing on the corner with "my buddies" on a warm August evening, drinking beer and believing that life couldn't get any better than it was at that moment. The feelings of being on top of the world that alcohol produced were exhilarating. I remember thinking I didn't need any of the socially acceptable bench-marks of success. In fact, I didn't need society at all! All I really needed was a six-pack, and life was good.

By the time I was eighteen, I was a daily drinker. I had graduated from high school and had no ambition other than to drink a six-pack of beer and find a loose woman. I fell into a small job that paid me enough money to purchase a car. I spent my days working and my evenings drinking beer and working on my jalopy. About every third day, the car would be in good enough condition to cruise the local hot spots to look for girls. Occasionally, I would see some girls, and on a few occasions, I actually talked to them. This never did prove to be a successful strat-egy though. Eventually, I would get so drunk and obnoxious that the girls would flee, and I would retreat to my safe haven—the corner with my buddies.

I believe I crossed the line into alcoholism at the age of eighteen, when I decided to cast off all the wisdom and life principles that I'd been taught. It became apparent to me that everything I enjoyed doing or thought I might want to try was illegal, immoral, or unhealthy. It was the era of the early seventies, and the hippie thing was still in full bloom. The tune-in-turn-on-drop-out mentality was at its peak, and that kind of life was much more appealing than the get-a-job-go-to-church-and-be-a-responsible-person thing. I openly ridiculed anyone who was living a responsible life. Booze told me I was an undiscov-ered genius with insight into the workings of the world and the myster-ies of life. I thought I had all the answers, but I was simply slipping into alcoholism.

I bounced through a couple of jobs, taking my increasingly cynical and sarcastic attitude with me. I would make a good appearance and a favorable impression when applying for work, but as soon as I was hired, I would immediately gravitate to the resident drunkards and malcontents. They were my kind of folks. I was never fired from a job for drinking, but I did quit a few as soon as it became obvious to me that the bosses were not going make me a vice president.

Eventually, I started my own business—painting houses. I became president, vice president, sales and labor forces, and the biggest mo-rale problem a company ever had . . . I almost had to fire myself!

Now, a businessman has to have a Cadillac. Everyone knows that. But a painter also needs a truck. I invested $50 in a truck, and $1500 in a Cadillac. It made sense to me at the time. During one of my many cash-flow problems, I neglected to reregister the work truck. The police were not very understanding of my dilemma, and they towed the truck to the auto pound and set a $135 bounty on it. I decided to let them keep it. It became necessary to turn the Cadillac into a multipurpose vehicle. It was the truck by day and the businessman's car by night. What a sight it was . . . a 1968 Coupe de Ville with extension ladders tied to the roof, the back seat full of drop cloths, and the trunk full of paint. None of my customers ever told me that the sight of this caused them any apprehension, but I'd never let someone like that work on *my* house!

Somewhere along the way, I had started dating a neighborhood girl named Carol. She was (and still is) one of those wonderful people who alkies seem to find and take advantage of. She had a certain character defect that left her unable to resist my charms and allowed this relationship to continue: she thought she could "fix" me. She also had a talent for asking me these unanswerable questions—the most difficult being "Why do you drink so much?" My response was "It's my hobby," or "I come from a drinking family." I don't think she believed those responses any more than I did. I had already started to suspect that I was drinking too much, or incorrectly, but I was not willing to acknowledge that to anyone else.

As the amount of alcohol I consumed increased, my behavior became more unpredictable. Although I had been experiencing blackouts on a regular basis since the age of fifteen, they were now becoming more frequent, and they seemed to last longer. Oblivion is the best word I've heard to describe where booze took me. The feelings of comfort and ease that I had once obtained from a few drinks were a thing of the past. It seemed I went from being stark-raving sober to hideously drunk with no in-between. I had developed a knack for getting insanely drunk at the worst possible times. Every time I took the first drink, I turned my will and my life over to the booze. There seemed no escape from the madness of drinking other than the worse insanity of not drinking.

By September of 1976, I had made several attempts at getting my drinking under control. I was motivated by my feelings for Carol and her sincere expressions of concern for my well-being. I made heartfelt promises to her and to my parents that I now know I was incapable of keeping. With every broken vow, the remorse and guilt became more intense. I had a sense that I was on a collision course with Armageddon. My mind raced with terrifying thoughts of how and where it would happen. Feelings of doom were with me every moment.

On one occasion, I drank a fifth of whiskey and passed out in my car before three in the afternoon. When Carol arrived to collect me for a social event we were to attend, my mother cautioned her: "My son is a drunk, and I've seen them all my life. Save yourself a lot of heartache, and just go on with you life and forget about him." Now a person knows for sure they are a drunk when their own mother says so.

I faced the next day with that awful anxiety. I would receive a lecture from the old man, tears from Carol, and a general attitude of contempt from everyone. I figured a phone call to Carol would get the most painful part over with first. I was stunned, when she informed me that she was going to heed the advice of my mom. She also told me that she had talked to a relative who was a member of Alcoholics Anonymous, and he had given her similar warnings. Things were looking pretty grim. The remorse and guilt were unbearable. I had a sense that drinking was destroying anything good in my life. It was no longer a pleasurable activity; I needed it to function. I knew I had to stop, but how does one do this? I needed a drink.

After about three hours of drinking whiskey and beer, I was able to make a decision. I would call A.A. I would make the leap, take the plunge, bite the bullet, or whatever it was they did in A.A. I had to do something. I made the call. The fellow on the phone said he would take me to a meeting. I took a shower and then passed out. I awoke to the shouts of my brother saying that there were two guys at the door looking for me. He thought they were police detectives, but I immediately recognized them as "A.A. guys." I had seen that look before.

They took me to my first A.A. meeting, and there I heard a man tell his story. He talked of all the trouble his drinking had brought about and how the program of Alcoholics Anonymous had shown him the way to live a sober life and rectify the damage he had done. I came away with hope.

During the next week, I read the book *Alcoholics Anonymous* and attended six meetings. Although I was convinced that drinking was the cause of my troubles, I figured that this A.A. stuff was a little bit drastic in my case. After all, I was only twenty-four years old. I wanted an easier softer way—one that didn't include all this "God" stuff. So although I didn't drink for the next six months, I made no effort to apply the principles of A.A. to my life or attend A.A. meetings.

By the spring of 1977, things had greatly improved. Carol and I had set a wedding date; I had managed to get a good job; I had money in the bank; I had a car with good tires and current safety inspection; and I had regained enough arrogance to be dangerous to myself. I was sure that my decision to attend A.A. was made in haste. I was just having a run of bad luck back then. Life was good. The only thing that could make it absolutely perfect was a few beers to celebrate. I remembered reading in the A.A. book about "controlled drinking." I remember it saying that alkies can't do it. It said if a real alcoholic tries it, he eventually will be drinking as if he had never quit. The book does say that if one is not convinced that he is an alkie then, he should try some controlled drinking to find out. I decided to find out.

My first experiment was on a Tuesday. My associates were somewhat surprised that I would start drinking again. It was obvious to them that my recent good fortunes were a result of my abstinence from alcohol. They were convinced already. But I told them it was going to be different now. After all, I went to A.A. and learned all about this alcoholism stuff, and I knew what the warning signs were. I also proceeded to give them unsolicited advice regarding the way *they* were drinking. So I had my three beers, and other than Carol being mildly disappointed, there seemed to be no ill effects. Strike one.

My next experiment came the following Friday when I had three more beers. Carol was cautiously optimistic. I suffered no blackouts, no wrecked cars, and no emotional outbursts. Things were looking better than ever. Strike two.

My third and final experiment with controlled drinking came one week later, again on a Friday. What a wonderful thing it was. I'm not sure where the three-beer idea came from. I guess it just seemed like a civilized amount of drinks for a "normal" person to have. I have since realized that "normal" drinkers don't think about numbers of drinks at all. They just drink until they've had enough. Once again, the experiment was successful. I suffered none of the negative effects that drinking had caused me in the past. I was now convinced that my decision to quit drinking was made during a moment of weakness. I was sure I was OK in the drinking department. Strike three.

The next day found me drinking whiskey and beer and watching the Saturday morning cartoons at my favorite bar. I was drunk by noon. The next few months were a tortuous succession of attempts to regain control of my drinking. I tried to determine exactly which drink it was that sent me into a blackout. I tried jogging, reading, motorcycling, and working and eventually found myself going to prayer meetings and Bible studies—still looking for an easier softer way. I had friends who had become "social" drinkers after attending the prayer meetings. Now that sounded attractive to me, but it didn't work in my case. I actually seemed to drink more!

In August of 1977, I took myself back to Alcoholics Anonymous. I knew I could stop drinking if I went to A.A. meetings, but I was not happy about it. I started to believe what the folks in A.A. had told me about total abstinence being the only hope for a real alcoholic.

For the next year, I attended one A.A. meeting a week. I viewed attendance at A.A. meetings as a sort of penance. I had abused drinking and therefore had forfeited the privilege of drinking normally. I was restless, irritable, and discontent. I was full of self-pity, resentment, and fear, but I would be damned if I was going to succumb to all of this A.A. brainwashing nonsense. It seemed to me that these A.A. people were old, weak, or stupid. I was young, smart, and willful. Although I would admit that I had drank myself into a state that left me unable to maintain sobriety on my own, I refused to believe that I was so incapacitated that I needed all this Twelve Step stuff. It all looked too much like the stuff I learned in grade school and had encountered again at the prayer meetings. My biggest fear was that if I ever did actually do the Twelve Steps, I would turn into one of those self-righteous people that I so intensely despised.

By late September of 1978, I had married, bought a home, and was once again self-employed. I was, from all outward appearances, doing well once more. Inside my heart and head, however, was a different scene. I felt as though I was slipping into madness. I was overwhelmed by everyday life and baffled as to what to do about it. I knew drinking would be absolutely insane. Booze no longer held the promise of comfort and ease for me. I had not yet reached the point of becoming suicidal, but I sensed that that's where my mental state was leading.

The thought came to me that I might possibly be able to medicate myself to ease my tortured emotional and mental state. I was not wanting oblivion, just a little comfort. On three occasions, I ingested some prescription drugs that I was able to pilfer from various sources. It was like taking remorse pills. It became clear that whatever I was suffering from, medication was not a solution either. I was starting to resent the fact that because I really was different, I did not react to medication normally either. With my whole being, I resented the fact that I was unable to drink normally. I felt as though I was trapped in some hostile reality with no resources to do battle. I was consumed with self-pity and rage. I was once again at the jumping-off place.

It is customary at local A.A. meetings to read the first part of chapter five of the Big Book at the opening of every meeting. This reading includes the sentence "If you have decided that you want what we have and are willing to go to any length to get it, then you are ready to take certain steps." It was unclear to me exactly what it was that A.A. was selling. I knew going to meetings was somehow keeping me away from booze, and I was aware of the so-called "program of recovery" contained in the A.A. Twelve Steps. But I was sure the Twelve Steps were for the more desperate cases, and I was not one of them.

On October 1, 1978, I became willing to go to any length—I surrendered. My spirit and my will were broken. I stopped resisting the direction of the folks at the meetings. They were talking of serenity, and I had none. They claimed to be contented, and I was chronically agitated. They told me that they had been able to grasp a Power that enabled them to live purposeful and productive lives, while I had a sense that life was futile and meaningless. I had never disbelieved their claims; I just wasn't willing to become another brainwashed A.A. automaton.

Although I was not particularly enamored with what they promised, it looked better than what I had. I deduced that it was better to be a sober, contented—albeit brainwashed—A.A. robot than to continue as I was. I started to attend more meetings and to talk with men who seemed to have an outlook on life that I admired. They instructed me to read the A.A. Big Book and to apply the Twelve Steps in my daily life.

My A.A. mentors advised me that making a decision to attend and participate in the A.A. Fellowship on a regular basis effectively put me at Step Four. There was none of that admitting and accepting at a deeper level stuff with them. I set out making a list of persons toward whom I harbored resentment, and I proceeded to victimize anyone who would listen with my Fifth Step tales of frustrated adolescent sexual fantasy, petty thievery, and generally obnoxious behavior. I continued to do this until it became clear to me that my problems were of my own making.

It is said that Steps Six and Seven separate the men from the boys. I was not sure I wanted to ask God to remove all of these things called "character defects." Developing an awareness of how my self-centered motives negatively influenced my life was an unexpected and very annoying result of my ongoing inventories. I figured a little lust was good for my sex life; a little greed would help out my bank account, and so on. I learned, however, that any time my actions are based on self-serving motives, they never have the result I had intended; in most instances, they have negative effects far graver than I can imagine. I have come to believe that all areas in my life must be guided by Spiritual Principles. I became willing to ask God to remove my shortcomings.

I had this weird idea that if I asked God to remove my defects of character that He was actually going to do just that. It has not worked out that way for me. Through the Grace of God I have come to see that the attributes uncovered in my inventory are character defects only when used for self-serving purposes. For example, when we are shaky in the early days of sobriety, the best thing we can do is to try and help another alkie. It seems to me that the urge or obsession to drink can be defined as a character defect only if it causes me to drink. If the drinking impulse causes me to go out and help another alkie, then I don't know how I could call it a "defect." It is proof for me of how all things work toward good for those whose motivation is to serve God.

Before their deaths, I was able to make amends to my parents, and I am thankful. They were able to see the type of person I was working to become and were proud of my work. What a wonderful gift that was. I continue to take inventory, and it has become part of my nature to promptly admit when I am wrong. Promptly realizing that I am wrong is still problematical. To the degree that I seek through prayer and meditation to improve my contact with God, I am able to more quickly realize and accept my responsibility.

I experienced my first miracle when the compulsion to drink disappeared. I don't remember whether it was two days, two weeks, or two months; I just remember noticing one day that it was gone. As I proceeded to work my way through the Twelve Steps, I became connected to what they were calling the "Higher Power." This contact has become the primary purpose of my life today. I have come to believe that only things that are inspired by that Power will ultimately prove satisfying. The realm of the Spirit has become the true reality.

I have come to know the meaning of the word "serenity." I know serenity is a by-product of my being right with God and the people around me. Rigorous honesty is essential for my continued peace of mind and contentment. I understand the bits of wisdom that my elders gave me. I have reconnected with the faith of my family and my youth, and it has become a comforting influence in my life. I have been asked by my pastor to involve myself in church activities. He sees me as an asset to the congregation. What a change that is from my drinking days. The A.A. program has given me strength of character and an outlook and appreciation for the things in life that I used to take for granted.

I have been married to the same gal for more than twenty years. She has taken the A.A. program to heart and is my partner in this journey called life. God is included in every aspect of our lives. We persist in attempting to apply the A.A. way to all things and to share what we have found with others who might be interested. We have discovered a way of living that works for us. I would never have willingly chosen this way of life. It was the threat of certain destruction that caused me to seek a different way. I have seen how God is able to take the worst of all situations and turn them to Good if I continue to seek His Will. This miracle continues to unfold before me every day.

The Miracle

Joyce W.—Missouri

I was raised by respectable, responsible parents and had no excuse for the direction I chose in life. I had no one to blame. Yet somehow, I failed to develop adequate skills for coping with life's situations, both social and familial. I lacked the ability to form a true and honest relationship with anyone. From an early age, I felt detached from my peers, especially socially. Instead of forming a personal identity, I became a pro at role-playing. My most noteworthy roles included daughter, sister, student, friend, employee, neighbor, wife, and mother. I never knew quite how to feel about those roles or my performances, so I measured my morality by how others viewed what I did or didn't do.

Even my first marriage was an exercise in role-playing. I suffered from the Cinderella Syndrome: I met Prince Charming, married, had children, and believed we'd live "happily ever after." My error, as I see it today, was in thinking I had anything to bring to any relationship. Since I lacked a true identity, there was nothing to share—except the fear, which consumed me and manifested itself in many convoluted behaviors.

During high school, I had discovered alcohol relieved my overwhelming social stress. As soon as I experienced the ease, which came with a few drinks, I became dependent on that release, and no further emotional development occurred after that first drink. Drinking became as much a part of my life as eating and bathing. It was automatically scheduled into every activity of my life from that moment on. I became a heartbreak and humiliation to those who loved me. I was vaguely aware of this, but alcohol had a way of activating denial and blinding me to reality. I had no idea how to live, how to feel, how to act, or how to be without drinking.

Today, I view myself as a prodigal daughter. Before I began drinking, I was given many treasures: youth, intelligence, beauty, opportunity, hopes, and dreams. I took these treasures out into the world and squandered them all. Then—when all was gone, and I was desperate to find something to live for—it occurred to me that I should try to stop drinking. It was alcohol, I figured, that had taken everything from me.

I had certainly lost many friends. I'd become a problem at my job and because I was such a poor influence on my children, my parents took them from me. Days and weeks ran together, and I neglected to eat. I was admitted to the hospital on several occasions for malnutrition and emotional/mental breakdowns and treated for several conditions associated with prolonged chemical abuse. I lost my self-respect and the respect of others; I lost my confidence, hopes, and dreams. I lost the will to live.

Some nights I was so desperately lonely that I tried to call old friends or family members, but they soon detected my level of intoxication and asked me to call when I wasn't so drunk. Some even asked me to stop calling all together. When that first happened, I was filled with rage, then confusion and despair. It seemed there was nowhere to turn. I was terrified of dying, and, at the same time, I couldn't imagine living even one more day. I was against the wall, so to speak, and tormented by the Four Horsemen mentioned in the Big Book: terror, bewilderment, frustration, and despair.

Driven by the mental anguish of my present and the overwhelming guilt of what I had become, I was squarely faced with a decision: either take my own life, or stop drinking. I had no idea how difficult life would be without alcohol, but I was ready to try. At that moment, I was willing to do anything necessary to avoid taking even one more drink. It was Sunday, January 17, and as my blurry eyes focused on a Christmas tree, I couldn't remember if Christmas was coming or past! I realized there were young children calling me "mother," and I had no recollection of how that came about! My decision was made. From that day to this, I have never taken another drink. My first day without alcohol was a good one. I had the sense I was doing something right, and that sustained and elated me all day long. I called my parents to inform them of my decision and ask if they'd help me.

Sometime in the next twenty-four hour period, I slipped into severe D.T.s. Doctors in the emergency room told me that I was seriously toxic and probably alcoholic; they said there was nothing they could do for me. They said I needed A.A. Geez! What a diagnosis! How could I be alcoholic? After all, I hadn't had a drink for nearly two days! I was positive they'd misunderstood and overlooked some serious physical problems. They suggested I go to a meeting near the hospital, and I did. After listening to some of the people there, I was equally positive I was alcoholic.

I had no idea alcoholism was a malady that included so many symptoms—other than drinking. As I listened to others describe their loneliness, their inability to stop after the first drink, their feelings of inadequacy and inferiority until taking a few drinks, I was fascinated by the similarities. I was overcome with hope and felt comforted to finally meet others who'd had all those same feelings I'd had all my life—the terminally uniqueness, the feeling of impending doom, the combined depression and anxiety, and the fear that I couldn't stop drinking. Wow, these were my people.

And when I finally began reading the Big Book . . . eureka! Here was my story, told by others just like me. I wanted what these people had. I wanted it now. Unlike some people I've known, I didn't have to struggle with the diagnosis. I was immediately overcome with gratitude to learn there was a solution to the painful and destructive way of life I'd been living. And it was free! I've heard some say it took courage for them to walk through the doors of A.A.. For me, it took desperation and having nowhere else to go. A.A. was the "last house on the block." And what wonderment: it turned out to be the home I'd been looking for all my life. I was welcomed with open arms and open hearts; they loved me before they even knew me, and they forgave me even before my errors were revealed. Yes, I must have this thing.

As I approached the Steps, they didn't seem unreasonable or difficult. After all, I had already admitted that I was completely powerless over alcohol and that my life was wildly out of control. Nevertheless, I had a lingering compulsion to escape reality or to knock the edge off the intense feelings I was experiencing. I wasn't accustomed to dealing with these feelings without alcohol. I was either morbidly depressed, or ecstatically elated, and often couldn't differentiate between the two. I needed to reprogram my thinking and learn to correctly and comfortably experience all my emotions.

As I approached Step Two, vague images were conjured from my past about God: the Ten Commandments, Sunday school clothes, sin, hell, but absolutely nothing spiritual. Little barriers went up. It seemed odd to me that a room full of people could speak of God and dependence on Him while chain smoking and profanely describing the hair-raising escapades of their drinking pasts. Surely, I thought, they didn't understand God or the proper way to view Him. I believed there was a God, but I just wasn't "righteous" enough to think seriously about Him.

I was reserving any actual contact with God or Higher Power until I could get myself better situated, but each moment without alcohol became more uncomfortable. Then the fear that this program wouldn't work for me would cause a knot in my gut and stark terror of where to turn next. I'd run to an A.A. meeting just to be in a "safe zone." I even tried to make the decision required in Step Three, which of course was impossible until I'd fully grasped and begun to apply Step Two.

My life was like a trickling stream of fresh water, constantly being fed by tributaries (age and life experiences). As I progressed through life, my character defects became little pebbles in the stream of my life. As time went on, certain experiences caused more unnatural flowing and eventually resulted in a blockage. The flowing river was now a pool that had no outlet and no direction. It began to stagnate and ferment, and the complexion of the surface changed and obscured the waters. I was a most unattractive and angry mass of miserable life!

Sobriety and the lack of an anesthetic to dull life's pain became so unbearable that I sought escape from the mental anguish and fear. This is the point I began to define the Second Step. Came to believe—arrived at a point of faith and trust. A power greater than myself—something that could accomplish what I could not. Could restore—has the capacity and inclination to mend or make new. Me—this affects me personally. To sanity—to a rational state or soundness of mind. And that's exactly what I needed. I was definitely unreasonable, irrational, and out of control. I was eager to tap into this source of power. But where and how to find it? Could this program be speaking of the same God I'd been exposed to as a child? The One of judgment and condemnation . . . the One who gave commands . . . the One who might exact rigid behavior . . . and yet the One who was love? It seemed a monumental undertaking indeed for me to call on such a God. It was only later that I realized why the Big Book speaks of a "simple concept." At this point, I became willing to accept God as a realistic and personal source of power accessible to me, rather than the obscure and unreachable entity I'd envisioned as a child. This realization enabled me to let go and place my will and my life in His care.

I was eager to begin on Step Four after I made the Third Step decision. It's apparent that a decision is not made until acted upon—which means, of course, doing the dreaded Step Four. I had begun to study the book in earnest but couldn't find anyone who could explain to me exactly how to make contact with, and get plugged into, this Higher Power or how to complete a moral inventory. But I firmly believed these things must be done, or I would drink again.

I celebrated my first year sober with much fanfare, of course. My sponsor was beaming, and I was congratulated. On the 366th day of sobriety, however, I felt let down and knew deep in my heart that I had made no forward progress in the program of recovery. Much more was required on my part.

After eighteen months clean and sober, I went to see a doctor and told him I was alcoholic but was unable to sleep. The old hustle came naturally. If only I had something for sleep, just for a little while, I just knew I'd make it in A.A. I never mentioned to the doctor that I was also a drug abuser. So he prescribed sleeping medication. It was not the kind I wanted, so I told him I thought I remembered having an allergy to that particular medication in the past. He asked me what I had taken before that worked. Just the question I was waiting for! I told him I "thought" it was Placidyl. (Heck, I knew what it was!) So, I left with a prescription and three refills. Then, I proceeded to visit two more doctors and get similar prescriptions from each using the same "hustle." I didn't take the medication right away. I was saving it as a cushion, in case the Steps were too hard. And I anticipated they would be.

I had a stash of twelve bottles of 500mg. Placidyl! I felt ten feet tall and bulletproof. I would get them out, look at them, smell them, and think about taking just one. Then, I stopped eating; this way when I did take one, the pills would hit me with the full impact. It was a firm plan. I knew an overdose would rescue me from looking at myself and discovering the hideous creature I'd become.

The night I took the first one I sat down at the table with all the bottles, a glass of hot water, and an empty stomach. About ten minutes later—when the drug kicked in—I took two more. Then two more. I took five total in about thirty minutes. The instant the effect kicked in, I didn't want to stop—I couldn't. After all, I didn't want to go through D.T.s again.

The very next day, I contacted a doctor who had supplied large quantities of the drug for me in the past. He had a brand-new bottle of

Placidyl—500 capsules at 750mg. each—and just gave them to me. My distorted brain told me God had answered my prayer: I was supposed to take them all. My plan took twenty-six days to unfold. I shopped for gifts for the kids, wrapped them, and put them under the bed. I got my hair done. I completely cleaned the house and got all my affairs in order. I was very calm and not the least bit sad with my decision. I continued to abuse the 500mg capsules until they were gone, not realizing I had forgotten to go to work!

The night I had planned to die, I put the kids to bed, took a bath, applied fresh makeup, and chose the new nightgown I would die in. I sat down at the table with my housemate (a young girl with no place to stay) and explained my plan. She cried and begged me to change my mind. She threatened to call the police or my parents. But I convinced her that my plan would be carried out . . . if not that night, then the next. But I would do it. She promised to put my kids on the school bus the next morning and go to work without opening the door to my room. She agreed to call my sponsor about 10:00 a.m. so he could take steps to have me removed from the house before the kids came home from school and then contact my family. I took a pitcher of hot water, a glass, and a 500-count bottle of Placidyl into my bedroom and locked the door. Because they are large and hard to swallow, I took the capsules a few at a time. After sixty capsules, I lay down and prayed myself to sleep.

I have only vague memories of the phone ringing, and my next recollection is hearing a man's voice (a man who was putting me on a hard table in the E.R. of a hospital) saying, "Please don't let this woman die." Apparently, I had become comatose and didn't metabolize most of the drug. When the phone rang, I must have realized I wasn't dead yet and took several more capsules. I was in a coma for nearly four days. I had lost thirty pounds in twenty-six days. The doctors didn't know if I'd recover from the extensive damage. I was in the hospital for seven weeks and only ambulatory for the last week.

After I was moved from critical care into my own room, a nurse came and asked if I'd like sleeping medication. I knew, then, any mind-altering chemical was exactly like alcohol, and I was determined to live and to live free. The nurse reassured me that declining the medication would not make me die; perhaps I'd want to die and feel I was dying, but I would not die. I declined medication, and she stayed the night to watch.

After the lights were out and all was quiet in the corridor—as I lay crying with tears crackling in my ears, knots in my stomach and legs, and a muddled and confused mind—I began to pray. I was angry that I had survived and was left to face myself (and yet another failure at exercising my will). I heard someone say my name very softly. I saw no one and chalked it up to my own insanity. As I continued to plead with God for answers, I heard the voice again. I sat up and looked around the room . . . nobody was there. I felt strangely warm but a little alarmed. I sat on the edge of the bed long enough to convince myself I was lucid and not half asleep. I took a drink of water and lay down once again. I began to pray again with more desperation than before. For the first time in my life, I was praying with actual belief. Not only did God exist but He had somehow thwarted my plan to die. "God, why can't I die?" I demanded.

Then, the voice came a third time, firm and clear. I got out of bed, walked to the door of the room, and looked up and down the corridor but saw no one. Suddenly, I knew who was speaking my name. It was as though He was there in the room with me, and as I turned back into the room, I asked my question again. The answer came in a firm, but gentle voice. He said, "Because, it's not time yet." Relief came at once. This brief exchange was so real, so very intimate. It was then that I flung myself into the waiting arms of God, and I've held firmly to that moment ever since. It was then that I realized I wanted my life and will to be in the care of God. It was then that my faith began to grow. I was ready and prepared to move forward into recovery with the Twelve Steps, and until then, it had been impossible.

I had a spiritual awakening much like awakening from a deep sleep. First came the awareness, then the alertness, then activity. From that moment, my life changed completely! If I was to live, I could not ever take another mind altering chemical into my body. Something happens when I do: I try to kill myself! After my failed attempt, I had no choice but to put each moment into the care of a God who had made Himself known to me by His intervention. His presence and power were no longer disputable or obscure. It was real.

Once I was out of critical care, a friend came to see me and brought with him a page torn from a book. It read, "Sometimes, God, like the rescuer of a drowning man, must render that man helpless, in order to save him." I had certainly been saved, and my old concept of God had been smashed. I met God squarely, and the reality of His power and

His presence entered my life, my mind, and my heart. His power began to do for me what I could not do for myself.

I suffered from a fatal malady, which had already caused much personal tragedy and heartbreak, and I was eager to stop the progression immediately and begin the recovery process. It seemed to me there was a critical time-element involved here, but some kept telling me to "take my time." The Big Book (and the method of embracing and applying the principles used on "A.A. Number Three") does not suggest a leisurely pace. Time after time I was learning that those who had recovered had not wasted time, but had diligently pushed on in the Steps. With pen and paper in hand, I set out to find someone to help me understand this "moral inventory." I didn't need to emphasize "fearless"; I was terrified of not making this inventory. It became clear to me that I had an inherent knowledge of right and wrong, but my drinking had distorted and corrupted those morals.

I wanted to find the right path, jump on it, and walk strongly and confidently into recovery. I wanted to rid myself of the demons inside me. I approached a few people whom I believed had a grasp of the program and an admirable way of life. Each time, however, I was shocked and dismayed to hear "I hadn't actually written it down," or "It is between me and God," or "I'm working on it and haven't finished it yet," or worst of all, "Maybe you're not ready for this Step yet." So, I turned inward and resolved to do this thing on my own with God's help. I opened the dictionary again and commenced to meditate on "moral." I already understood that an inventory was a written list of everything about me, but moral? So I began to make a list of all the things I believed deeply in my heart and soul were right and wrong between God and me.

Until this commission to paper, I only considered right and wrong as dictated by the legal authorities, the religious leaders, the patriarchs of my family, and the influence of society and culture. As I wrote, however, I began to understand that without God, there are no moral issues. I realized why the Big Book writers had written a book which was "spiritual as well as moral," and "it means of course, that we're going to talk about God." Why couldn't the people in meetings just tell me this? Perhaps it was God's will that I should study the book, meditate, and come to understand for myself. At any rate, that's exactly what I did. While committing myself to a code of morals, I was building a foundation for my personal recovery and a methodology that would be necessary in order to apply Step Ten—when I reached that point. As this "personality/ character" profile of myself began to develop before my eyes, my mind was busy recalling all the many ways I'd violated my own beliefs and standards.

The word "honesty" became vitally operative, and I was elated to learn I could mend these flaws in my character and recover from this insidious condition with God's help. While developing my own understanding of Step Four, I first needed to commit to certain standards and then focus on how my behavior violated them. This process went hand-in-hand with the "admission of my grosser handicaps" and forming a new list of the defects in my character. I needed to differentiate between "moral inventory" (the list of my defects), "nature of my wrongs" (genus, beginning, or seed), "shortcomings" (how these wrongs caused me to fall short of my own standards), and "defects of character" (flaws or imperfections in my character development). They are four distinctly different terms, each describing something different! I won't attempt to suggest another's moral structure or point to any specific defects in anyone else. These vital applications are very personal, intimate, and definitely individual.

After I'd thoroughly listed my moral standards and begun to write down all the times my behavior was in conflict with those standards, I had a better idea of what my defects were. I noticed that the same moral wrongs were committed time after time only with different players and varying results. I also noticed my underlying defects were almost always fear and selfishness. I imagined a tree with the taproot being fear and the trunk being selfishness. From the trunk, many branches depicting various other defects (such as greed, jealousy, guilt, and vengeance) leafed out in hundreds of other ways. And the fruit of this tree? It was rotten. Under the tree, there was a pile of broken relationships, lost hopes, and withered dreams, and the tree was ugly.

When I approached the woman who would hear my Fifth Step, I had identified and labeled the "nature" of the majority of my wrongs. She helped me label and accept the others by sharing with me how she identified her own defects. And you know what? None of this was nearly as difficult or frightening as I'd heard some say in meetings. In fact, it was most enlightening and relieving to learn I wasn't an evil person, just someone who hadn't developed proper coping skills or practiced any kind of self-analysis. Instead of admitting my wrongs, I had defended my actions and rationalized my behavior.

During my Fifth Step discussion, I saw a completely different person than I ever dreamed I was or ever wanted to become. In addition, this inventory resulted in a list of people who'd been harmed by my behavior, and some amends were in order. Steps Four and Five introduced me to myself for the first time in my life, and I noticed the fear was beginning to slip away. As a matter of fact, I was feeling pretty darned confident that I could realize some of the "promises" of this program.

The promises began to materialize during the inventory process. I knew a new happiness, and the new freedom from alcohol was making me stronger and more resolved every day. I did comprehend the word serenity, and my moments of peace increased. I was entirely ready (meaning not only prepared but also willing) to have God remove all these defects of character. As I approached Step Seven, I realized He'd always been aware of my shortcomings. He just wanted me to know and be willing to let Him remove these damaging and undesirable things from me. As I knelt—fully prepared to let go of all these things and knowing how many they were and how helpless I was to change—I actually felt humility for the first time ever. I'd made a mess of my life: I'd squandered all my treasures, spent all my personal resources, and was emotionally bankrupt, helpless, and very much ashamed. At that moment, I felt worthy somehow. I felt relieved and grateful for being afforded such an opportunity to present my sorry self to the God who'd loved me, provided for me, and protected me all those years. I know He always knew the truth about my actions and me. I imagined He must have looked very sad and distressed at some of my decisions and actions in my past. But at that moment—in my mind's eye—God was smiling, and I smiled too. I was ready to go out, find those I'd harmed, and try to set things right. I wasn't afraid. I knew I'd be making payments on this tremendous debt of gratitude I owed to God and Alcoholics Anonymous—a program I believe He inspired.

I had my list of those to whom I owed amends; I'd made it in Steps Four and Five. It is important not only to apologize but also to actually verbalize what humiliating defect in my character motivated me to harm another person. By making this admission, it certainly helped me to prevent having to repeat this repair process again. Perhaps others didn't find it necessary to apply Step Nine in that manner, but it was helping me to focus a more accurate picture of what I'd been like and allowed me to include my wish to change. And by doing this, I was making direct amends to myself. My progress accelerated when I studied the Big Book and other A.A. literature. I had to stop depending on people in meetings (who were, perhaps, sicker than I) and begin to seek the information from the sources others had used to recover.

In attempting to make direct amends, I discovered my ego was still allowing me to believe that I'd done great harm to many people. When I approached some of these people, I discovered that at the time of my ugly behavior—when my motive was purely evil and I'd acted out in a most unacceptable manner—the incident was viewed completely differently by others involved. My ego was undergoing further alteration. I was shocked and often humiliated to learn that I'd appeared as a pathetic drunk and was laughed at when I approached some of the people on my list. I was learning that the damage done to others was not nearly as great as the damage I'd done to myself. Still, I had to exercise discretion and prudence, especially concerning incidents that would cleanse my conscience at someone else's expense. Other times, I learned that the best amends I could make was to leave people alone!

When I'd finished my amends as best I could, I moved onto Step Ten feeling confident: I was aware of my major difficulties, and God was helping me become more suitable for relationships of all kinds. Since all my needs were being satisfied by Him, I was no longer accompanied by those Four Horsemen. I became emotionally stable, and gratitude replaced the anxiety and depression I'd lived with most of my life.

Steps Ten, Eleven, and Twelve have become a way of life for me. Cleaning up the messes I created in life made it simple and easy to apply these Steps on a daily basis. Of course, there are moments in the day when I'm agitated or irritated, but that's something that can be repaired immediately as long as I stay in "practice." I've also come to understand that the phrase "when we were wrong" allows me to make alterations and additions to the original moral commitments I made in Step Four. For me, this is spiritual growth. I open the gift of each new sober day with thanks and a request for God to walk with me through the day, showing me the way of patience, tolerance, kindliness, and love and guiding me to do His will.

Step Eleven suggests I improve my conscious contact with God through prayer and meditation. I prayed "for the knowledge of His will for us and the power to carry that out." How simple that is! I no longer have to decide what God wants me to do, or when and how. I've come to know that His will—even though at times may seem unjust—always works out best for all concerned. His timetable can't be improved upon. I've found surrendering to God's will and depending on Him has made me strong.

Today, I feel like a child of God. He is the parent, and I'm the child. He takes care of all my needs while I participate in His plans. This is a new freedom and brings me much happiness. When faced with a decision or a baffling situation, I read the St. Francis prayer and reflect back on page eighty-six of the Big Book, asking that my thinking be divorced from self-pity, dishonest or self-seeking motives. When I do this, I find the right action or decision has already been made. When I honestly identify my motive in a thought or action, there is no decision to be made but rather a right or wrong thing to do or say. And when viewed in that manner, what can else my decision be?

The last Step offers the loudest and most effective message of all: "to carry this message to alcoholics and to practice these principles in all our affairs." The way I live my life—the decisions I make, my compatibility with others, and my sane and calm behavior in all areas of life—is a demonstration to all that the miracle of recovery exists. It's much easier to think and act rationally while in an A.A. meeting, and I like to shine like an A.A.-star while sharing on a topic, either from the podium or one-to-one with a newcomer. But it serves me well to keep in mind that there are vast numbers of suffering alcoholics who are not in A.A. and may be reaching out for help. I want to be vigilant and prepared to sparkle and shine as an example to anyone, anywhere, who may be looking for a way out of a seemingly hopeless sea of alcoholism.

Living along the guidelines suggested for recovery and adhering to my own code of ethics has taken the wrinkles out of my face, the knot out of my stomach, and the conflict out of my mind. For all my years alive, I find the A.A. way "the easier, softer way."

Jail Was a Disguise in Blessing

Doug B.—Southlands

For the first couple days, they kept me in an infirmary cell with an epileptic. My mind was in a daze—this being my first day of sobriety—but I dimly wondered why I was in the infirmary instead of the jail proper. Certainly, I wasn't about to complain. I was too thankful the judge decided I only needed a little jail time, not a long prison term.

Right then, I decided to make the best of this first opportunity to finally, at last, break free of forty years of bondage to the bottle. My first son was an epileptic, so I knew what to do when the other prisoner fell down in fits. He was a most unsavory and unfriendly human being, foulmouthed and unappreciative. Thankfully he was a loner and kept to his end of the room. Each time he had a fit, I'd tap on the unbreakable plastic panel that served as a window to summon a guard or nurse, and we'd help the guy. This happened several times each day, so bad was his epilepsy.

After a couple days, my mind cleared enough for me to inquire of the guard, "Why am I in the infirmary?"

"Suicide watch," he replied.

I broke out laughing. It seems this convinced them it was safe to let me out into the jail population. The institutional wisdom of the jail was to put every drunk in the infirmary first to sober up and get over the first couple days of the shakes, a dangerous time for any alcoholic.

A guard marched me down one long corridor after another until we reached a big room where I was assigned a twelve-by-six foot cell with a view of a pine forest beyond the wire-topped, chain-link fence. How thankful I was to see trees, for they made it easier to imagine my cell was a cabin in the woods. I would not have minded staying there the entire time, so nice it was to see trees and birds.

But I was urged to come out and mingle with the other prisoners. What energy! Everywhere men were releasing a tremendous store of energy, doing exercises, and working out with weights made by slipping a broom handle through the handles of mop buckets full of water. Even card games were played with much gusto and energy; the guys preferred to play standing up so they could spin more force to their playing, slamming down cards with an air of "There!" It was a fearsome sight for an old man among powerful young bodies, but for the most part, they were all kind to me.

Later, a jail job took me into the "dungeons" where they kept the dangerous criminals, the real sociopaths. It was a frightening experience! I never again want to look in the eyes of a real sociopath. It chills one to the bone.

Most of the prisoners were there for the same reason I was: run-ins with the law stemming from their alcoholism or drug addiction. All that energy came from the restlessness brought forth by withdrawal. It was not until much later I realized the sociopaths who were locked up in deep cells were a much more relaxed lot than the prisoners I was in contact with! I was so restless that I paced out the distance around the big room. It was one-fourteenth of a mile, so I began a daily routine of a mile walk after cleaning up after each meal. In the six months I was in jail, I lost forty pounds!

Yes, the food was horrible. Fortunately, they allowed us to buy fourteen candy bars each week, and I was able to trade my meals for apples and oranges from other prisoners. The only other edible foods were the dry cereals with milk and bologna sandwiches. Freshly roasted chicken at Thanksgiving, Christmas, and New Year's Day were just about the only full meals I enjoyed during my time.

The turning point for me was the sight of the wet brains. I was in this vast area where the inmates are housed for only a week before the prison guards and warden noticed my love of work and transferred me on to the trustee wing. One man spent entire days preaching to a bare wall, bible open in hand; he could see a congregation where no one else could see. He would've made a great preacher, if not for his wet brain—the term for the final phase of mental deterioration in the progression of the disease of alcoholism. He was certainly zealous about his religion. But it was the sight of one man tiptoeing around, his eyes wide with terror at the sight of snakes on the bare floor, that convinced me I must never take another drink.

Luck was with me—there was an opening for a helper in the jail library! There I found the Big Book. The sight of the wet brains had already primed me to seek a solution to my alcoholism. I read through it twice and convinced myself that I was indeed an alcoholic and that my disease was serious enough that I should never take another drink. I did not realize it at the time, but after reading the "Doctor's Opinion" and "More About Alcoholism," I already completed the First Step. I had known for years that I had a drinking problem, and I thought of myself as a stinking drunk. The pages of the Big Book showed the true nature of my problem: that it is a disease that held me helpless in its power. The chapter entitled "There Is A Solution" even provided me with a name for the kind of drunk I was, a Dr. Jekyll and Mr. Hyde, and brought me face-to-face with the fact that I needed a Higher Power to help me out of this insanity.

Dear God! Now I have to believe in You! I never accepted the concept of a mean, petty, and small-minded God, but somehow, somewhere in the deep recesses of my mind persisted a notion that nature was too wonderfully designed for there to be no Creator. My training was in the sciences, and I was familiar with the inner workings of nature and how everything intertwined so that the Earth became a living, breathing being in and of itself. There has to be a God behind all this wonder. Yet, I could never quite get it all together, so the concept of God remained vague and unformed in my mind. I often joked to myself that if the Christians were right, I would eventually come face-to-face with my Maker. I had a ready excuse: "What can I say? I was drunk all these years, God. . . ."

So technically, I was an agnostic and read "We Agnostics" with the intense interest of a man who knew he had to find a Higher Power, if he was ever to get well. Even then, my concept of God remained vague and formless. Somehow, I became spiritual before I knew it. At least I had somebody to talk with during the frequent opportunities for meditation that jail certainly provided. Though I did not realize it at the time, God was right within me the whole time!

The job with the library took me into all areas of the jail, where I saw the terrible effects of alcohol and drugs on otherwise fine people. The lies, the denials, the delusions, the hopelessness, the degradation, and the despair could not mask the deep yearning I could discern from the books and magazines they picked from the book cart. The most popular were the romances! Even burly men liked them. Other favorites were the fables, fantasies, and even good literature. The most popular magazines proved to be of the home and gardens variety! Many of these people never had a good home. Only in the deep cells of the hardened criminals were crime stories popular. Most chilling was their fondness for anything about Jack the Ripper, Ted Bundy, and other celebrated mass murderers and predators.

Before I knew it, my growing spirituality got me withholding women's magazines from the men. You see, women's magazines were very popular among the men and for selfish reasons; the underwear advertisements and the perfume samples were a big turn-on for lonely men. Female inmates housed in other areas of the prison were not allowed to work in the library, so they depended on male library workers for their reading material. Ah, the library workers held a power over the other inmates and enjoyed a scam where they could trade women's magazines for candy bars and the like. By the time the men were finished with women's magazines, they were torn and a big disappointment to the women who received them.

I did not realize it at the time, but the reading of "We Agnostics" had already got me submitting to God's will. Even the librarian seemed to notice, for he made me responsible for unpacking new magazines and seeing to their timely distribution among the jail populace. I hid the women's magazines in a store room until the day the cart was scheduled to go into the women's area. What can I say? God made me do it. I had unwittingly begun to apply the Third Step in my program.

Actually, I had already taken the Third Step when time came to face the judge and surrender to his judgment. I prayed to whatever God was out there, saying that I would take my medicine like a man and accept whatever the state decided. Never mind that I have no memory of anything that happened during my blackouts, I still made a deal with God that I would go along with whatever plan He had in mind. He certainly kept his end of the bargain. He saw to it the library had a Big Book. It was up to me to read it, and read it I did.

By the time I reached "How It Works," I knew alcohol had brought me to the door of death and disgrace, and I had full faith that the program would give me back my life. I knew the nature of my disease would never allow me to take another drink again in my life, and that I had to RECOVER, if I was ever going to enjoy the rest of my life. I thought I had only a few years remaining in my life, due to the damages alcohol had inflicted on my body, and was determined to make those few years the best of my life. So it was with eagerness I began the moral inventory of the Fourth Step. It was the first time I had consciously begun a Step and actually worked one.

There being no A.A. program in that jail and no other inmates who seemed interested, the Fifth Step could not be fully completed until I got out of jail, but my inventory was complete. I was ready for God to remove most of my flaws and defects. Already I sensed them melting away, as promised in the Big Book. I did not know it at the time, but I had already subconsciously completed the Sixth and Seventh Steps.

The Fourth Step is a ready basis for doing the Eighth and Ninth Steps, the making of amends. I immediately wrote letters to everyone I could think of at the time. One stumbling block was my resentment at my last wife, which I handed over to God to hold for me so I could get on with my recovery. I know someday He will let me know when it is time to take care of that issue in the way He thinks best. By then, I was already doing the Tenth and Eleventh Steps every day, and the Twelfth had to wait 'til I got out in the world.

At long last, after six months, I walked out into a beautiful winter day, looked back, and said a silent thank you. Never once since have I felt any desire to drink, but still need the fellowship of A.A. and the daily practice of Steps Ten through Twelve to learn how to handle feelings that I had sought to drown in drink in the far distant past.

The Lost Child

Jackie A.—California

Growing up in a family of seven children was not easy. My father was a functioning alcoholic and a drug addict; he always worked and provided for his family but was physically and sexually abusive. My mother was a co-dependent, trying to raise her seven children and her husband alone. Our home was full of chaos; there were no clear-cut directions on how to handle problems. Instead, we usually met tough situations with anger and hostility—a traditional dysfunctional response. Most of our problems became family secrets, and there wasn't much of a chance to resolve them.

To my family, God was a fleeting thought at best. There was no prayer, no Bible study, and no church. God simply didn't have any part of our lives—until my uncle asked my dad to play softball for a church team. My father had played semiprofessional baseball in the 1950s and played for several community teams. In order to play for this team, he had to attend church three weeks a month. And if he had to go to church, he planned on taking the entire family hostage. We had to go with him. I was about nine or ten years old.

Life started to change a little. The pastor visited and talked to my parents. He prayed in our house and with my parents. The chaos and dysfunction calmed down a little. There didn't seem to be as much yelling, screaming, or fighting. I looked forward to going to church on Sundays. There, I felt safe and peaceful.

The Sunday school teachers encouraged us to spend a few minutes each day alone with God and to talk with Him as we would anyone else. They said He understood us. But being alone with God was difficult in my house; with seven children and two parents, we didn't have much "alone" time. But I did try. That is how I learned to pray, to talk

101

to God. It seemed as though He only listened during the day: my dad was still drinking and abusive at night.

I don't remember how long my dad played for that team, but I do know it was long enough for some of us to get to know God. Then, we moved to New Mexico. This was difficult for me because I saw that the hope for my family was lost. We went back to being the family we were before going to church. Not only did we go back to being that family; things got worse.

My dad's drinking increased, and he added moonshine to the beer and liquor. He was out of control, and the abuse became unbearable. I hated that place but could not escape it. I wondered why God didn't help me. The very people who were supposed to teach me trust and goodness did terrible things to me. I prayed for someone to help.

When we moved, I met my great-grandparents; they were in their late seventies and were very religious people. I started going to church with them and spending all my time with them—all the time my parents would allow. But that didn't last long either. We moved back to California in two years. I was twelve then, and the sexual abuse seemed to just stop. I hoped all other bad things in our home would stop too.

I started junior high school and met some new friends. School was much different in California than in New Mexico. It was the late 1960s or early 1970s, and everything moved much faster. I grew up in a matter of months: I wore makeup, dated boys, and experimented with drugs and alcohol. And I found it—the "solution" to all my problems. Since I couldn't drink and use drugs and serve God at the same time, I decided to give up on God. Besides, I figured He had already given up on me. I was doomed anyway; I believed I was a dirty, used child who had no right to ask Him for anything.

I was a full-blown alcoholic and drug addict by fourteen, and I didn't stop until I walked into the doors of Alcoholics Anonymous on March 7, 1981. I was then twenty-six years old and had two children. I had done most of the things that alcoholic, drug-addicted women did in those days. More than ever, I felt lost and didn't know how to survive. I wanted a better life for my children. I didn't want to do to them what my parents had done to me.

My last drunk started on March 5th of that year. As I came out of a blackout, some people were taking my kids and my car to my parents' house and yelling at me. I stumbled into their house to find a beer. (I was living with them.) My father came into the kitchen and suggested that I go to a hospital or to an A.A. meeting. Ironically, he probably saved my life that night. I know I needed help, yet I left the house and headed to the liquor store. When I came back, I sat on the curb and asked one more time for God to hear my prayer for help.

I went to my first Alcoholics Anonymous meeting on a March 7, my first day sober. I felt so out of place, so different. I remember they prayed and told me to keep coming back. I did not know I was an alcoholic, but I knew I was in trouble. Some people introduced themselves and welcomed me to the meeting. I was scared to death. They didn't ask me if I was alcoholic, only if I was new. I could deal with that. They talked about what God did for them and about the Big Book. I was both afraid and amazed, but I bought the book and started to read it. I looked forward to meetings. It was the rest of the week that was hard.

At my fourth meeting, a man sat down next to me, introduced himself, and asked if I was an alcoholic. I didn't know. He asked if I had a Big Book, and I explained that I had one but couldn't understand it. Then, he offered to help me. I am so grateful for that individual. God just seemed to bring a teacher when I needed one. I started to study the book once a week with this gentleman.

At once, I knew I was an alcoholic. God instantly revealed my disease to me. I was not a bad person; I was a lost child who had a disease called alcoholism. It was not hard to see at all. Once I became willing to be open-minded, God brought me hope and help. I set about trying to get well. The book started to make sense, and I started to find myself in the words on the pages.

Soon, I became frustrated and angry. I wanted answers and felt that God wasn't listening to me. I talked to Him the only way I knew how: I talked, yelled, and cried to God to make me well. I would throw my book across the room, only to have to get it and try again. If there really is a God, why didn't he save me as a child? Why did I have to go through all this? I don't want to be an alcoholic, an addict, a child of an alcoholic, a survivor, and who knows what else. I wanted to just belong somewhere, to go to college, to do something with my life.

This was a difficult task, considering I was only talking to newcomers in the Fellowship. We didn't have any answers, but we gave our opinions to each other on a regular basis. Eventually, I realized I couldn't get better if I didn't change the people I associated with in the rooms of Alcoholics Anonymous.

Old-timers often said, "When the pupil is ready, the teacher will appear." I have had many teachers in Alcoholic Anonymous. Some were good, and some were bad. I needed them all. They all taught me the things God wanted me to know—how to stay sick or how to live life; how I could help others when I thought I had nothing to offer; and how I could be of service in meetings by washing coffee cups, mopping floors, making coffee, and cleaning toilets. God did give me the answers to my questions, and I almost missed them.

It was my sponsor, Judy, who taught me the three basics in Alcoholics Anonymous: study the Big Book, go to meetings on a regular basis, and work the Steps of recovery. She introduced me to the Steps and told me they are to be done in order. I was asked to imagine climbing a ladder with one foot on First Step and one foot on the Sixth Step. How could I proceed with my legs stretched so far? I couldn't.

The First Step was easy—I was completely out of control when I drank, and there was no manageability in my life or household. I knew before I ever came to Alcoholics Anonymous that the first drink always meant a drunk and usually a blackout.

The Second Step was more difficult. I could admit I was sick, but I had always been afraid of being insane. My sponsor explained that insanity meant doing the same thing over and over and expecting different results. I had been doing that all my life, especially with my drinking. Before coming into A.A., I didn't know there was any other way, and I refused to believe my way didn't work. Soon, I was shown just how painful old ideas could be. I needed help only God could deliver. The Second Step doesn't say God would restore me to sanity; it simply says that He could. I started to believe He could.

The Third Step is a decision, one that might make the difference between life and death, a decision to turn my will and life over to Him. My greatest concern was that God would have me do something I didn't want to do, and I balked. I didn't want to make decisions at this point in my sobriety. What if they were the wrong ones? I didn't realize I could change them until my sponsor pointed this out to me.

There came the day when I could not find my sunglasses. I was so angry that I stayed home from work. I ran around in circles all day, literally circles. Later that night, I went to a meeting and heard the answer that worked for me: God would never give me anything that He couldn't get me out of. So I needed to give my life to Him. I could do that tomorrow. I left the meeting and ran more circles.

I knew I looked silly, and I could just imagine God laughing at me. Then, I just collapsed and cried, ready to turn my will and my life over to Him. The next day, I called my sponsor, and we got on our knees and asked God to take all of me. What a relief! I didn't need to be perfect, just willing to trust God. He has done a better job than I ever could have done. I am so grateful God took that burden; it was too big for me.

Step Four: the dreaded inventory, sweeping off my side of the street. When I was new to the Fellowship, I took the phrase "clean my house" literally, and I did. I had no idea how much freedom comes with this Step. I heard people say how scary and hard it was, and I procrastinated until I could not stand the pain. I watched myself live certain patterns for twenty-six years before I came to Alcoholics Anonymous, and I wasn't happy with what I saw. God had a plan for me, and I needed to clean my side of the street for it to happen. For several minutes, I prayed that God would help me be honest; then, I started to write. I wrote for five or six hours—everything that came to my mind. Just like the Big Book says, God put it all in order for me.

At that time, several approaches to the inventory were floating around A.A. They had nothing to do with the Fourth Step—not the one described in the Big Book. I had to make a list: people I had harmed, my fears, resentments, and sexual conduct; and how my defects affected me. I had to be honest and thorough because "if we are not sorry, and our conduct continues to harm others, we are quite sure to drink." I never wanted to drink again, and I was willing.

People said I'd never have to feel that way again, and I didn't want to. God was so gentle; it was He who made me willing, He who guided my pen. I could not have done this on my own. I wasn't brave enough, but I was tired of being sick. God just took over, and my baggage was cleaned up.

Having to admit all this to another human being was a difficult task. I was so afraid of someone finding out all my secrets. I thought if they truly knew who I was, I would be ruined. I had built some relationships in Alcoholics Anonymous, but I was still afraid that the hearer of my Fifth Step would tell everyone. This was such an unfounded fear. I decided to continue my journey and made the appointment to do this vital Step. The person I chose asked me if I would read my list aloud. I was embarrassed at first, but I did it. We discussed the patterns of self-destructiveness and selfishness I had created. Now that I knew what I had to work with, it was time for me to get to work.

I went home, opened the Big Book, and began to consider whether I had kept anything to myself. I hadn't. God gave me the willingness to put all my character defects down on that paper. I knew I was building a foundation that would last me a lifetime, and I didn't want it crumbling when the road got tough. Step Six says "Were entirely ready for God to remove all these defects of character," and I was ready. There was nothing I wanted to keep. My defects only caused pain. I asked God to remove everything that did not benefit Him and to restore me for His use. I wanted to be of maximum service for Him. I had finished Step Seven.

Now, I had to make amends. I wanted to be free of guilt. I had a list of the people that I had harmed; I had made it when I took inventory. I decided I would start with my friends and family, then I would look for people I hadn't seen for some time or couldn't find easily. I was uneasy about doing so but was willing to continue. Some amends could not be made. Those are the amends I have to *live*. I couldn't make some financial amends, so I put extra money in the basket at meetings, or at church, or in the pocket of a hungry man. This is what worked for me.

Our book gives us a list of promises that will happen after Step Nine. I have received them. I have a freedom I never experienced before. I have forgiven my father. He is a sick man in denial, and I leave him to God. I have no more secrets, and the weight has been lifted.

I am not in recovery. I am recovered, and God has restored my sanity. To keep this freedom, I do a daily inventory. If I owe an amends, I make it promptly. I don't much like the word "prompt." I don't like admitting I was wrong, but I like the freedom that comes with honesty.

Prayer and meditation has been my saving grace. If I am having difficulty or I am bothered by something, I know God has the answer for me. All I need to do is pray. God will give me wisdom if I stay tuned. I work on my conscious contact with Him, so He can communicate with me. It is one thing to ask, and another to listen.

As a result of doing these Steps, I have had a spiritual awakening. I now walk with my Creator, and I ask His guidance in all things. Without God, I would not be on this Earth. Without God, I would not have been able to clear the emotional scars of my childhood. It took work, love, understanding, and outside help, but those scars are long gone now. I owe my life to God and Alcoholics Anonymous.

Twelve Step calls were plentiful when I got sober. We went on calls at all hours of the day and night. I miss those days. There aren't many of those calls anymore, but there should be. There are things we must be willing to do to help the man who still suffers: go to bars to pick up a willing drunk, nurse him with a bottle of booze, or be willing to do whatever it takes. I am willing to go to any length to help another alcoholic who wants to get sober. I try to freely give what was so freely given to me. That is my job in Alcoholics Anonymous.

An old-timer once said it was his job "to get the new members ready to be sponsors to the new members coming behind us." That is what I am doing now—preparing those who have come after me to help those who come after them.

My Name is Bill R.

Bill R.—Brandon, Florida

I have recovered from the "seemingly" hopeless state of mind and body called alcoholism. I'm telling my story; it is not an attempt to tell anyone how to recover from alcoholism. A book published in 1939, titled *Alcoholics Anonymous*, better tells that story.

My childhood was normal. I did not have alcoholic parents. I was taken to church every week, whether I liked it or not. As a teenager, I didn't drink but did feel inferior to, and different from, my classmates.

The first time I got drunk was at an office Christmas party in 1965. The sickness and the hangover the next day convinced me that I would never get drunk again and it was two years before I experienced this state of mind and body again. Then I drank socially for six years, and my tolerance for alcohol increased and the suffering I endured from getting drunk wasn't as painful as I remembered.

It was around this time in my life that I began to question the values I had been taught. Finding some of them untrue, I cast almost all of them out. In September of 1972, I sat under a tree in my front yard going over in my mind what I had been taught by society. A good job, a house in the suburbs, a wife, five kids, two cars, and a dog—is this what life is about? They say you have succeeded if you obtain these things.

Well, I had all of them. I was twenty-five years old and extremely unhappy. *Is this all there is?* I thought as I opened a bottle of wine. Once again in my life, I was different, the rules of life didn't work for me. What was I to do? Like any intelligent being, I rid myself of all these burdens. The house and dog first, then the wife and kids.

In 1973, I began working as a contract engineer on temporary assignments. This gave me freedom from the control of a full-time employer, plus higher wages. My drinking was on the increase, along with my arrogance. Free time was drinking time. I loved the bars, the excitement, laughter and the people. Nothing dramatic happened. I ate, slept, worked and drank.

In 1974 I married the love of my life. She was everything I could ask for in a soul mate. A beautiful, intelligent, free-spirited person. My drinking slowed for a while, she was all I needed. Surely she would fill all my needs, or so I thought.

Alas, my needs turned out to be so great that no one, no matter how wonderful, could fill them. My drinking began to increase again. We moved from town to town and bar to bar. She drank and partied with the best of us. We were enjoying life but somewhere in the mid-1970s I started to lose control of my drinking. Once I began a drink, I would end up drunk. Being prompt and on time became a trait of the past. I could not understand why I could not leave the bar. The only way I would leave was to promise myself that I'd continue the party at my next destination. I believed life was meant to be one never-ending party, the great quest for happiness.

Deep down inside, I knew this wasn't true. The emotional and spiritual pain I suffered was growing to be unbearable and the only way to quiet it was to drink. My arrogance and anger was on the increase. There were, I thought, only two types of people in the world: those who were with me and those who were against me. The latter being the majority. I did not trust anyone who didn't drink and party as much as I did.

This continued into the early 1980s, then one day my wife, Linda, made a statement that sent a shock wave through my body. She said, "Aren't you tired of all this drinking and partying? It is the same thing every week. The same people, the same stories over and over, and the wasted weekends." She moderated her drinking from that point without any effort whatsoever. I had lost my drinking buddy, plus she was no longer tolerant of my behavior and drunkenness. Her decision probably saved my life.

Although she had moderated, I continued on the same path. Alcohol and my defects of character were driving a wedge between us, but I was too drunk to realize this. We moved to Florida with a new plan to settle down, buy a home and maybe get a dog. Does this sound familiar! I guess I was trying to go back to the old pursuit of happiness, since my way wasn't working!

This time it was different. I brought alcoholism with me. More and more time was being spent away from home. I had to work sixty hours a week to accomplish what I used to be able to do in forty. My reward for hard work was the bar. Alcoholism had me baffled. Why couldn't I have just two drinks and then go home? I used to be able to. Why was I getting drunk so quickly? What were these strange mental states all about? What had happened to my memory? By then I had started to have blackouts and large chunks of time were missing from my memory.

Eureka! I finally figured it out! It was the extreme heat of the Florida summers! At last, now I could devise a plan! New hope for the future! My spirits were flying again.

I stepped into the bar that evening with a new confidence. The bartender asked, "The usual, Bill?"

"No, I will have a glass of water first," I replied.

The extreme heat of Florida had made me thirstier than normal, I had concluded. Therefore if I would only quench my thirst before having a drink, everything would be OK. The first glass of water went down quickly. I ordered another. Then a third. My thirst was gone! I felt full! Surely this was the answer!

Tim, the bartender, asked, "Now are you ready?"

"First, a beer," was my answer. I had to make sure. Surely I wouldn't get drunk on a beer. Many times I had sobered somewhat by drinking beer. Ah, my plan was working, now I can have one scotch and water. Easy on the water, please. By the way, the ice melting in the drink will be enough. Hadn't I had enough water already?

The scotch went down easily and quickly. I had time for one more. This one eased all of my tensions and worries. One more will be OK: Hadn't I already found the remedy to my problem?

Once again, I closed the bar. The great water experiment was a failure. It went on the list of all the other failed attempts at controlling my drinking. My wife had become a cold, bitter person. I could not figure out why. If only she would meet me at the bars as she used to do, everything would be OK. She was moving to the list of people against me.

My boss was becoming intolerable. What a jerk! A person who works as many hours as I did couldn't be expected to show up at work on time. So what if occasionally I didn't come back to work after lunch?

On awaking in the mornings, I faced the Four Horsemen: Terror, Bewilderment, Frustration and Despair. What did I do last night? How am I going to work all day? I hate my life. I am doomed to this useless world, to tolerate all these idiots and put up with the misery dished out to me by God. All because I could not live up to the demands He placed on me. Who possibly could? His Creation was no more than a joke played on mankind for His amusement.

Desperate for a solution, I started to pray on the way to work every morning, pleading for God to help me control my drinking. Praying was something I hadn't done in years. After one week of prayer, I was arrested for an alcohol-related incident. As I sat in the jail cell, I thought, "Well, this proves it—God hates me! He did not answer my prayers, as usual. Why should I think He would do anything for me? No one else ever has."

Linda came to bail me out. There wasn't much discussion on the way to find my car. I knew she no longer cared about me. I received no sympathy from her. The date was October 16, 1986, my fortieth birthday.

I started to think maybe the problem was not her, but *me*. "Am I going mad?" I asked myself. Maybe, just maybe, this has something to do with my drinking.

The most miserable week of my life was about to unfold. With all the power within me, I resolved to quit stopping at the bars and limit myself to two drinks a night at home. I made a pledge to Linda to turn over a new leaf. All went well with the new plan for six days. No bars, two drinks a night, and I was miserable.

On the seventh night, October 23, 1986, Linda went shopping with a friend. In the house was a liter of scotch given me on my birthday by Linda's friend and her husband. My mood was dark. The thought of suicide had flashed through my mind several times that week. Two drinks is all I am going to have, I told myself as I sat at the kitchen table. The first was gone in a flash. During the second I began to think of my useless job and boss. The ire started to rise in me. The next thought was "Who is Linda to tell me that I can only have two drinks?"

The pain and misery of last week was dim in my mind. The resolution I made now seemed stupid. This is all God's fault for creating me. Within two hours the bottle was almost empty. Everything was blurred. The blaming of anything or anyone that came to mind was rampant.

Suddenly, out of nowhere the fog was lifted. It was as though I had not taken a drink. My mind was clear, I could see clearly. This thought came to me: *Bill, you need help. It is not the fault of anyone other than yourself. You have created this situation. You are an alcoholic and your life is out of control.*

What an awareness this was! It wasn't an idea or a plan. It was a "knowing," running through every fiber of my body.

As quickly as the moment of clarity came, it left. The alcoholic fog returned but the "knowing" stayed. I knew I had to do something and it had to be now. If I waited until tomorrow, I would justify this knowing away as some stupid idea that had entered my mind. All I could think of was a movie I had seen sometime ago. Carol Burnett had played an alcoholic woman who had quit drinking through A.A. I knew nothing about A.A. other than that. It was strange for me to watch such a movie, but once I had started, I couldn't turn it off.

I grabbed the phone book and started looking for a number for A.A. I remembered in the movie she had called someone in A.A. Being as intoxicated as I was, I could not spell alcoholic. Despair set in. The phone number was nowhere to be found. I was doomed to this alcoholic existence. This must be my punishment. Self-pity overwhelmed me. Doomed! I started crying, putting my head down on the table. The phone book I slammed down on the table was in front of me. I lifted my head and saw the book had opened to the "Frequently called numbers" section. At the top of this list of numbers was simply A.A. and the number.

With great difficulty I punched in the number. As the phone rang, I hoped I'd not dialed the wrong number. Then to my surprise there was the voice of a woman on the other end of the line. For some reason I had expected a man. Immediately I began to tell her my tale of woe. When I would stop to catch my breath, she'd ask for my number so she could have someone call me. I was reluctant to give out my number and continued to tell her what a mess I'd made out of my life. Eventually she convinced me to give her my number. She said she'd have someone call and she hung up.

Going back to the table, I sat down thinking, "So that was it. She didn't care. Don't call us, we'll call you." I imagined that someone would call in a day or two. By that time, it'd be too late. Once again no one understood me, no one cared.

As that thought was completed, I lifted my glass to my lips and drank deeply.

The sound of the phone ringing scared me so much I spilt my drink. I answered and heard a voice say, "Is this Bill?"

"Yeah."

"My name is Jimmy and I am a recovered alcoholic."

At the time his statement "recovered alcoholic" did not mean anything to me. But later I became very grateful for the fact that he was recovered. Also, I am glad he did not believe in the adage that had crept among some in A.A. of "never talk to someone when they're drunk. Tell them to call the next day." If Jimmy had done that with me, I probably would be dead today. He listened to me. I immediately told him about what was going on within me, all the horror I was living in, how I was drinking against my own will.

Jimmy asked if he could come over to my house. I said "NO!" He began to tell me about himself, his state of mind and drinking problems before he stopped. He showed no intolerance of me or my drinking. Never did he lecture or demand I do anything. I found this odd. This was the first person I had known who understood.

I asked how he had stopped drinking. He stated that he'd come in contact with a man that knew all about the drinking game and had a full knowledge of himself. This man had offered a solution.

Jimmy then asked, "Bill, do you want the solution?"

My thought was *Of course, isn't this why I made the call.* But I said, "I guess so."

He then described alcoholism to me as, I found out later, it is described in "The Doctor's Opinion" and chapter three "More about Alcoholism" in the Big Book of A.A. For once in my life I listened. How had he said it? Yes, "a man that knew all about the drinking game." That's who I was talking to. I don't remember much else about our conversation except he asked me to meet him the next night at a meeting of A.A. He also asked me not to take a drink the next day before the meeting. I said I could and would do this.

As I hung up the phone Linda walked in from shopping. She took one look at me and I could see the disgust on her face. I immediately defended myself by slurring out, "Don't worry, honey. Everything is going to be OK, I called A.A. Tomorrow I am going to one of their meetings."

This didn't impress her. She turned without a word and went to the bedroom. How could I expect her to believe anything I said? The silence was deafening. I drank no more that night, but passed out.

The next day began with the all-time worst hangover ever. On the way to work, I thought about what I'd done the previous night. As I had prophesied, the "knowing" was leaving me. Had I made a rash decision while drunk, based on some screwed up emotional state, and in fear of what Linda would say when she came home? The Great Debate ran all day in my mind.

I arrived home that evening still sick from the night before. "Strange," I thought, "This hasn't happened to me in a long time." I hadn't drank at lunch, although I'd wanted to. When I walked in the door, Linda asked, "Are you going to that meeting tonight?" I was afraid to say no. Mustering all the confidence I could, I said, "Of course, I told you I was last night." No reply.

The directions to the meeting I had scribbled down last night were barely decipherable. After taking a shower, hoping to wash the smell of alcohol out of my pores, I prepared for the meeting. I barely touched my dinner. I imagined Linda was smirking at me. She knew the physical misery I was in. Knowing of all the pain and misery alcohol had caused me, knowing the problems it was causing in my life, I still wanted a drink more than anything in the world.

On the way to the meeting as I was driving down Palm River Road, I was struck with a thought of brilliance. The directions stated that I was to turn left on 78th Street. Across that street was a bowling alley with a bar. That was it. I was insane that night: One drink and I will feel OK. I was starting to feel better already! A plan was forming.

As I approached the traffic light, my mind was made up. Straight through the light to the bar. It came to me that I'd better make up a story before I started to drink. I'll tell Linda I went to the meeting and went with some of them to the bar afterwards. Made sense to me.

The light turned red. Sitting at the light all I could think of was the drink I was about to have. The light turned green and I turned left. Amazed that I'd turned left, I decided to go on to the meeting. This would make my story better. I'll drink afterwards. At the church, the parking lot was full. Getting out of the car, I didn't know what to expect. I wandered up to the door and looked in. People were laughing, drinking coffee and generally having a good time. It puzzled me why people would be drinking hot coffee on a hot humid night in Florida. Didn't they understand that today is Friday, the start of the weekend, time to unwind and relax?

A man met me at the door and led me to Jimmy. We walked away from the group he was sitting with and chatted for a while, and how glad he was that I came. I did not reveal my plan to get drunk. Jimmy poured me some coffee, I was thankful it was only half full, because my hands were unsteady. Soon the meeting started. I introduced myself as a newcomer and to my surprise everyone welcomed me. The topic did not focus on me. A man in the group had just lost his son to AIDS and he was of course very upset.

The topic focused on acceptance. As the people spoke I was amazed at their understanding. Near the end of the meeting, Bill Z. spoke directly to me: "Bill, you are the most important person in the room tonight." Then he talked about alcoholism as Jimmy had the night before.

Somewhere during that meeting, I forgot my plan to drink. Something changed in me; I simply wanted to stop the nightmare.

After the meeting Jimmy and I talked some more about alcoholism. He asked if I believed I am an alcoholic. I had to say, Yes. Are you ready to quit drinking for the rest of your life? Yes. Then he asked, "Bill, do you want to get well and are you willing to go to any length to do so?" I began to cry, and said yes.

He gave me a copy of *Alcoholics Anonymous* and explained that this is the textbook of A.A. and that inside are the clear-cut directions for getting well. He told me to read this book from the first page that has printing on it, through chapter three, and to meet him at the church Tuesday evening for a test.

The next day I read the book through chapter eleven. I found myself in the book and wondered how could they have written this about me in 1939! The decision to follow through with this program of recovery was an easy one to make. Nothing else had worked.

Five days without a drink and miserable, I met Jimmy for my test. I hoped the test would take away my pain. Jimmy was there when I arrived. With the Big Book in hand, I pronounced myself ready for the test. To my surprise he said I had already passed the test, for I had shown up. Many times he has waited and they never came. This same experience would come to me many times, too, later on, after I had done the Steps and recovered.

In a small room off of the main meeting room, we spent five hours, he reading the book to me as I followed along in mine. He'd stop to emphasize certain sentences and paragraphs to answer my questions. Often he'd pause to ask me questions such as "Have you admitted to your innermost self that you are an alcoholic? Only after I had answered to his satisfaction would he proceed.

When we read "that I must find a power greater than myself to live by," I remarked that I had heard in a meeting that a higher power could be anything, a table, a chair, tree, light bulb or doorknob. I joked I'd decided on a fire hydrant. He said, "You have been misinformed. There is a lot of stupid misinformation in the fellowship of A.A. Bill, if you continue with this stupidity you will die drunk."

I opened my mouth to respond, he held up a hand. We continued with the reading, on the next page it said, "and that power is God." He said I did not have to believe in the God of my youth. But I must find an understanding of God that I could live by.

We finished the night in chapter five. Without realizing it, I'd done Steps One and Two while going through the first four chapters. After the ABC's in chapter five it states, "Being convinced, we are at Step Three." I was convinced.

We read through the Third Step prayer, and we said the prayer aloud together. At once I felt different, I felt light and happy. Then we read through the Fourth Step description and discussed it. He stressed the importance of doing this Step quickly. We reread where the book warns the effects of Step Three would not last unless at once followed by Step Four. Again, he told me Step Four was to find out what had blocked me from God.

Elated at the feeling I had received from Step Three, I returned home. Everything looked different to me. I saw that I was the one who was cold and bitter, not Linda. At that time, the obsession to drink had been removed. Never again was I to experience the mental blank spots and twist of thinking the alcoholic has toward alcohol. It had been removed.

But I didn't do Step Four at once as I was instructed. I cancelled appointments with Jimmy for some trivial excuse or other. Then came the day when emotional and spiritual pain reappeared. Now I remembered his warning! I knew the obsession would return if I didn't get to work on Step Four.

I met Jimmy and begged him to continue with me. He asked, "Bill, are you sure you want to continue? Wouldn't you prefer to live in the comfort of your misery?"

We did go on, and I admitted the exact nature of my wrongs to him and God in Steps Four and Five. Now we read the Step Six paragraph and he asked me if I wanted to hold on to any of my character defects. Those things that had blocked me from God. "He can have them all!"

was my reply. I was willing. Had not the past two weeks shown me the consequences of being blocked? Now we read the Seventh Step paragraph before I prayed with Jimmy asking God to remove all my defects.

Then Jimmy asked, "At this moment do you feel you have any of these defects?"

I thought for a moment, and said, "No."

He warned me that God had removed them, but I could and probably would, pick them up again and use them. When this happened, they would produce extreme pain within me for I no longer owned them and they no longer owned me. Ah, later experience would prove him right.

Steps Eight and Nine were done quickly as I now knew what had to be done. Three days later he led me through the rest of the Steps, and now I had the "design for living" referred to in the book. Jimmy said by doing the first nine Steps, I gained an understanding of God, learned what had blocked me from Him, set up a new life with God and straightened out my past with my fellow man. I was now at the beginning point. The slate had been wiped clean. Now it was up to me whether I wanted to go back to my old way of life or create a new one by practicing Steps Ten, Eleven, and Twelve every day the rest of my life.

That was more than twelve years ago. I am living proof that the "design for living" works. I continue to go to A.A. meetings, not to stay sober, but to carry the message that is in the book *Alcoholics Anonymous.*

Sad to say, for many years I was ridiculed and told that the Steps were a long process, and that I would get drunk from believing I was recovered from alcoholism. I almost left A.A. during those years. One night while talking with Jimmy, he asked, "Bill where might you find an alcoholic who wants to get well? Not in the bars or streets. The treatment centers have told you they don't want you back because of the message you carry. But what about the rooms of A.A? They can't throw you out."

During the first nine years in A.A. I found three that wanted what I had. All three are sober, but left A.A. At the end of those nine long years, one night I walked into a meeting of A.A. and it has never been the same since. I summoned up courage to speak about my experiences. Of course I was bashed by some people in the room, but it didn't matter any more. Afterwards, a lady came up to me and said she's been drunk the past three years after being sober for seven before that. She had never heard that she could get well and recover. "Please tell me more!"

I opened the Big Book and pointed to the subtitle on the title page where it states: "The Story of How Thousands of Men and Women have Recovered from Alcoholism." Her mouth dropped open. She was in total disbelief at what she had just read.

Today she has recovered and now works with many others.

From that time there has been a revival of the message in the Big Book in our area. Many people have recovered through the process I have just described. Now there are four meetings in our county that are labeled: "Recovered Meetings." The Original Message is the only topic in those meetings.

Since 1939, when the book was written, alcohol has not changed, the Steps have not changed and, most important, God has not changed. The only thing that has changed is the fellowship of A.A. From my study of A.A., the watered-down message seems to have started in the 1950s. It is *not* the fault of those in the rooms. They are only doing what they have been taught.

This is not an attack on A.A. I owe my life to the program which is in the book. This is a plea to anyone suffering from alcoholism to try what is in the book with the aid of a recovered alcoholic.

Please contact us.

Relief

Edy G.—California

Neither of my parents were alcoholic, and there was no alcohol kept in our home. My thoughts on the matter were simple: alcoholics were mentally incapable, uneducated people living on skid row. It never occurred to me that alcoholics were regular people or that I could be one.

I took my first drink sometime in college. But I was thirty years old and married with two children before I experienced my first drunk. The neighbors were having an end-of-summer party, and we were invited over. I didn't drink very often, so I didn't realize how sneaky those tasty frozen drinks could be. I stood up to go home, and it hit me! The dizziness, the loss of control. I went home and spent the night on the floor with my head in the porcelain god! I felt so helpless. I couldn't get up off the floor. I told myself I would never do that again. Little did I know.

When I was thirty-four, my married life was becoming unbearable, and a divorce was in order. I was very restless and discontent. I thought the best thing for me to do was to get rid of my main problem—the man—and everything would be OK. That was not the case. Now thrown into single-parenthood, I found things astonishingly difficult to handle. I had to work long hours to support my children, and I needed some form of relaxation to take me away from my life.

I stopped at the bar every day on my way home from the jail where I worked as a correctional officer. I could only spend one hour because I had to pick my children up from day care. If I picked them up late, they would be kicked out, and I would have no place to take them. I often tried to come up with excuses that would sound plausible to the child-care worker, so I could stay and drink more. I never came up with one, so I always picked them up at the last minute.

I felt I had to work closer to home, so I left my job at the jail and took two in its place: as a geriatric nurse and as a bartender. I used to joke that I would make you sick (as a bartender) and make you well (as a nurse).

The first time I got in trouble with alcohol was when I was thirty-six years old. My boyfriend had given me a thirty-day notice that he was leaving me for someone else. Because I felt so sorry for myself, I immediately went down to the bar to get some attention. I ordered a double shot of tequila, and in the next four hours, I drank at least twenty-two shots. I remember all this because I was not one of those "fortunate" blackout drinkers. I have the distinct "pleasure" of remembering my drunks!

After four hours, I went home and passed out. When I awoke, I headed back to the bar. I had two more double shots and then got in my car to drive home. As I was turning into my driveway (with my signals on and my arm out the window), a man, who was exceeding the speed limit, passed me, crossing over the solid yellow line within one hundred yards of an intersection—and I hit him. He was so mad he followed me up my driveway cursing at me. I couldn't get rid of him, so I called the police.

When they arrived and smelled alcohol on my breath, they asked me to step outside and take some tests. Somewhere around L-M-N-O-P, I messed up. They took me down to the police station, and I took a Breathalyzer. They told me I was not under arrest and—true to their word—they took me home and instructed me not to drive. I had gotten lucky, but I was angry. It seemed to me that the other guy was in the wrong and should have been in trouble.

The police did turn their report in to the district attorney though, and he decided to prosecute. I had a jury trial which resulted in an acquittal. I pled out to a "wet reckless" which has virtually no consequences—unless you get another drunk driving charge and I was not planning on getting another one of those. This could have been used as one of many ominous warnings I received during my drinking career, but I was unable to tell the true from the false. I was living in a lie and had no idea.

In the next four years, my alcohol consumption picked up. As both a bartender and a drinker, I traveled around from bar to bar. I had three "home" bars in three different counties. I stayed in service to those bars.

One day, I was leaving one of my home bars on my way home when the brand-new tire on my car blew out. I hit the center divide and did a 540° spin. I drove my disabled car back to a gas station to call someone for help. When I walked out of the telephone booth, the local sheriff put handcuffs on me and said he was arresting me for driving under the influence of alcohol. I told him that I wasn't driving the telephone booth anywhere. He told me he was arresting me for driving my car. I told him that he hadn't seen me drive my car, and therefore he had no right to arrest me. Apparently, the gas station attendant had smelled alcohol on me and had summoned the sheriff. In this particular county, when someone turned someone else in for driving under the influence—and the driver arrested was successfully prosecuted—the person that turned the driver in got a one hundred dollar reward.

The sheriff took me into the county jail and had me do a Breathalyzer test. I had passed the field sobriety test, but the Breathalyzer showed results of .37–.39 BAC. The jail staff put me in the "rubber room" for the night. I think that they were expecting me to go into seizures. Alcohol wired me, so I was awake all night watching them watch me. They finally transferred me to a holding cell where I was able to make a phone call, and I called home for bail money. I was very indignant because the jail staff were making me bail out of jail. After all, I had owned my house for fifteen years and was not a flight risk. I thought I should be released on my own recognizance.

My friend showed up at jail about 6:45 A.M. and bailed me out. As I was getting out of jail, I remembered that they had taken my car to car jail, and I would have to bail it out, too. I figured car jail wouldn't open for another two hours, so we headed over to the local bar to have a few pops before we drove up to get my car.

I still did not think I had a problem with alcohol. I found out later I had a broken "thinker." Insanity viewed through an insane mind looks sane. I thought that I had a problem with people—not with alcohol—although, my probation officer didn't agree. He ended up giving me a choice between 120 days in jail or thirty days in rehabilitation; I took rehab.

I learned a few things about alcohol in rehab which I figured would help me if I ever decided to work with alcoholics. I learned alcoholics always drink more than three drinks and call it a couple, that they start drinking and can't quit, and that they never plan on getting drunk—they just do. None of those things were applicable to me (at least in my way of thinking). All I needed was to stay away from the people who were giving me grief.

Two years later, I was on one of my "not drinking" binges in a local bar when I figured this thing out. The problem was my car! If I got someone else to drive my car, I couldn't be arrested for drunk driving. I asked a drunk at the bar if he would drive me and my car to a friend's house after I had a few drinks, and he graciously agreed. In the next fifteen minutes, I downed about seven shots of 100-proof alcohol and went outside to warm up my car, so I could be driven to my friend's house. As I was getting out of the car to get the man in the bar, I was arrested by the local police. The charge: "In or about a vehicle while under the influence of alcohol." DUI number three.

I knew I was in big trouble this time, so instead of waiting to be told that I had to go to a program, I checked myself into a drug and alcohol rehabilitation program. I paid attention to what they said in those twenty-one days: ninety meeting in ninety days; get a sponsor; work the Steps; and get into service. I did those things. I knew that if I ever got in trouble around alcohol again, I would be doing state prison time. I wanted desperately to stay sober.

All went well for six months. I went to more than five hundred meetings in that time. I did service work for every meeting I went to— even if it was just picking up coffee cups. I called my sponsor every day and faithfully worked on a First Step work sheet she had given me. I heard others talk about getting a new feeling—the relief Step One offered them. I was doing everything humanly possible to achieve that feeling, and nothing seemed to be happening. I felt the same.

One day, I went to my third meeting of the day, took some people home as part of my service commitment, put gas in my car, and went over to a friend's house to watch comedy on T.V. I had been to this house several times in my "sobriety" and had never found it to be a problem. As I entered the house, my friend asked me if I would like something to drink, a normal question. I did want something, so I went to the refrigerator to help myself. When I opened the door, I saw a gallon of iced tea, a dozen colas, a half- gallon of orange juice, a half-gallon of grapefruit juice, and a half- gallon of milk. Way in the back, there was a bottle of gin and one of vodka. I filled my cup with ice and poured myself a vodka and orange juice.

You need to know at this point that drinking was the farthest thing from my mind. I was not drinking to escape anything. I was happy and content with most of my life at that time. I didn't even think about what I was doing. I went to the living room, sat down, watched the comedy, drank that drink as if it were iced tea. I finished that drink and poured myself another. About one o'clock in the morning, my friend informed me that he had to get some sleep since he had to work in the morning. He said I could stay in the spare bedroom, but I decided I needed a clean T-shirt for work. I got in my car to drive home.

I did not head home immediately. I went out of my way to stop by one of my home bars. As a bartender, I knew that closing time is a terrible time to stop by a bar, but I went anyway. When I got there, I rolled the bartender dice for a drink, and I won. I drank that drink right down and rolled for another drink. This time I lost.

All of a sudden, I remembered I wasn't supposed to be drinking and driving (even though I didn't feel intoxicated). I looked around the bar to see if there was someone there who could drive me home. There was a guy sitting at the bar who needed a place to stay for the night, so I struck a deal with him. If he would drive me home, I would drive him back in the morning before I had to go to work. After making our deal, we went out and got in my car for the ride home.

I awoke hours later on the ground outside my car. It was dark and cold. I found a nasty knot on my head, and my chest hurt terribly. Obviously, we had been in an accident. I couldn't see the extent of damage to my car, but when I crawled back into it, the keys were still in the ignition. I tried to start the car but was unsuccessful. About that time, the lady whose fence my car had run through came out of her house. She said she had called the state police, and they were on their way. I knew I was in trouble—big trouble.

When the police officer put the handcuffs on me and put me in the back of his car, I has this sinking feeling. I felt as if I had lost everything that was worthwhile in life. I knew I was going to prison for three to four years, and I was bewildered and confused.

When they booked me at the county jail, they charged me with felony drunk driving. They set bail at $15,000, and I believed my life was over. All of my life, I had been taught to suit up, show up, buck up, and keep my nose to the grindstone. No matter what, things would turn out OK. That seemed virtually impossible in this case. I was in a place of hopelessness and helplessness. No matter what I did, I was facing a wall. Other people were now in charge of my life. I was at the mercy of the department of corrections and on the other side of the bars.

While I was in jail, my son (who was fourteen and staying with his dad) came to visit me. It was the first time I had seen him in six months. He didn't know I had been in trouble before. I had to tell him—through glass—that his mom was looking at prison for the next four years. Tears were running down our cheeks. I felt totally demoralized. I felt hopeless and powerless. I felt like a complete failure. My unmanageability hit me like a ton of bricks. Fortunately, this was the beginning of the end of all those feelings.

I stayed in jail for four months, making bimonthly appearances before the judge. We were waiting for a piece of paper from another county that said some technicality of the law had been upheld in the conviction of one of my previous DUIs. Finally, the judge became irritated, overlooked that previous DUI, and reduced the charge against me to a misdemeanor. After five months, I walked out of jail—time served!

Right then and there, a major miracle in my life occurred. I am pretty particular about my miracles. Some people think miracles require hard work. To me, a miracle is something I had nothing to do with. All I have to do is show up and recognize it as a phenomenon over which I have no control.

I knew I needed to continue to stay sober, but I was still very, very confused about why I had actually drunk that last drink. I thought I had done everything that was told to me to do. But I drank anyway. I was powerless.

Under those circumstances, I met a guide who told me that there were one hundred people who had successfully recovered from a hopeless state of mind and body. These people had probably gone deeper into their alcoholism than I had and had found a way out. They had written a book which laid out precisely what they had done to recover. My guide told me that if I did exactly what those people did, I would get exactly what they got. Relief. I really wanted that.

I had to be willing to read the book *Alcoholics Anonymous* word for word, page by page. As we were going through the book, I was told that every time it says "we," I should imagine one hundred people standing before me saying the exact same thing. That impressed me. I had never seen one hundred people agree on anything much less one hundred alcoholics!

The book's main stated purpose is to help us find a Power greater than ourselves that will solve all our problems. That is exactly what I was looking for. I was tired of trying to solve my problems, and I was willing to try just about anything. This was a relatively "painless" way to get rid of my problems and move on with my life.

I wanted to jump right into Step One, although I had no idea what it was all about. I knew my life was not manageable—at least not by me. In fact, other people were managing my life for me—three probation officers from two different counties, two judges, and a few community service programs. As you can imagine, I wasn't allowed much latitude in the managing of my own life. I was told that as far as Step One was concerned, there was much pre-Step work that had to be done.

We started with the second appendix in the back of the book. I was told I needed to start there for a few reasons: to see that I didn't need a huge miraculous apparition to appear before me in order to have a spiritual experience; to see that I needed to have some sort of spiritual experience in order to recover; and that in order to recover, I had to be willing, honest, and open-minded.

When we finished reading the appendix, we started in the front of the book on the fly leaf which read "The Story of How Many Thousands of Men and Women Have Recovered from Alcoholism." This gave me the hope I needed. I realized that I, too, could recover if I did precisely what the first one hundred people did.

With the help of an excellent and patient guide and a huge encyclopedic dictionary, we worked our way through the forewords, the "Doctor's Opinion," "Bill's Story," and "There Is A Solution." I felt some hope and understanding start to take hold. I realized that I could not "just not drink." I was starting to understand what had happened to me the last time I took a drink. I came to realize that no matter how much I didn't want to drink, no matter how many meetings I went to, no matter how much service I was in, I still didn't have the needed power to "just not drink." What a sense of relief that was! I really wasn't a failure. I really wasn't a bad person. I was just a person with a malady for which there was a daily reprieve.

I was a person who had insanity in my life, and I needed to do something about that. I had been trying for a long time, but everything I had tried had failed. Then, it was pointed out to me that Step Two could offer me a solution. This Step gave me two requirements: I had to believe in some Power greater than myself, and the Power must have the ability to restore my sanity. If I could believe, then I could start to get on with my life.

After recognizing my insanity, wanting to get rid of it, and recognizing that this Power could, I decided to turn my whole life over to this Power and see what happened. If this Power could restore me to sanity, then I had better turn everything I had over to It. That was everything. My will, my life, everything. I did have some second thoughts. What if this Power messed up my life? What if it didn't do good things for me? I took a look at my life and decided this Power couldn't do any worse than I had. Then and there, I made a decision to turn my will and my life over to this Power, trusting that I would be taken care of.

A decision without action is a total and absolute fantasy. I was told the only way I could demonstrate my decision was to jump immediately into a fact-finding, fact-facing process—a searching, fearless and thorough moral inventory of myself. Not anyone else's morals but the ones I had adopted for myself. I was to write down everyone towards whom I had felt anger. I wrote down six or seven people. I was so proud of myself, and I figured that my guide would be proud of the wonderfully free life I had lived. I really believed that I couldn't care less what anybody thought of me. If I didn't care what you thought of me, there was no reason to be angry with you.

Then my guide threw me a curve ball. I was told to look up the word "angry" in the dictionary. I found out it meant a feeling of displeasure directed at something or someone. My list grew from six or seven people to more than three hundred pages! I must interject right now that anytime I was not relying on my Higher Power, my life went upside down as I did this inventory. When this happened, I was reminded that I needed to get a conscious contact with that Power and get back on track.

When I finally got all the people, institutions, and principles down on paper, I got together with my guide, and we started to go over these wrongs. My eyes were opened. I saw I had been only interested in myself and had tromped all over the toes of others trying to get what I wanted. I had total disregard for the feelings and thoughts of others. It was pointed out to me that my way of looking at something was not the only way to look at something and not necessarily the right way. What a concept!

When I was through telling someone else all this garbage and listening to their input, I began to realize the promises that came to me as a result of doing all this strenuous work. I could face life head on, and I could be serene doing it. I could feel the closeness of my Higher

Power, and that represented to me a spiritual experience. My fears—even the fear that I would take another drink—began to slip away. I was starting to feel free!

After doing the Fourth and Fifth Steps, I had a list of all my character defects. I had to be willing to turn these defects over to my Higher Power and be willing to let that Power have them all—lock, stock and barrel. Believe you me, I was willing to give these things over. I liked this feeling.

Next, I was instructed to go to all the people that I had hurt—as a result of my selfish self-seeking actions—and try and make things "right" with them. I was to amend my life so that this wouldn't happen again. Here again, I was told to look up the word "amend" in the dictionary. I thought all I had to do was go and tell people that I was sorry and offer to pay them what ever they thought I owed them. I found out there was much more to this part of the process. By taking a look at the defects which caused me to do these things to others, I could change. My life could, would, and did start to change dramatically.

As I started to face the people that I had harmed, I could feel the nearness of that Power working with and through me. I felt as if a huge weight were being lifted off my shoulders. I was willing to look at the past, so I would not repeat it. I began to know true and absolute peace and serenity. I was not afraid to face these people. Somehow, I knew just what to say without trying to make them feel sorry for me or trying to make myself look like a useless, helpless person. It was a truly amazing experience for me.

I knew I would continue to grow, but—since I am human—I would slide back on occasion. I needed to be vigilant, especially watching for fear, dishonesty, selfishness and resentment. My guide pointed out that I could do this by reviewing my day to see if there was anything I had done that I needed to clean up. I noticed I had stopped fighting and arguing with others. I felt as though my sanity had returned. My own will was starting to become one with that of my Higher Power.

I needed to keep this conscious contact new and fresh in my daily life. I learned how to pray (talk to my Higher Power) and how to meditate (listen to that Power). I had, without a shadow of a doubt, found that Power deep down inside of me. What an amazing revelation. It had been there all along.

Today, I start my day off by asking that Power help me to be of maximum service to others—just for today. As I go about my day, I pause to see if I am really implementing the Twelve Steps in my life. Because the Power is in me and because I am hooked up to it, I am able to tell the true from the false. I don't have to live in the lie anymore.

I practice all these principles in all my affairs and can effectively transmit the program of Alcoholics Anonymous to others. I have a working knowledge of a Power that is bigger and more powerful than me. I have been to the pits of hopelessness, helplessness, self-pity, and selfishness. I have, in effect, been lifted up and set on a Broad Highway, and for that I am eternally grateful.

I express my gratitude by giving away what was so freely given to me. I work with others to show them the path I have taken, a path outlined for us in the book *Alcoholics Anonymous*. When I finally was willing to follow directions—I received what the people who wrote that book received. I recovered—completely, from a hopeless state of mind and body.

I am sure that if you do what I did, you will get what I got. Perhaps, as the Big Book says, we will meet each other "as we trudge this Road of Happy Destiny."

I Didn't Know that I Didn't Know

Joe N.—Texas

The assigned counselors at the treatment center spoke of Alcoholics Anonymous (A.A.) constantly, and talked openly about their own previous drug- or alcohol-addictions and how the programs of A.A. or Narcotics Anonymous (N.A.) had kept them clean or sober for some time. The doctors said that, according to medical understanding, addictions, such as alcohol or drugs, and obsessions, were diseases. The counselors and doctors diagramed the progression of chemical dependency, learned or inherited, within my own body. They spoke of some of us who had been gifted with turbocharged processors: livers and other vital organs. This inherited or natural ability to adapt allowed me to use all I wanted. I was genetically encoded to self-destruct, once I started to use alcohol or, most likely, any other addictive substance.

Of course, what I heard in all this was proof that I was unique after all. Until these genetically souped-up processors failed, I could drink, God, could I drink, successfully achieving that desired balance point of appearing to be "here" while I was actually "there." My fear and anger grew in direct opposite proportion to my diminishing self-esteem while I behaved in ways that served to distance me from who I truly was, and from those I loved most. Drinking alcohol rebuilt my imagined self image each day. I felt better with the first drink, which set up a physical craving for the next, which spurred the undeserved feeling of well-being, which in turn justified the next round.

During those first days in the nut ward, I spoke often of all the things I'd done in my forty-eight years—things the average person only dreams of. I'd done them successfully while drinking daily. In fact, if it weren't for my drinking, I'd say, I'm not sure I could have accomplished these successes I so frequently pointed to. I knew my drinking had caused some problems, but I was sure I'd gotten more out of alcohol than alcohol had gotten out of me. Besides, I wasn't hurting anyone else but me, and then only now and then.

Finally returning home, I felt I had mostly recovered from the physical toll that daily drinking had taken on me. I approached my wife with a renewed, nearly adolescent love for her. She looked to me from her usual chair in front of her desk and I froze. I must have given her a long curious look. She said, *"Are you all right?"* Those were the words, but the message wasn't anything like the words. Fear took over the space I'd just given to all those thoughts of joy, rebirth, learning, changing, hope and love. There was none of that in her voice or her eyes. She, in a week, had become a threatening stranger to me.

For seven days I'd been lavished with affection and unselfish caring from some fifteen human beings struggling with fears and outrages similar to my own. We huddled together to form a protective shield. Each would ask the other, *"Are you all right?"* What we meant was, "Don't break down, keep going, I'm with you," and our fears were, "If this one breaks down, I might, too." This collection of alcoholics, drug-addicts and psychotics had grown to love one another in a matter of hours. It was a kind of caring I'd never known and it was shared among most of us.

Foraging for food turned out to be disappointing. I stole close to her again. "Uh . . ., would there be anything around to eat that I don't know about?"

She remained focused on her work; it was around 8:00 P.M. "I don't know," came her dry response.

I had two choices: Rage at her for her indifference to my homecoming or go to an A.A. meeting.

Seated in my car in the dim-lit parking lot in front of the darkened A.A. room for the next hour, eating a McDonald's Happy Meal, gave me time to cool down some.

There should have been a celebration, brisk talk about the future, resolve to forgive and forget the past, ending in a joyful rush to the bedroom. I paused on that thought. My God, is all this rage because I simply wanted to get laid? The next thought struck me with the most overpowering sense of shame and something I must call grief: I could not honestly say that, in the twenty-eight years of our marriage, we had ever made love without me or both of us having had at least one drink. I absolutely knew I had not had sex with that woman when I was sober in at least the past twenty years. In fact, she had never seen me sober after 6:30 P.M. in all that time after. The rage left me, yielding to a hail storm of feelings: sympathy, self-pity, shame, guilt, embarrassment, remorse, loss, demoralization and depression. I shouted inside the dark muted indifference of a late-model four-door sedan, "My God! What have I done!"

I had never been there. I showed up for the wedding and soon left looking after my own self-serving ends. I drank to go somewhere else or went somewhere else to drink. I was always in the process of leaving, never comfortable where I was. So why shouldn't the cupboards be bare? For the past twenty years or more I'd seen myself as a seventy-five percent partner and head of a household in which I was present ten percent of the time and had contributed nothing more than money. Why, for heaven's sake, did she stay?

I saw the pathetic picture of her where she retreated to the safety of her solitary desk and chair in the stark defined light of her desk lamp night after night. She'd been there for years and had long ago lost hope for relief. I couldn't release all these emotions and I couldn't accept them. I understood I'd been a contributor to her personal misery. It was too soon and these truths were too horrible to face.

"Old Bill" had shown up a few minutes after the meeting opened. A squat Texas redneck in his late sixties, he walked with a heavy cane and sported a belt buckle the size of a Buick hubcap. It was forced forward toward the ground by an ample gut. He eyed me coolly as he pulled up a chair and lit a cigarette. He scared me. I figured he had his own parking place out there and I hoped I hadn't taken it.

Toward the end of the hour the chairman called on me for my input on whatever the topic was. Knowing my state of mind, I probably brought up the past days in the treatment center, probably mentioned I was an employer, probably implied much material success (I was still stuck on reconciling that) and I most certainly mentioned "her."

Old Bill was called on after I finished.

"Bill, alcoholic," he introduced himself, and continued to look right at me while he spoke.

"I've been a sober member of Alcoholics Anonymous for over thirty-six years. Now, I hung around rooms like these for a couple of years, madder'n hell. Drove my sponsors nuts with my whining and complaining. My third sponsor finally sat me down one night and said, 'Bill, ya know what yer trouble is?'

"Yeah," I said, "*She* won't leave me alone and she won't do what's good for her neither."

"'No, Bill,'" he said, "'your problem is that you're double-dumb.'"

"Jimmy," I said, "what in the hell are you talkin' about?"

"So he proceeded to explain: 'There's folks like you, Bill, who *don't know that they don't know.* They're double-dumb. Until men like you figure out that ya don't even know enough to know you don't know nothin', this program, the people in it, or even God can't help you and yer gonna stay miserable. Yer gonna make others miserable, yer gonna get hateful, yer gonna drink, yer gonna kill yerself, or worse, yer gonna kill someone else. You got the only known disease that kills people who don't know they have it.'"

"I got the message. I was here to learn somethin'. Still don't know what it is, really. But Jimmy helped to make me teachable. By doin' that, he helped saved my life."

Driving home, I repeated the phrase, "double-dumb." "I didn't know that I didn't know" about the empty cupboards, the absent man in the house. What else was out there that I didn't know I didn't know about? With those conscious thoughts surfacing as I pulled into the drive beside our house, I had become, for the first time, "teachable."

She was still seated in her place of refuge. I believed the best thing for us now was my silence. It had been one hell of a twenty-four hour day—the seventh without a drink in my adult life. I was numbed by the sensory assaults of the past few hours. I filled a large coffee cup with water from the kitchen tap intending to heat it in the microwave for instant coffee. Instead, I opened the refrigerator door, placed the cup on a shelf and closed the door. After a couple of minutes, I wondered why the microwave hadn't toned "ready." I looked inside it and realized I'd associated the refrigerator with "drink" for so long, I'd opened that door instead of the oven door. I started again. If this is what sobriety had in store for me, I realized I'd better find a sense of humor, quick.

Our only son was a senior in high school. He played trumpet. Best in the school. Best in the region. Best in the state. In fact, if it had not been for his school and extracurricular activities, we never would have attended functions as a family, outside of rare occasional dinners together, even at home. It seems we always had to have more than just us around to justify being together. Whether twenty or more for a party at our house or a few hundred at band contests, concerts, football or Little

League. We have pictures and memories of these. I don't recall family talks, with just the three of us, when I didn't lecture them both on matters of proper conduct, behavior, religions of the world, politics, the faults of the neighbors down the street or how to properly wash and prepare vegetables. We had never taken a vacation that didn't include the distraction of another family or acquaintance. Bringing other people along inhibited me from occasionally taking the two of them hostage during the trips.

I walked past her desk on the way to bed with my book and instant coffee finally in hand; I paused long enough to ask where he was.

She answered, "At band practice." This comment had long ago been established as our code for "He's safe and probably not getting into trouble right now." After petty theft and public intoxication arrests some time ago, she worried about him constantly. I had disapproved of her attitude and resented her concerns about his behavior for years. I saw her as doting and obsessive over her only child. I knew he was as smart as I was and only lacked the experience that life would soon enough present him. I dismissed her opinions and settled easily for this coded communication with which my own angry responses to her intuitive concerns had reduced us.

On page one hundred twenty-two of *Alcoholics Anonymous*, a doctor is quoted: "Years of living with an alcoholic is almost sure to make any wife or child neurotic. The entire family is, to some extent, ill." Well, I had it. She took it. He got it. It was to be another year and half before we could begin to stop speaking in codes and tongues and to become aware of what it was that each of us had become.

Deliberately and regularly recalling the definition of double-dumb through each day caused me to actually ask questions of others without manipulating them in ways to provide me with the answers I wanted to hear. I then allowed that they might be right and started altering my actions according to their responses.

I settled into the routine of attending nighttime meetings, reading each chapter in the Big Book, returning to the treatment center daily, calling this God-nut of an A.A. sponsor each morning, remaining self-absorbed when at home, and, for all I was worth, doing my utmost to avoid death by alcoholism.

After three more weeks of outpatient treatment at the center, I returned to my *other family*—the workplace. Just as I had as a husband and father, I also behaved as a boss. The effects on my employees were remarkably similar to those on the family at home. We spoke in codes, sidestepped issues, arrived and left angry, were subject to angry flare-ups, outbursts, isolation, rejection, depression. There were starts without finishes, resolutions without resolve, broken promises, hopelessness and a tolerance for unacceptable behavior that was, of itself, intolerable. And why did *they* stay?

All had retreated into their own version of a personal safe haven and protected it menacingly. By all appearances, they seemed to be *here* while they were really *there*. Now that I had been exposed to a few healthy types, I had developed a sense of humor about my own shortcomings and was experiencing life with a little less self-reliance, I began to place more emphasis on learning from others. I recognized that something was rotten and I had to take some of the blame while I understood that I also had to take some action. The suggestions in A.A. to save my life might work to save my livelihood. So I got a *business sponsor*— properly titled, business consultant.

For the next three months I was subjected to my reeducation in living with the help of A.A. at the rate of a dollar a meeting while my "business sponsor" sat side by side with me forty hours a week at the rate of a dollar a minute. Both messages were the same: To receive help, I first had to accept that I needed it. Once I asked for it, I had to take on the responsibility of implementing suggestions to identify and break the old habits that continued to get in the way of my happiness and that of others. Most importantly, for me, I had to admit to my innermost self that, on my own, I had no real power to change these things. When I became willing to learn, hope and self-esteem began to surface in me and my sense of self worth began to increase at the comparative rate of about twenty-five cents a day. It was a very poor return on the investment but I began experiencing some recognizable personal gains after a lifetime of loss. It is called progress.

Things changed. Business got worse. So did the marriage. Loneliness set in. My A.A. sponsor was spending long weeks out of town and out of touch. My son began spending less time at home, coming in at 3:00 A.M. or dawn. My wife shrunk farther into depression, hitting "happy hours" and coming home drunk on occasion with a female companion—a drinking partner who replaced me for a time. A kind of post-alcoholic depression set in. I stayed close to A.A. and buried in the new workload assigned by the business consultant. Without alcohol, I became paralyzed. Wave after wave of unfiltered feelings provoked the impulse to take action on this or that issue while those in A.A. parroted the unwritten edict to make no major changes, unless a situation was life-threatening, for one year. The medics in the treatment center told me it would take all of three years for a drunk like me to begin to be the person I might have been before crossing over into alcoholism. The business consultant said it would take three to five years to unlearn my worst habits practiced for a lifetime. I was stuck. Prone to reactions instead of responses, I couldn't prioritize my next moves—there were too many next moves. I was one gigantic cramp. And I was ready to blow or implode.

Somehow I stayed plugged in. I attended those 9:30 P.M. A.A. meetings faithfully. I drove to the one-hour-long follow-up group meetings at the treatment center twice a week. After five months, I couldn't contain it anymore and, at a treatment center meeting, I once again asked for help. I had lost contact with that first sponsor. The business consultant had been a surrogate and was now gone. I had been using the business issues to avoid my living issues. I was miserable and said so during that meeting. I was honestly enjoying some parts of my life without alcohol but I wanted peace and peace of mind and finally asked for it. A counselor made a call on my behalf to a man whom they knew had sixteen years of active A.A. sobriety.

The first question Dave asked me when I met him in the coffee shop was, "What Step are you on?" When I replied, "Step Four," he responded, "Good, we're gonna start on Step One. But first I'll tell you a little about myself."

Dave's decision to attend his first meeting of A.A. sixteen years ago came one night shortly after ripping his wife's blouse off her back and moments after she kicked him in the groin. They were both drunk. She found A.A. first and he, the day after. She's kept twenty-four hours ahead of him ever since. His second son surrendered to A.A. when a moment of clarity came to him in a three-foot by three-foot by seven-foot concrete container behind the walls of a southern state penitentiary. He's doing well and sober today.

Dave allowed me to share some of my issues. To the problem of "Her," he set his face in squarely in front of mine with these simple instructions: "Leave her alone! She's ahead of you and gaining."

Addressing the employee and morale problems, he said, "That's the *doing* part of you. I can't address that. We're dealing here with the *being* part of you. The doing follows. I attend one particular meeting a week on Wednesdays at 7:00 P.M. Show up there, do what I do, we'll have coffee after the meetings each week and we'll begin to work the Steps after we've visited a few times."

Dave seemed to be in no hurry to watch me do my thing. As he said in the first meeting, " I'd say that one appropriate slogan for you to adopt right now is, 'Easy Does It.' If it took thirty years to do what you did, it might take more than a few months to undo the worst of it. Just slow down."

Things then began to get better. Every week he and I would talk. He allowed me to proceed through the first three Steps again and filled in some of the missing pieces. I revisited the initial fears of emotional and spiritual suffocation and death with him. The fear of the desire to end it, the hopelessness . . . all the stuff that had lead me to pick up the phone and ask for help from that local treatment center, with his help, became part of a stronger spiritual fiber.

I had come to realize early in my recovery that my life was unmanageable and that I had no power over my desire to drink alcohol or my reaction to it, once I did. The notion of Double-Dumb permitted me to admit that there were others, individuals or in groups who were more experienced or who had more power over things that simply baffled me. I became willing to accept that I did not have to be alone, reinvent the wheel of commerce, or recreate the concepts of marriage, fatherhood, small business, spirituality or religion. I simply needed to understand that recent history did not commence with my birth and my subsequent takeover of this planet.

I became willing to borrow bits and pieces of the good in others and the God they trusted until I had assembled a God of my own that I trusted. As He became whole within me, the hole within me diminished and whole me began to emerge—the one I was at the age of fifteen—vital, optimistic, hopeful, spirited and hungry to learn. I had to review and learn of the damage I had done to others and myself and then share my view of my part in these wrongs openly with another human being. I came to understand that I could forgive them and myself and be free of the shame and guilt resulting from my actions so long as I held to my resolve to never act in the same ways again. I admitted I had to grow up.

When I had made a list of the people I had harmed, Dave and I reviewed it to be sure it was fact and not the fantasies spawned from my over-reactive and manipulative mind. We discussed how my behaviors might be changed to make it up to those I'd harmed and with whom I should offer a humble apology and reparation.

I saw how my reliance on my sarcasm, skepticism, and fears of failing and a defective sense for relationships could hurt others, whether or not I poured alcohol into the mind that believed they had served me well at home and at work. Through a constant and conscious association with a piecemeal God, I learned to focus, as often as I can remember to, on my reactions to things that fit in a world I haven't made and to realize that all things have a purpose. I am no longer judge and no longer juror; I am a steward.

Alcoholism is also called a disease of social isolation. It was practiced so long in my immediate and extended family that, when I finally reached out for help, those I had touched had all insulated themselves from me, from each other and from the rest of the world. In a sick ritual and dance, at home and in the workplace, we exchanged spit daily, each contributing something to what the other had who in turn supported the worst in the ones next to them.

Circumstances arose permitting my son to agree to a week of voluntary confinement in a local treatment center where he became educated, as I had been earlier. He participated in A.A. for a brief time, entered the job market, and undertook a certification program in a computer-related field, and is employable today, at the age of twenty-one. He's on his own and at livable wages. His self-esteem and free will were delivered back to him quickly and we enjoy a closer, more loving relationship than was possible before taking this new road. He may not find it necessary to again experience life in a three-foot, by three-foot, by seven-foot concrete container in the middle of a penitentiary yard in a southern state. He may not find it necessary to return to A.A. for further education in a way to live without alcohol. However, he now knows he has a choice of one over the other, should he ever reach that fork in the road.

Out of twenty-two original employees at the beginning of my recovery, within two years, we maintained an efficient staff of eighteen. Three of the originals remained.

My wife attends occasional Al-Anon meetings and accompanies me to A.A.-related conferences. Together, we often attend family group meetings and other A.A.-related events. She still prefers her nightly place of refuge, but has cut back on the later night hours more often lately. We're attempting to date again and the overall anger in the house rises, then falls when I remember to avoid my own old reactions that causes it in either of us.

The healing of the family will come, perhaps never as completely as I want it. I understand that. Upon visiting the Tenth and Eleventh Steps of A.A. daily, I am reminded to review my actions and to appreciate those actions having beneficial effects on others and me. I am instructed to, and therefore, promptly and humbly apologize to anyone whom I might have subjected to my old behaviors and adjust my alignment on the new path I walk in God's world daily.

Things are better now, but not perfect. I've learned patience. I sometimes remember to think about what I'm thinking about before I act on the originating thought. As I change my behavior, the family's responses change too. With the closest family members, this takes longer. We developed more elaborate response rituals, rooted in complicated personal survival fears. It takes a while for such time-worn responses to erode, even when we know they are destructive and hurtful because they have protected us for years.

The issues for me are no longer related to alcohol use but to alcoholism, which I experience daily. The desire to have a drink left long ago. It visits me occasionally, asking if I'd like to reconsider this absurd decision, like an annoying telemarketer from a credit card company calling at the dinner hour. I still hang up politely. I continue, however, to experience frequent spells of long-term obsessive thinking, usually focused on getting things done, getting them done now, and getting them done my way, which, of course, does nothing to nourish growth in partnerships in a family, the workplace or society in general. My mind, however, did then and continues now to carry me away to a place where I prefer to apply quick fixes, impatience, self-righteous indignation and my array of trusted flight, fright and fight remedies when things are not going the way I want them to.

Often now, things crop up—things I didn't know I didn't know about. Someone has pointed out to me that the process of gaining knowledge is actually a violent and destructive procedure within us. In order to receive a new thought on a subject we know about, we never *unlearn*, we must *destroy* what we know. It is only then that we allow in new information and recreate a new understanding with which we create new knowledge. I react with fear toward a process that represents painful change and results in new understandings that recreate me. Without Alcoholics Anonymous, its simple Steps, its members and the help I receive from a personal God, I would never have come to know that I didn't know that. I would never have permitted the daily, sometimes painful, healing and recreating that occurs within me now as I follow twelve simple suggestions that my life and the lives of others now depend upon.

Fifteen Years Old, an Alcoholic and a Drug Addict

Amy C.—Pennsylvania

No knocks. No warning. Just the sound of stomping feet, smashing shoulders, collapsing hinges, and scraping wood. I managed to make it to the bathroom before the police broke the door down. They stormed my friend's apartment with extended guns and stern faces, kicking at empty beer cans and whiskey bottles. My drinking buddies sat on the sunken couch, pushing the coke bags deeper into their pockets and hoping that they wouldn't be frisked.

When the commotion faded, my parents emerged. They seemed to have walked right out of the wall to present me with a few choices—none of which were attractive. Jail, institutions, or an alcoholic death. The reality was that I had no choice. My parents chose for me, and they chose an institution. At three o'clock in the morning on January 13, 1990, I was admitted to Charter Fairmount Institute. I was fifteen years old, an alcoholic, and a drug addict.

During my thirty-day stay, I learned very little about the disease of alcoholism. Sure, I learned the classic phrases: "People, places, and things." "Think, think, think." "Meeting makers make it." "Just don't drink." "This too shall pass." "You never have to feel this way again." "Keep coming back." "No relationships for the first year." "It's a selfish program." I could spout any one of these on command, but I still knew nothing of alcoholism's causes and conditions. I was without defense.

I made ninety meetings in ninety days. My mother monitored my attendance (which sometimes included drafting a schedule for me). She knew that I had earned my seat. Slouched in a folding chair, I would sit in the back of the room and chain-smoke. I didn't ask anyone's name, and when someone asked mine, I lied. Sharing was out of the question. If pushed, I would announce my feelings but never the causes. I didn't want any of these people to know anything about me. I had worked very hard at veiling myself, and I wasn't about to stop now. After huffing through the Lord's Prayer, I hurried out of the room, refusing rides and phone numbers.

During this time, my old friends would follow me in their cars (at drive-by speed) and throw beer cans at my head. The dented cans were like daggers against my temples, the foam like my blood. I heard A.A.'s predict that old friends fade quicker than an alcohol-induced fog. This was not the case with me. I was caught between two worlds: one that demanded total abstinence and one that jeered at the thought. I was petrified of both.

I foolishly tried to forge a compromise: A.A. at night and old friends during the day—an attempt which sent my friends into mania. They quickly became tired of and bored with me. I owed most of them money, stash, or "favors." They had no tolerance for the slice of conscience I had gained in those ninety days. Eventually, their world rolled on without me, flattening my ego and leaving me unconnected. After the dust cleared, it was only the hand of A.A. that remained. I reluctantly grabbed at it.

I became very active in what I then thought was the program. I made an average of six meetings a week, subscribing to the "living in the rooms" approach to recovery. I bowled, went to dinners, played pool, danced, shuffled cards, and cleaned ash trays. Occasionally, someone would ask me to share my experience, strength, and hope—at which point, a gray-haired man might profess that he had spilled more than I had consumed. A very sloppy drunk, I'd think. The thought of speaking always made me tremble. The experience part I had down; it was the strength and hope that I lacked.

I was often restless, irritable, and discontent. To "get out of my head," I began sponsoring anyone who asked me. (Many wouldn't because I was so young.) When asked about recovery, I gave vague answers and sometimes changed the subject. I could not explain how the obsession would pass because mine had not. I tried to give assurances that I myself did not believe. All of these suffering alcoholics drank again, except me. (If any one of you are reading this now, I can only offer my deepest regrets and apologies. I have prayed for you many times since, in the hope that you will return.)

Being around these alcoholics did not comfort me. I struggled with the idea of being one of them, of never being able to drink again. I searched for loopholes but found none. I could relate all too well. "This too shall pass, " the old-timers said. "Just don't drink." And that's about all I did.

To appease my sponsor, I made an uneducated and halfhearted attempt at a moral inventory. "If you don't do a Fourth, you'll pick up a Fifth," he said. I listed all the people who hurt me and read them aloud arrogantly. They were the reason I was so screwed up, I assured him. Together, we lit the corner of my paper on fire and watched the names disappear. The ashes floated through the air like wish weeds. My resentments, fears, and desire to retaliate remained. They festered and grew into a thick wall, which would block me from God for many years. I was bound.

With nearly three years sobriety, I went away to a small college where secrets had a short shelf life. It did not take long for people to discover that I didn't drink and why. On many weekends, rogues would line up empty beer cans in front of my door and write "Drink Bitch" on my message board. It was a very lonely first year.

There was a pernicious hole in the core of my stomach, and I decided that a man would cork it. I found several willing participants who marveled at the idea of being my stopper. I demanded that I be the center of their universes. When they failed to act as I prescribed, I became angry and hurt, and many of the relationships ended soon after. Occasionally, these relationships would drag on long after they should have, long after bitter resentments had materialized. John was the last and most momentous of them all.

We were introduced in the rooms by a mutual friend. He was confident and aggressive with a thin face and a steady eye. He asserted that he already knew who I was, that he had known for awhile. There was something about him that I liked immediately, something unnamed but instinctual, something conveyed in the tone of his voice. Much later, I discovered that a date with me won him a small amount of cash, no more than twenty dollars—a bet wagered and lost by his cousin. Soon, we began to date each other exclusively; I have since wondered if he was further rewarded for that.

After a few months, he exhibited all the signs of relapse: erratic behavior, stiff smells, the constant need to explain, shaking hands and a fast-beating heart, and possession of other people's money. He would sober up for a few days here and there but always ended up on the street with a crack stem in his pocket. I would save him, I thought, and we moved in together. In return, I expected complete devotion and dependence. He did not comply.

I came home to floors covered with glass stems and empty Bud cans, missing blank checks, pawned furniture, and eventually, another woman's clothing in my closet. Still, I stayed. We had heated arguments constantly, during which I became violent and destructive. I threw knives at his head, broke dishes against his body, sliced phone cords, chased his new girlfriend down the street with a metal bar, and lit their clothing on fire. (I had always been a violent drunk. Merely removing the alcohol from my system did not change that.) Fueled by this anger, my obsession to drink was growing, oozing out of my ears and crawling across my face. I was faced with two alternatives: to go on to the bitter end or accept spiritual help. Not easy alternatives to face! I decided to persist for a little while longer.

Again, the police intervened, this time with raised pistols and threats of conspiracy charges. John was wanted for several thefts and burglaries (including robbing my college roommate). "Aiding and abetting is a serious charge," they said, and I talked. I never had a problem doing that—talking—even in my active drinking days. I had adopted the better-you-than-me attitude very quickly. After all, I could not go to jail with five years of sobriety. What would people think? Today, he sits in a lonely jail cell waiting for AIDS to steal his breath. I pray for him daily, in the hope that he will find the courage and the need for repentance.

For my fifth-year anniversary, I was asked to speak by my first sponsor. I sat next to him in the front of the room on a hard wooden bench and bawled. I charged A.A.s with lying. They had said I would never have to feel that way again—hopeless, angry, insane, suicidal, and afraid—but I did feel that way. I did, and the golden coin they presented me that night did not mitigate those feelings.

"Keep coming back," they said.

Instead, I locked myself in my dorm room for several days and did not eat or shower. With my knees to my chest, I recited a few quickie prayers, the kind we pray when all else fails: please help me God, because I don't know what to do anymore. I expected something drastic, a blast of lightning, an epiphany. Bobby, my new friend from A.A., called the next day, when I had grown particularly pitiful.

"Amy, you don't have to feel that way anymore," he said. He must have been at that meeting. "I know how to make it OK."

"How's that?" I asked arrogantly. I knew he had only been sober for about nine months. What could he tell me about recovery?

"You have to do the Steps."

"I already have," I said, but I hadn't—not all of them, not any of them honestly.

"If you had, you wouldn't feel this way now."

I lazed in that bitter morass of self-pity for a few more days before I took him up on that offer. When I did, he promised that my fear and my drink problem would virtually disappear. I was skeptical but willing to hear him out.

He provided me with a Big Book, highlighters, and a dictionary. We opened the cover and he asked, "What's on the first page on this book?" I stared down at a blank page and said, "Nothing."

"Exactly," he said. "That's what you know about this book."

I was insulted by his comment but too tired to argue. Besides, I had nothing to base an argument on. I took long, deep breaths, trying to inhale as much willingness as I could. My chest rose and swelled, and I stole a sliver of comfort from that repetition. Willingness was all that was required of me, he said.

As we read, I highlighted the parts I could relate to. When we reached page twenty-one, the brief description of a real alcoholic, the corners of my mouth rose to my cheeks. At this point, I hoped to tell Bobby that I had made a mistake, that I was not alcoholic, that we need not continue. But I could not. My page was saturated with yellow ink. I am a real alcoholic, and I conceded that fact to my innermost self. I suffered, he said, from an illness which only a spiritual experience would conquer. But how and when? We read on and talked of God.

I had always believed in the existence of God, but I could not see the personal relevance. What did He have to do with me? I thought of him as an onlooker, someone unwilling to intervene in the destruction of His own people.

"How've you stayed sober all these years?" Bobby asked.

How had I stayed sober? It certainly couldn't be contributed to anything I had done. I had encouraged my defects to blossom and often enjoyed their reign. I danced around booze, trying to snatch vicarious pleasure from others. My sobriety had been nothing short of a miracle.

"Are you willing to believe in a Power greater than yourself?" he asked.

I nodded.

Now, how to turn my will and my life over to Him? In those first five years of sobriety, I had heard many interpretations on how to do this Step: pretend my problems were in my hands and lift them to God; write down my problems and stick them in a jar marked "God"; repeat "God's will, not mine" to myself several times in a row. "There are as many ways to do these Steps as there are members," some A.A.ers said.

"If that was the case, " Bobby said, "A.A. would be dead indeed. We share a common solution, Amy."

There was only one way to do the Third Step: I had to quit playing God, dictating plans to unwillingness listeners, and indulging in self-pity and anger. I had to quit making myself the center of everything. "Selfishness—self-centeredness! That, we think, is the root of our trouble." Bobby held my shaking hands, and we kneeled in the middle of his living room. He propped my Big Book on his couch and instructed me to read aloud the following prayer:

"God, I offer myself to Thee—to build with me and do with me what Thou wilt. Relieve me of bondage of self that I may better do Thy will. Take away my difficulties, that victory over them may bear witness to those I would help of Thy Power, Thy Love, and Thy Way of Life. May I do Thy will always!"

This prayer and decision would have little permanent effect, we read, if not immediately followed by action—a moral inventory. How true that was! How many times had I asked for help and then declined when the situation lessened? Now was the time, when my hands were still bruised from crawling back to A.A. If I would have waited until the "fog" of insanity lifted, as some suggest, I might not be here today.

I did exactly as the Big Book outlines: I listed my resentments, fears, and harms done and got right down to the causes and conditions. For the next week, I wrote and wrote and wrote until I couldn't anymore, until I could honestly say that I had not skimped or omitted anyone or anything. When I was finished, pages and pages of harbored feelings stared me in the face. I had always thought that I had few defects of character, that others had been the problem, that people got what they deserved from me. My long inventory was proof of the opposite.

I shared it with Bobby the very next day. "You have swallowed some big chunks of truth about yourself," he said.

Again, we knelt and thanked God for allowing us to know Him better. I was on my way to finding a sweet relationship with the God of my understanding. I could see the ways in which I had been blocked from that Power, the part I played in my own spiritual destruction. It was like looking in a mirror and watching your reflection shrivel before your eyes. Things are not always what they seem. I was willing to have those crippling defects removed, and I prayed for God to do just that—to remove them, each and every one. The Sixth and Seventh Steps were completed. "But faith without works is dead," he said. Still, more action—amends!

Before working the Steps, I always qualified my apologies with explanations. "I'm sorry I did that, but you deserved it," I'd say. Or, "If you wouldn't have done that, I would have had to. . . ." Nothing was ever really my fault; hence, my apologies were never quite sincere. The problem was that I had never forgiven anyone else their harms done. Resentments ignited my insides like a torch in a cave. I wrapped them around my body and felt the warmth of their familiarity. Making amends required the destruction of such comfort. I had to be rid of it. I had to, or my defects would eat me alive, sending me back to alcohol in skeleton form. I prayed for the willingness to forgive others.

I had a list of those to whom I owed amends; I made it when I took inventory. There was plenty of debris that needed cleaning. Humbly, I went to my family first. They obviously knew of my struggle and had prayed for its end. Many of them saw me as an habitual apologizer. I had to explain the difference, that I was not simply saying "I'm sorry," that I was committed to change, and that I was searching for a spiritual experience which would conquer my alcohol problem (and any other for that matter). Skeptical and still smarting, they held the "don't-tell-me, show-me" stance. I have worked very hard since to show them that I mean business, that I am recovered. Together, we thank God.

And so it went, the clearing away of my spiritual, emotional, physical, and financial wreckage. However, not all my experiences with the Ninth Step were so pleasant. I have watched many A.A.s twist, manipulate, and justify the Ninth Step tag—"except when to do so would injury them or others." How easy it is to label ourselves as an "other," claiming that a particular amends would hurt us. I am guilty of such a justification.

Carol, the woman for whom John left me, was at the top of my amends list. Since I had no idea how to contact her, I prayed for the willingness to set matters right, if we ever met again. Late one evening, just outside the doors of my home group, Carol approached me and asked me for directions. I stared into her squinted eyes, knowing that she knew me, that God had sent her to collect my amends. Fear had once again squeezed my shoulder. I spit out her directions but no amends. She disappeared into the darkness, and that fast my opportunity was gone. I had waved it away.

This proved to me how easy it is to rest on my laurels, to let up on the spiritual program of action. I must be vigilant, continue to watch for my defects, ask for them to be removed when they crop up, and make amends when necessary. This is essential for my daily spiritual maintenance.

After reviewing my actions (or should I say inaction) with Carol, I asked God to forgive my procrastination and to provide me with another opportunity to measure my willingness. To date, such an opportunity has not presented itself. (Carol, I look for you in the shadows, hoping that you will come once again to collect what is rightfully yours.) Next time, I will not shrink. God will guide me in word and thought.

The Big Book assures us that He "does not make too hard terms to those who seek Him." Released from an alcoholic coma, I have embraced God and come to call Him by name. I ask every morning for guidance, for the right thoughts and motives, for strength and courage; I thank him daily for all that He has given and all that He has taken away. "Gratitude is an action, not a feeling," a friend of mine once said. Therefore, I have begun to work for Him, with His children, my brothers and sisters, to share my experience, strength, and hope with those who still suffer. I testify of His power and love. It is my honor and pleasure.

In return, He has done for me what I could not do for myself—released me from torture and bankruptcy. God brought me to Alcoholics Anonymous; Alcoholics Anonymous brought me back to God; God led me to Freedom. I am reborn and recovered!

My Story of Recovery

Bill R.—Apollo Beach, Florida

I have learned, from speaking at A.A. meetings, that the preferred format to follow is "what it was like, what happened, and what it's like now," so that is how I am going to approach telling my story.

I grew up in an average middle-class Irish-German family in the New York City area. Early on I learned that drinking was an acceptable method for relaxing after a day's work or for getting people "oiled" and getting a party really rolling. With the exception of a little marijuana in college, I never got into the drug scene. I had it in my mind that doing drugs was stupid and could kill you, but drinking alcohol was a normal part of being an adult. We had a pretty good family life, except that sometimes Dad, who was probably a good, functioning alcoholic would get a little too loaded, and holidays could get crazy.

I was a straight-A student, scholarships to high school and college. In my sophomore year at college, I joined a fraternity that was the biggest drinking and party frat on campus. I later served as president of that fraternity for two years. In looking back at it, I guess I had found a group where I belonged.

In spite of all the partying, I managed to graduate with a degree in chemical engineering in 1972. Life was great; I had a good job, money in my pocket, and lots of good friends to party with.

I continued on as a good, "functioning" drunk for quite a few years, advancing in my profession, traveling, doing consulting and service work throughout the USA and some foreign assignments. I felt I could function and think better half-loaded than many people did when they were stone sober.

Sure, there were a few rough moments, like one Monday morning when a vice president at work noted that I kind of reeked of booze and asked what I had been up to all weekend. I told him that I had been to the weddings of college buddies, on both Saturday and Sunday, and it had been a "pretty tough" weekend. There was one really long drinking lunch around Christmas 1977, that ended up with me and a college buddy sitting at my desk chatting and polishing off most of a bottle of scotch. When I was leaving, around 6:00 P.M., my boss commented that it might be better if I didn't come back to the office after such lunch meetings. He didn't seem really mad, he just thought it didn't look good to the other employees. *But*, I thought, *how mad could this guy get?* After all, I was one of the most productive guys in the company.

When I traveled on business, I always carried some booze in my luggage, since I never knew how late I might get in to the hotel, or if I might wind up in a "dry" county. I liked to be prepared. It never occurred to me that normal people didn't worry about having a sure supply of liquor.

There were other rough moments, but all in all, I functioned pretty well, and in over ten years of steady business travel, I only missed two planes as a result of my drinking. I thought that was an admirable record.

I first learned about Alcoholics Anonymous in 1975. One of my best college drinking buddies was hitting bottom, having problems at work and with his marriage. He obviously needed to do something about his drinking. One piece of A.A. literature he showed me was a pamphlet of twenty yes-or-no questions to determine if you were an alcoholic. If you answered yes to any three or four of the questions, you most likely had a problem. I answered yes to about five or six of them, but I discarded it with the idea that they probably made the questions intentionally easy since they were looking to recruit new members. By the time I got to A.A. in June of 1985, I could answer yes to about eighteen or nineteen of the twenty questions. I carried the checked-off question list in my wallet during my first year of sobriety to serve as a reminder of how much worse I had become since 1975, in the event that I should start to feel that I could go back and start drinking "successfully" again.

In January of 1979 I was moved from NYC to Los Angeles to open the company's west-coast office. Later that year, the girl I had been dating for several years in New York moved to L.A. We became engaged, and were married in December of that year.

In December 1980 I got arrested for my one and only drunk driving. The judge ultimately reduced it to a "wet reckless driving," since it was my first offense and my blood alcohol level reading of 0.11 was not terribly high. Frankly, the low blood alcohol amazed me since I got pulled over around 11:00 P.M. and I had been drinking most of the day, since we had a Christmas party at the office. I got off with a few hundred-dollars fine and attendance at some educational films. My wife was really upset because I was being so irresponsible by driving a company car drunk; if I had a wreck I could have lost my job. At that point, my problem was not my being an alcoholic; my problem was getting caught. So we made an agreement for the future that if I were going to get drunk, she would drive.

In mid-1984 the company I had been working for during the past two years decided to shut down the small division that I was in, and my boss persuaded me to purchase the local account base for a few dollars down and a percentage of ongoing sales. So, in June of 1984, I became my own boss. Things went well for the first six months, but by December I was starting to have problems showing up and keeping commitments to customers.

Unlike some people, I did not have one specific event that I would call the "bottom" of my alcoholic drinking. I just went slowly downhill from January to June of 1985, losing my ability to function. At first I was able to get up in the morning, get showered, shaved, dressed, and put on the appearance of going to work. My wife might come home and find me slightly drunk and ask if I had been drinking, and I would reply that I had gotten done early at the customer's, and come home (my office was in my house) and had a few "pops" while I did some paperwork. Later in that six-month downhill slide, in spite of my best intentions, she would come home and find me drunk, unshowered, unshaved, and in the same clothes I had put on in the morning. Meanwhile, I am going nuts, because every time the phone rang in my office at home, I just knew it was some unhappy customer getting ready to cancel their account.

When I looked in the mirror, I felt what I call "the death of a thousand cuts" as I slowly lost one customer after another. I often wished that I worked for a company and had a boss who could fire me and end the pain. I was paranoid, thinking that everyone knew how far I had degenerated and was talking about me. I was suicidal. I wanted to end it all, but first I would have to get current on my backlogged work and then I would have to think up a really unique method of suicide, something that would get written up and presented at a coroner's convention. Is that insane pride and ego or what? But most of all I was tired. Tired of achieving stuff, climbing mountains for others, only to find when I got to the top there was a bigger mountain on the other side.

My wife became pregnant in early 1985, so she quit drinking. By then she could clearly see how far downhill I had gone. She told me that I was an alcoholic and that I had better do something about my drinking, otherwise she was going to leave since she did not intend to bring a child into the kind of marriage that we had.

While she had complained about my drinking in the past, this time, for some unknown reason, I really believed that she was serious about leaving. (I later found out in A.A. that this is called a "moment of clarity.") If she divorced me, my entire "veneer of social respectability" would be stripped away. I would lose the house, the family, and what little was left of the business.

So I called A.A. and got some meeting information. When it came time to go to the meeting that night, I told her that I was too tired. She insisted that I go and even drove me. To this day, I don't know if she drove me because she wanted to make sure I went, or because she saw that I was a bit drunk and could have been arrested for drunk driving.

I was a bit loaded at that first meeting, but I didn't seem as bad as the guy who was the speaker. He had a funny laugh, and some nervous twitches, and I figured he had only been recently released from a mental institution. I found out later that he had been sober for three years. I went to a "beginners" meeting the next night.

I still remember that beginners meeting. The people made me feel welcome and some guy, about my age, told his story, which sounded a lot like mine. He and another man invited me to go for coffee after the meeting. The other man, Bill H., seemed even more mentally defective than the first speaker I had heard did. Bill had a Texas drawl and talked kind of "marble-mouthed" with an odd cadence to his speech. And though he appeared to be slightly "wet brained," Bill had as much love in his heart for the newcomers as anyone I have ever met in A.A. That first night, he went out to his car, came back with a directory of A.A. meetings and wrote his name and phone number on the cover. It made me feel connected, or special, or something, since I was so naive, I thought that an A.A. meeting directory was top secret, confidential information. It was at that meeting that I purchased my copy of the book *Alcoholics Anonymous*. I figured it would give my wife the appearance that I was really serious about my "studies" in A.A. That was June 14,

1985, Flag Day (I used to say that they put out the flags to celebrate that I had quit drinking), and I have not had a relapse and gone back to drinking since that day. I never went through a hospital detox or rehab program; I think I felt that it would have been too embarrassing to have to explain to people that I had to go to rehab. I can sure relate to the concept that alcoholism is a "disease of denial" and that "alcoholism is one disease that *no* hypochondriac will claim to have."

Though I was attending daily A.A. meetings and raising my hand as a newcomer, I did not really intend to stay sober for the long haul. I just wanted to stay sober long enough to get my wife and customers off my ass, and eventually get back to the point where I could drink a few cocktails in the evening after work and limit the serious, heavy drinking to the weekends. My target was to stay sober until the birth of our first child in October, because I knew that surely I would have to have a few drinks to celebrate the birth.

I attended a daily meeting at 7:00 A.M. The people there taught me how to "live sober," how to put up with all the day-to-day aggravation and nonsense of spouses, families, customers, jobs, etc. and not have to take a drink to cope with life. There were some great, loving people in that meeting, including my first sponsor, Jim G., and they became a wonderful source of support and encouragement in my early sobriety.

God must have known that I was going to need that support, because on September 20, at three months sober, my daughter was born and she was a month premature and almost died. She spent ten days in newborn intensive care and had some problems during her first few years, but today, by God's grace, she is a thriving A+ student and a roughhouse soccer goalie. In addition to my daughter being premature, my wife had problems with the delivery and almost bled to death on the delivery table. Amazingly, A.A. people started showing up at the hospital to look after me. I could not understand why people who had known me for just a few months would spend their time to come and look after me. I came to learn that they were just giving back of the time and support that was lovingly given to them when they were newcomers. All they wanted to do was to help me stay sober.

I learned so many things during my early years in A.A. I will try to touch briefly on some of the highlights:

That alcoholism is a disease, and not a moral weakness. And that it may be a genetically transmitted disease; I could have gotten it from my dad, without my permission.

That there are three stages to the disease: 1) Fun, 2) Fun and Problems, 3) All Problems. And that just about no one hits "bottom" until the final stage.

• My life in early sobriety got better, just because it wasn't getting "worser" as a result of my drinking.

• That the act of Surrender is not necessarily a cowardly act. That in war many brave men had to be asked by their general to surrender, lest they keep fighting a greatly superior force, and wind up all dying for nothing. That was a major revelation for a guy like me who was raised with the notion that being pigheaded and obstinate were character assets.

• That while I was self-conscious and felt like a bit of a "lightweight" for not having a really horrible drinking history, I should be grateful that I had gotten sober at the relatively young age of thirty-five.

• That for me there is *no fun* left in the liquor bottle—I used it all up years ago.

• That the First Step in recovery was to "concede to my innermost-self that I was alcoholic." Which to me means that no matter where I am in the world, and no matter how long I have been physically sober, I will always have a bodily allergy to ethyl alcohol in any form. As a chemist, it became rather easy for me to do my First Step when I put it in the context of being powerless over the biochemical reactions which take place in my body.

My first sponsor, Jim G., had eighteen years sober at the time, and had managed not only to stay sober but was able to keep his family together and hold onto his job. That was the kind of stuff that I wanted. Plus, I think I figured that with eighteen years sober, he could write the essence of the A.A. program on a matchbook cover and he would be a good guy for me to pick his brain and learn everything real quick and get done with it.

I learned from him that I could not just absorb the life experiences and lessons of his eighteen years of sobriety. After he got to know my flair for being "a genius," he told me that I could probably memorize the entire Big Book of A.A., and that while that might do me a lot of good, I would still have to spend the rest of my life living the program.

I would talk to him about my life problems and he would steadfastly refuse to tell me what decisions to make. What he talked to me about were the principles that I was to use in making my decisions. He said it was not his job as my sponsor to make my decisions, rather it was his job to teach me some principles for good living, so that when he was gone, I would have something by which to live my life.

He made no big demands on me, and didn't threaten me that I was going to get drunk if I didn't move along in working the Steps of the A.A. program. When I was dragging my heels on writing my Fourth Step Inventory, he would say, "Well, Bill, how long do you want to put off feeling good?"

When I was finally ready to do my Fourth Step he didn't jump for joy. Instead, he sat me down and asked me how I felt about my Third Step, about the God that I had turned my will and my life over to. I was kind of insulted, since academically I have always been on the fast track and didn't like being "put back a grade." Turns out that was one of the best things he ever did for me. He had me review my Third Step, looking at the kind of God that I had. He suggested that it was important to have a loving and forgiving God to take with me into the writing of my Fourth Step. A God who already knew all of the terrible stuff that I had done, and who still loved me enough to give me the gift of sobriety, the moment of clarity. About the only thing I can recall him quoting out of the Big Book was the part about "there will come a time when you will have no effective mental defense against getting drunk, the only thing that will save you is your relationship with the God of your understanding."

After latching on to a loving and forgiving God, I was able to write my Fourth Step over just two weekends. At that time, Jim was getting ready to move out of the area, so I had some extra motivation to get it done before he left. We went to a quiet local park for him hear my Fifth Step. He listened and jotted some notes on an old envelope. It probably took about four hours to get it done. When I was finished, he looked at his notes and said something to the effect "Well, it's all there . . . a lot of B.S., along with a lot of truth." I was devastated. No congratulations for having written the best Fourth Step he had heard in his eighteen years of sponsoring people. Plus, I did not feel any great lifting-of-weight off of my shoulders, like some people do. I talked about my disappointing Fifth Step in meetings and was relieved to hear that other people had also not experienced any great relief when it was done. Fortunately, I had experienced some major spiritual feelings in doing my First and Third Steps, so I was not totally disconnected from my God. Gradually the feeling of disappointment faded as time went by.

During my first two years in A.A., I had a lot of "life stuff" happen to me, besides the stuff with my wife and daughter. At fourteen months sober, the doctors thought I had a bad appendix, so they put me in the hospital. I wound up having surgery for diverticulitis and woke up eighteen hours later in intensive care, with a temporary colostomy, and near-dead from peritonitis. I was mad as hell. I was a nice guy, working a good A.A. program and my wife was pregnant with our son. After eighteen months of doctor visits, tests, and procedures, and three more major surgeries (including another temporary colostomy), they finally got me put back together. It was certainly not a pleasant thing to go through, but looking back it was a powerful period of learning a whole lot about acceptance, surrender, and humility. Someone in A.A. told me that it was a blessing. After I told them where to go with their stupid idea, I backed up and asked them for their definition of "blessing." They told me a "blessing" was anything that forced me to work on my conscious contact with my God and grow in my relationship with Him. Well, it had certainly done that. The guy who became my second sponsor, Danny A., told me that God must really like me since He was sending me so many challenges in my early sobriety. He encouraged me by telling me that if I could stay sober and learn something through all of this stuff, I would probably be able to stay sober through anything.

After I got done with my Fifth Step, I gradually started to see some of my defects of character. I was envious and fearful of others' successes; I was controlling and manipulative; I was shallow yet prideful, and though I was a people-pleaser, I was dishonest in my relationships with other people. I also learned that I was never grateful or content in the moment or with the things that I currently had. I just knew that things could be or should be better down the road. I had lived most of my life being "hopelessly lost, but making great time." I immediately identified with an A.A. friend who talked about being a "chronic malcontent." There is an ancient proverb about it being better to light a candle than to curse the darkness, and somehow while growing up I had forgotten about taking action on the candle and instead had gotten the idea that if you just complained long and loudly enough, someone would light the damn candle for you.

While I had glimpses of these character defects in doing Step Five, their repetitive nature was really highlighted when I sat down to look at the people and relationships on my Eighth Step amends list. In the

A.A. book, *12 Steps and 12 Traditions*, in the chapter on the Eighth Step, there is a part that says in essence: We find that our defective relations with people were the principle cause of most of our woes, including our alcoholism. The *big* piece of information I got out of that is that if I don't learn how to get along better with the people in the world, there is a good probability that I am going to go back to drinking. Drinking to kill the recurring pain and frustration.

When I was working on looking at those relationships and talking (or complaining) to my sponsor about them, he was relentless in asking, "Bill, what was your part in this deal?" To this day I thank God that my sponsors never rubber stamped my alibis and excuses.

Those sponsors taught me that the Ninth Step was where I get to go out and change all my defective relationships by behaving differently. I was taught by experienced A.A. people that "amend" means to change, not to apologize. I see a lot of confusion on that in the meetings that I sit in today. Go look up the word in the dictionary if you want, it might prove helpful.

Not that I didn't have some apologies to make for my drunken behavior, and the related neglect and abuse. However, since I was not a major felon, thief, wife beater, child abuser, etc., etc., I was a bit confused about how I needed to make my amends. Jim told me, "Bill, you are gonna have to make yours the hard way . . . you are gonna have to *live* them by behaving better." He pointed out that if I am six-months or two-years sober and still standing there on Monday morning apologizing to my family for having been a horse's ass the whole weekend, that family is probably not going to much impressed by my sobriety. Jim would ask: "What's really different in your behavior, other than you haven't gotten drunk in quite a while." Damn good question.

I learned to live my amends to the customers I had abused (because my disease of alcoholism had kept me from keeping appointments and doing what I had promised to do) by arriving on time and doing a little extra, without letting them know it. The little extra part was between me and God, and that it was part of what is called "the *inside* job." The same concept was to be applied to my wife, family, and friends. I was directed to try to be the best husband, father, friend, or engineer that I could be today, in sobriety. And to trust in God that over time my improved behavior with people would slowly mend those relationships, better than could ever be done even with the most sincere apology.

I had one major financial amend to make, regarding back payments owed to the company that I had purchased the account base from to start my business. I owed them more than $12,000, and in the first years of sobriety I truly didn't have the money to pay them. I got some wise direction in being told not to put myself on the cross by immediately contacting them, since that might risk losing my business and my ability to support my family.

After being sober a few years, I had put away enough money to pay them in full. Since it was a legal matter, I was told to get my business attorney involved and I think that was wise advice. That attorney knew about my drinking problem and my recovery, and when I explained the "spiritual nature" of my amends Step, he said something to the effect that God and I could take care of the spiritual stuff, and he would handle the legal end. Bottom line was that so many years had elapsed that none of the people who had been involved with my deal were still around. My lawyer sent some letters and directed me to put the money aside until the statute of limitations had elapsed. We could have really gotten into it and tried to dig up the people and the records, but it was a really large company, and I was told that digging too deep might damage the reputations of the people who probably should have pursued the matter of collecting the money from me years ago. So, I never had to pay them. But I didn't really get to keep the money either.

About that same time, I had a customer who owed me about the same amount of money and who would not or could not pay me. Rather than go through the legal expense of trying to collect from them, I was advised to "let it go" and just consider it God's way of evening out accounts. So that is what I did. Funny how God works sometimes. As Jim used to tell me, "God almost never works in a straight line." You do bad stuff and it sometimes doesn't get you right away, it may take weeks or months or years. Which makes it very hard to see cause and effect, and leaves me with the delusion that I maybe got away with something. The same concept applies when I do good things, I don't always see the immediate pay off. This spiritual way of life I have been taught to live can sure be interesting, and confusing.

In starting to do regular personal inventory (Tenth Step), I was taught to "Clear away the wreckage of the past, and try like hell not to create too much wreckage of the present."

There is a part in the A.A. "12 & 12" book on the Tenth Step that says, in effect, "Whenever I am disturbed, no matter what the reason, the problem is with me." I still remember how much I hated that when I first read it. I asked Jim how long I had to be sober before I got to blame other people. He replied that I had probably been doing *that* most of my life, and that I could start doing it again immediately. *But*, it would never get me any relief. I would just remain a perpetual victim. He told me that the only one I could ever hope to change was me and that I got to do that by taking inventory on my character defects and the defective relationships and situations which they created. Trying to change other people was a futile effort that would just leave me frustrated and discontented.

I was advised that when I am behaving the best that I can and other people continue to abuse me, lie to me, or generally give me a hard time, it might do well for me to just move away from those people and situations. That has proven to be excellent advice. It has kept me from constantly being frustrated by going back and trying to outmaneuver them. It has also helped me to stop being a perpetual victim of circumstance. A situation which can only lead me to carrying resentments toward my abusers. God knows, I see too many perpetual victims, with years of physical sobriety, sitting in A.A. meetings.

I think that part of the reason I see so many victims is that people do not know there is a difference between anger and resentment. I was taught that resentment is "chronic anger." It stems from never telling people that they stepped on my toes and that I don't like it. I encourage the people I meet in recovery to allow themselves to be angry and to look at the cause of it. But then, and this is most important, to get into the solution. Channel the anger, get mad enough about something to *do* something about it.

When I was in my first year of sobriety and struggling with my concept of God, an A.A. buddy suggested I try an "Eleventh Step Meeting" on Sunday mornings. The meeting format consisted of reading the "Prayer of St. Francis," then five minutes of silent meditation with the lights out, then reading from the Eleventh Step Chapter in the "12 & 12" book, with people sharing about their relationship with their God, or whatever else they had on their mind. People talked mostly about their relationship with the God of their understanding. I got to hear a lot of wonderful, spiritual things and I got to borrow bits and pieces from them in constructing the God that I understood.

The Eleventh Step talks about praying for knowledge of God's will for us and the power to carry it out. I have come to substitute the word "courage" for "power." Many times when I know in my heart what God wants me to do, it seems like a scary thing to do in a material world. So I have to ask Him for courage to face situations that look, in my small view of things, like sure disasters. Having been through a few of those situations in sobriety, it is now easier to face new ones as they come up. I can now review the places that God has put me in the past and I gain courage for today, or sometimes just for the next five minutes, by looking at how God has helped me in the past when I was challenged to do the "right thing."

Once I got into the regular practice of prayer and meditation, I thought that if I just prayed and meditated real well for fifteen minutes in the morning that I could stay on the "spiritual beam" all day, what I like to call *"unconscious* contact" with God. One more time I was looking for the cheap, quick fix and found that it doesn't work that way. I usually have to pause many times during the day and ask for help. The simplest thing I have learned to say is "God is with me." This is especially comforting in times of great fear. It slows down the frightened, thinking part of my mind, which is projecting nothing but death and disaster, and causes me to be reminded that God is *truly* with me, even in the midst of the most appalling mess. I find it much more effective than asking "God be with me," since that phrase, at least for me, gives me the idea that God at some point abandoned me and I have to beg Him to come back.

I have also learned that I have to keep working on "balance," whether it is mental, emotional or spiritual balance. I used to think that I should be able to get balanced for once and for all and stay that way. Kind of like becoming an expert tightrope walker. However, even the world's best tightrope walkers carry a very long balance pole and constantly sway from side to side. What makes them "expert" is that they keep moving back and forth enough to average out somewhere in the middle. I have come to accept "somewhere in the middle" as a reasonable goal for me.

I have come to look at my life as if it were a long journey by car. And on those long journeys, the radio station that was crystal clear when I started gradually starts to fade and pick up static. I sometimes feel totally tuned in with God and His plan for me, and then the signal fades. I lose touch. I can either do some work and adjust the tuning, or just keep going and be annoyed by the increasing static. Meditation is a way for me to call time-out and tune back in. I find that the music may be different, and the channel is certainly changed, but ultimately the Source is the same, a loving God as I understand Him.

I have had to give up a lot of my perfectionist, straight-A attitude and come to understand that in most of life, a C is a passing grade. I have also been helped by other honest, loving friends in recovery to see that what I thought was A+ work, was really only a C. That does not mean that I should slack off on using the talents and abilities that God gave to me. It only means that while I should strive for "excellence," I need to see that there is a distinct difference between "excellent" and "perfect." One is attainable for me; the other is God's domain.

As for the Twelfth Step, I know in the very deepest part of my heart and soul that I have had a spiritual awakening in my program of recovery; several of them as a matter of fact. Some of them were undeserved gifts from God, like the first moment of clarity. Others I believe I received because I did the spiritual work necessary, that is working the Steps, to prepare myself to receive them. Some were major awakenings about God's plan for me, and others were just like minor insights into what I was doing wrong in a defective relationship.

That is the message I try to carry to people in early physical sobriety who are new to the process of recovery. That seems at times difficult to do in some meetings that are full of sick, unrecovered people. But I have come to understand that they are just like me when I was new—either angry because they are frightened of the future (or the past), or just ignorant of the fact that the program and process of recovery will always produce the desired result, if they do the required work. They are lacking in faith. So I try to share some of my story of recovery with them.

I understand that speaking about spiritual solutions to worldly problems will not always make me popular. But I learned long ago that recovering from the disease of alcoholism is not about being popular. Hell, I wasn't particularly well liked by people for my drunken, abusive behavior. I sometimes say in meetings: "This is *not* the Elks Club, this is not about being popular; we play a game here where the losers die or go insane from this disease."

I was charged, by some wonderful, recovered people who have helped me over the years, with the responsibility of carrying the message, as undiluted as possible, to the people who are new. In my heart I owe a debt to those wonderful people that I can never fully repay. It is a debt of time, and patience, and love. So I try to do that, knowing from my experience, that whatever group I may be in, that there may be one or two people who are ready to recover, who want what I have received and are willing to go to any lengths to get it. To let the newcomers know, as Jim and others taught me, that "if all you get out of this deal is just *not* drinking, you have missed the boat."

If you who read this story are ready, I welcome you aboard the boat. It may seem small and unsteady to you at first, but it sure beats being in that cold water with the sharks, and I promise you, that if you stay the course, the boat will magically grow in size and take you on a journey that never ends, to a place that is ever changing.

Jump in or Back Away in Fear?

Robin K.—Illinois

As a child, I was shy and quiet. I was sad most of the time and terribly afraid of people. My two brothers and I were raised in a Christian home and we went to church every Sunday. I had a real zest for God then and was active in church activities. It was there I learned I could see God in everything and that He could see everything in me. But I also learned that He would punish me for being bad, and my father reinforced that. I remember being jealous of the kids at school who were "bad," believing they had more fun than I did. I wished I had their guts.

By the time I was thirteen, I figured out that if I smoked and used drugs, I would have instant friends. Because I was too afraid to use drugs, I just smoked and pretended to be high. In the meantime, I would go to my brother's room and practice smoking his stash of pot and hash. Soon, I was able to smoke with my new friends but still didn't feel connected to them. So I started drinking and using drugs more. I felt I could get away from the guilt ingrained in me by the church.

In no time, I was drinking and using daily—so much in fact that my new friends didn't want anymore to do with me. I was a "stoner," they said. I was forced to find friends who drank and drugged like me, so I did. Somehow, I managed to graduate from high school.

Shortly after graduating, my best friend introduced me to her older brother when he got out of prison (a man five years my senior). She and I decided to take him under our wing to keep him out of trouble. It wasn't long before we abandoned our friends and began hanging around with his. We went to parties with bikers, ex-cons, and needle-heads. He got me all the drugs and booze I wanted.

I was eighteen and had never had sex. I suppose I feared getting too close to someone and feared what God would do to me if I had sex out of wedlock. But her brother and I were in a full-fledged relation-ship now. Finally, the booze outweighed my fear, and I entered the worlds of sex and motherhood all in one night. I was sure God had punished me.

I thought the only way to make it right would be to marry the ex-con and stop drinking and drugging. I tried it for a year and a half, and during that time, I was a shell of a person. My husband and my friends were at the bar, as I sat alone and waited for my baby to be born. When he was born, I put him in his crib and wondered, "What now?" I con-tinued to wait—alone—with my drapes closed and a phone that never rang. I was afraid: to drive my car, to go outside, and to watch televi-sion. I was swallowed by fear, alone in an empty pit of despair.

Finally, I couldn't wait anymore: I drank. But it was all different now. The party was over. The drink became my lifeline, my tool for survival. I had a new guilt now, wondering how I could do this to my baby, wondering why God had punished me so. I kept waiting.

At twenty-two, I had a baby girl. When I brought her home, I could hardly live in my skin. I knew it wasn't right to bring these babies into such a house. Something had to change. If my husband changed, I decided, all would be well. So I went to Al-Anon. After a few meet-ings, I knew I had a problem too. Since I didn't want to go to A.A., I figured I could work Al-Anon's Twelve Steps and get the same results.

It only took six months for Al-Anon to sabotage my drinking. I tried to convince myself I was too young for this crap. I believed I could straighten out long enough to help my husband. Then, I could drink again. Instead of drinking, I smoked pot, thinking my sponsor wouldn't know the difference, and I was floored when she told me she knew. I thought I hid it well. "Get rid of the pot," she said, and then I might have a chance to recover. I accepted that my life was unmanage-able and that I was powerless over my husband's drinking, but I had a hard time accepting my own powerlessness. I thought I had some good drinking years left. . . . I relapsed.

I couldn't get my head straight and was consumed with thoughts of suicide. Under the advisement of a friend, I committed myself to a treatment center. When I awoke the next morning, I felt the effects of my pride. One week prior, I had been running a bridge group on that ward. How could I face anyone? That was the beginning of the miracle. I needed to be humbled. I needed to surrender before I could feel God's gentle hand guide me through the Twelve Steps. I found I was sick and in need of healing. I found I could only survive with complete reliance on God.

I was worried about the safety of my children. My husband was a heroin addict, and I worried he would neglect them. In addition, I discovered that he had been drugging me for months; he must have hoped to get rid of me so he and his girlfriend could have the kids. Then and there, I learned to pray. Up to this point, I had a hard time relating to God on a personal level. But as I prayed, I came to believe—believe that God was watching over my children, and I believed that He would give me the strength I needed. I felt God working in me and realized I was no good for my children until then.

When I closed my eyes, I saw myself standing on the edge of a cliff above a mass of clear water. I had to make a decision: jump in or back away in fear? I decided to get my feet wet; I jumped and found the water cool and refreshing. Making the decision to work the remaining Steps was quite similar. I decided to jump right in—to turn my will and life over to the care of God.

Since making this decision I have acted out on self-will. I used to get frustrated and beat myself up about it. But I learned this is an ongoing process. When this happens, I am reminded of the story of the little boy who brings his toy to his daddy to fix. Crying and stomping his feet, the boy wonders why his daddy will not fix the toy. His father waits patiently for the boy to quiet down and then says, "Son, you have to let it go before I can fix it." I find great peace in living His will.

It was time to write my inventory. Because I was unsure about what to write, I looked to the outline in the Big Book. When I put pen to paper, the magic happened. I wrote about how I operated, connived, and conned, and how I used people and benefits to benefit me. I wrote about my darkened soul, my defects, and the moral decay of my being. Then, I shared them with another alcoholic. I learned fear had ruled my every move and caused me to lie and distrust others. Sharing my defects with another person brought me a step closer to losing that fear.

My sponsor and I then talked about the Sixth and Seventh Steps— about the removal of my defects. After seeing them on paper, I was willing to let them go, one by one, and knelt down and asked God to remove them all. I knew God, in His infinite wisdom, would turn them into strengths.

In all honesty, because I was a quiet, stay-at-home drunk, my amends list consisted primarily of family members: my mom, dad, brothers, husband, and children. I have heard over and over in meetings that people put themselves first on their lists. I have a difficult time with that. For this drunk, I spent most of my drinking years trying to pamper myself and make situations go my way. Had I put myself on my amends list, I might have never gotten to anyone else. Instead, I went humbly to my family, and they accepted me graciously. I am lucky to have such a loving family.

While working the Steps, I was in the middle of a divorce and a custody battle, and my husband, bound by his disease, was threatening my life. I feared one of us would not survive this dangerous time. I know God carried me and directed my every move. On April 10th, 1986, he died of a drug overdose; at least that's what the death certificate said. He didn't even get the whole needle into his body before his insides ruptured like a chain reaction—starting with his lungs, working its way through his organs, and ending with his brain.

At twenty-three, I was a widow with three children, all under the age of five. I fell apart and was unable to function, wondering why I had sobered up and he had died. It was the A.A. fellowship that carried and comforted me, maintaining that God would relieve my pain. But I fought that relief—with clinched teeth and angry sobs—until I almost exploded, until I could not fight anymore. With my hands folded tightly and tears flowing down my face, I pled with God to take my pain. He showed me a picture: my husband stood in front of me as his body fell away like ashes. From that emerged a small child with a radiant face. The child opened his arms, looked up to the bright light that came from above, and was lifted up. God showed me that my husband had been brought home. I began to heal.

When I let go, God penetrates my life. At night, I review my day, asking God to show me where and how I might have harmed others. If I have, I make amends. Making mistakes and admitting them is not as frightening as it once was—I have learned that I will not shrivel up or die. I have learned how important my relationship with God is. I used to have to remind myself to talk to Him; but now, it seems to come naturally, and I do it many times throughout the day. With a soft heart and a sense of humor, He is the friend who's always there. I trust Him and am never lonely.

Humbly, I pray I can share this miracle with others. Unfortunately, many alcoholics in the fellowship do not want help, and in that case, I do not waste my time. Instead, I look for those who do want my help, those who are willing to go to any lengths to recover. I know God will embrace and give them peace, if they are willing to have Him.

Prayer, meditation, and work with other alcoholics keep this program alive for me, and I can see it working in every aspect of my life. I am no longer the same person. I have rejoined the mainstream of life. Today, I am a whole person. Today, I feel joy. The turmoil has vanished. This is not to say that I never feel pain—I do. But now, I know what to do about it. I know where to turn for answers; and if I turn to Him, all will be well with me. I will eventually leave this world, meet my Maker, and see Him smile. That is what I live for, and I hope I can bring you with me.

My Life Story

JILL D.— Atlantic Coast, Florida

My life had been a self-created prison, unbeknownst to me. I had myself locked in a bottle, and had no idea how to get out. I thought I had control, but I had no choice. Booze and pills had me in their grip and there seemed no way out of this prison. I could not find the key no matter where I looked. My feelings were hopeless and helpless, despair being my main sentiment and the void in my gut was growing increasingly greater at every turn. I drank and took the pills to provide the safety of living with secrets, running as fast as I could from the past that seemed to be right behind me, closing in.

I grew up going to a Catholic school, which seemed to be good. Mass was required in the morning before class and it seemed to be the only time I felt safe. A little peaceful feeling way down in my gut, as the priest said Latin mass and we all responded back in the same language. I didn't understand it, but it was so mystical. It gave me a warm fuzzy feeling that would one day draw me back to God. So this part of my life was essential for the long journey I was about to create for myself. If it's true that we are created in the image and likeness of God, then it seems true that I can create. And create I did.

From childhood on I felt like I never fit in. In fact, I used to ask my parents if I was adopted. I had an obstinate side that would fight to fit in but there was also a hopeless, abject part of me. It was to be my lot in life to pretend to be happy-go-lucky yet feel all alone in a crowded room. I was the only girl in the family including my cousins.

Growing up, my grandmother and Mother wanted me in any activity a girl could be in. By the time I was eleven, they had me in modeling school and before I knew it, I was on the runway! My only hope was that I could crawl into myself and become invisible. By the time I hit twelve the magic of booze came into my life and transformed me into a more tolerant person. I met my childhood sweetheart who would become my husband at sixteen *and* become my best drinking buddy. Beer and beer parties on the weekends became my lifeline to living. I could lose myself in the feeling of nothing and do just about anything I was asked, knowing that the weekend would bring the joy of release from this troubled and hopeless world I had to endure. Alcohol became my release from feelings that kept me from enjoying my life. It would take me on a journey, I know, God never intended me to go on. But as I said, I was creating my world which was to begin to be a series of doors, slamming shut and never allowing me out.

By age sixteen I was married to Terry, and acting grown-up in a child's body. Playing house, cooking dinners, planning that weekend party full of booze. Yes, this was the life. I had no idea within a year I would start to experience physical and verbal abuse beyond my wildest dreams! Did I say dream? Nightmare is a better word to describe the next nine years. I was always taught as a child, what goes on in the house, stays in the house. So when the atrocity began, the lies did too. I fell down steps, bumped into walls, lost my balance walking. I either was really believable, or no one wanted to really know what I was enduring. I decided that to save this marriage a child should be conceived. The next ordeal to be encountered was a sterile husband. Before you know it alcohol had me having my first affair. I say alcohol purposefully because without it I would not have had the courage to expose myself. Sex was a meaningless act and repulsive to me. So alcohol gave me the audacity to almost fool myself. As soon as I was pregnant the affair was over, and another secret was born.

Within the next three years the beatings became unbearable but I felt each was totally deserved for the indiscretion that had taken place. I had to get out and had no idea how. I had to tell someone and I just could not breathe the horrible words. My parents were over one night and Terry and my dad were drinking up a storm. My parents had no sooner walked out the door, when Terry began flinging beer bottles at me. The moment of truth was at hand. I ran to the driveway and begged my parents to come back in the house. As they walked through the door I begged my dad to stop Terry from hurting me. My dad looked at us and stated bluntly, I probably deserved a good beating and ordered my mom back to the car to leave. The feeling of impending doom turned into what felt like my death sentence.

I was showing collies at dog specialty shows and began to flee on weekends with my dogs. Grasping onto this to keep me into reality and out of the insanity of my everyday life. The end of January is my birthday and I met the most understanding and compassionate man. We bonded almost immediately and I felt safe and supported by this man, Tony. He gave me hope that I could escape the depths of the hell I was living and I believed for the first time it was possible for me to find happiness in a world that had been ajar for me for a long time. As we sipped our cocktails and talked that false courage began to arise in me and tell me I deserved better than the life I was leading. By the end of February the final abuse came to pass. Every piece of glass had been broken in my home and as I was on the phone with my brother for help, the phone was yanked out of the wall. I knew this was my final night to live. As I was holding my son who was frantically crying, my husband came at us with his shotgun. Never in my life has my heart skipped beats as it did then. A miracle happened. My brother drove into the driveway with the police. A quick thought that there was a God not sentencing me to death that night raced through my thoughts. I packed all that I could get into my station wagon and was out of there, vowing never to return. I had escaped and I did thank God for my brother's timely arrival. I called Tony in New York to thank him for his encouraging talks and thanked him for making me believe I could have a better life. He asked me to pick him up at the airport the following day so that he could just be sure I was really unharmed. He arrived with two suitcases and never went back. We felt like God had put us together to save us from our pasts. Little did we know how that would truly come to pass in the years ahead.

We got through our divorces, mine was again another molestation of basic human rights. As we stood before the judge, I was ruled alcoholic since I drank scotch and he only drank beer. And the temporary custody was turned over to him since I could not prove abuse. I had no witness. Only God, and He failed me entirely again. My dilemma now became more entangled as I chose to run from the order and refused to turn my son over. I took him to Europe and left him with my relatives and came back for the final decree. When I returned to the States I was told by my lawyer the final decree had taken place when I fled the country. No appeal could take place unless the baby was turned over to my ex-husband. I was in contempt of court and could be locked up if I did not heed the judge's order. I drank and found doctors who had magical pills to quiet my nerves. I ran from the state and refused to return the child. A year passed and Tony and I were married and now out of state and my son returned from Europe. I hated God, and most of all I loathed myself. I was out of control and I knew it, so I stayed in the confines of my home and hid from the world. In the next years I managed to have two beautiful children with Tony, and his son came from New York to live with us two weeks after our daughter was born.

Within a year I was attending Al-Anon with my sister-in-law. Never in that whole nine months did I see my part in the struggle living with such an abusive alcoholic in my first marriage. And never once did I see my drug habit or drinking as a problem. I had convinced myself I was locked in my home hiding from the courts and my ex-husband. I finally locked horns with my own disease on April 18, 1982. I found myself at my dining room table at 2:00 A.M. smoking a joint with a glass of B & B in front of me. I didn't know how or when I had arrived at that table. Nor did I know how I had written the poem laying in front of me entitled "The God Of My Understanding." I felt like I became sober instantaneously and feelings were changing within seconds. The real fear set in as I could not stifle the feelings. I drank down the glass and no relief, total bewilderment set in. Suddenly the door bell rang! My heart was pounding, my adrenaline ran and total dread set in. I peeked around the dining room into the foyer and through the front door I saw Jesus Christ, staring downheartedly through the pane of glass. I knew at that moment that my secrets were getting me drunk. It wasn't Terry, the abuse or running from the courts. It was *me* and I was using alcohol to drown any attempt for sanity to enter my life. I had to stop drinking and drugging and this experience was my motivation.

I knew a girl named Alice from Al-Anon. She was in A.A. also, and I knew she could help me if I could just make it through that morning. I called her and it happened she was having a meeting that night at her house and she invited me to come. I accepted and as the day wore on, I began to feel sick. I tried to cancel but she came and picked me up. That was my introduction to the kindness and help these people offer each other and new persons coming in. I sat through that meeting and trembled. I don't remember a word said, but I felt that same little feeling of my childhood, sitting in mass in the morning. I connected with that long-forgotten feeling and knew I was home. I knew A.A. was my answer. I realized that the problem was me and that God was the solution, and my last hope.

Three days into recovery after my nightly meeting, I had been given a blue book they called The Big Book. I, to this day, do not know who to thank for giving me this book, nor who to thank for telling me where the Third Step prayer was in the book.

I sat in my family room and opened the book to chapter five. I read the First Step. I knew I was powerless over alcohol and having locked myself in my own home for the past years, I knew, deep within my gut, that my life was unmanageable. Convinced from the depths of my soul, I read the Second Step. "Came to believe that a Power greater than ourselves could restore us to sanity." The feeling in my gut that I had felt as a small child in mass came over me again and I knew God could do this. I had seen it in the rooms of A.A. and I believed it could happen to me, too. With that, I knew that I could make the decision Step Three talked about, and I turned to page sixty-three in that book and over and over I read the Third Step prayer. Tears streamed down my face and I prayed it aloud: "My Creator, I offer myself to Thee, to build with me and do with me as Thou wilt. Relieve me of the bondage of self, that I may better do Thy will. Take away my difficulties, that victory over them may bear witness to those I would help of Thy Power, Thy Love and Thy Way of life. May I do Thy will always. Amen."

Crying through it I wanted God to know I meant business, and I even asked Him there and then for not just sobriety, but sobriety and beyond! I had no idea how that prayer would be answered. Nevertheless, I prayed it and I meant it and I know it was consummated that night as I went into my kitchen and dried my eyes and picked up a pencil and paper and began to write. I knew at that split second that my secrets were getting me drunk and keeping me that way. And by picking up those writing tools and writing I was breaking free of the old ideas taught me growing up. It was drilled into our heads that you never write anything down on paper that could be used against you. Hell, I had been using my secrets against myself my whole life. No one could do to me what I had not already done to myself with the lies and secrets I held inside me. By praying that prayer it was like a divination had occurred. Ideas began to come to me I hadn't thought of in years. Visions of actual events played out in my head, and I wrote them all down. It was like this outflowing of the truth was setting right all the wrong. The saying, "Know the truth and the truth will set you free," kept replaying in my head. I felt different; I didn't want to drink or drug all of a sudden. The compulsion had been lifted. I felt free of that old have to do it sentiment. I was amazed how easily it was to finally face myself. Of course, the hard part was going to be telling someone all of this. However I did not have to do that right now and I wouldn't worry about it. I wanted to get all of the trash out. I wanted to be rid of the old me and I didn't care how bad it hurt. Even the people I was sharing with at meetings were encouraging me to continue. Not once did someone say, I was too new, or I should wait until I was sober longer. They kept telling me to pray and ask God for help, and keep writing. You see, this was a miracle unfolding, and the miracle was that I was taking the action and not just thinking about it. Wow, what a rush! Even my drugs didn't give me this much of a release. Now I had to do this Fifth Step thing, telling this whole mess to someone. And I had heard a girl named Natalie share her story at Alice's meeting. She had such a peace about her and I felt a strange connection. I felt that my gut feeling was God telling me to use her! So I called her up, embarrassed to bother her, and asked if she would be my sponsor and hear my Fifth Step. I was happy the answer was yes, and we made the date for three days from then, on April 29th, 9:00 P.M.

I felt a cramping start as I would have to wait three whole days. April 29th came and we did the whole thing. She shared information about herself while pointing out how I had set a lot of my problems in motion myself! She would stop me at times to point out what she called a deadly sin . . . and, with her help, I came to understand what these sins were and to see all seven of them in myself: Pride, greed, lust, anger, gluttony, envy and sloth.

Pride was a big one, it had made me make demands upon myself and others that could never had been met by *anyone*, of course. But my fears that would stem out of this would keep me drinking for sure, and I could see it so clearly as she talked! It was as if someone had taken a blindfold off me and let me see the world and myself for the first time. Anger was one I had to look at in a different way, because my anger had been turned inward and I would stay in states of depression. And she showed me how that was happening, and how anger was something I must be constantly watchful of. Lust, greed, envy and yes, sloth— they were all right there on paper, but not put in those words. And she gently took time to show me how they played havoc in my life without me having a clue that this is what would set off all my fears. Fear would be the boogy man that would keep me drinking and hiding out from playing an active role in the world around me.

She was right, and I felt happy as I finished up but afraid to go home and have this feeling end. Then she asked me if I was ready? I thought, *for coffee or does she want me to leave?* It was 3:30 in the morning and she probably was really tired. She looked me in the eye and stated, "Jill, are you ready to have God remove these defects of character?" I wondered, *Who would say no after just laying myself out wide open like that?* I said yes, I was absolutely ready to have God take all my garbage from me.

So she told me to get down on my knees; we were going to do a Seventh Step prayer together! And we did! After that prayer we went down in her family room and burnt my Fourth Step. As the ashes went up the chimney, I felt the terrible doom lift. I felt released and free of the old me and I was at peace, felt clean inside, and I had never felt this way in my life. I felt "new!" I had thus completed Steps Five, Six and Seven that night with my sponsor, and I felt the release as I left her house to go home. I was told to turn to page seventy-five when I got home and do as it said. I did just that. I reviewed everything when I got home that night, well, morning. And I reread Step Six and prayed again that Seventh Step prayer to God in my family room. I knew the next day I would write the names of everyone on my Eighth Step list and review this with her, later in the week.

She told me to read only spiritual books for the next two weeks. She said to treat myself as if I had just been vacuumed out. I wouldn't vacuum and then throw dirt on the carpet. So no T.V., radio, newspapers, magazines, no negativity. Only the positive: The Big Book and *Sermon on the Mount* by Emmet Fox and the Bible.

I made my list for the Eighth Step and was reminded by her that I left out myself and God. I needed to make amends to God and myself. Staying sober and finding a spiritual way of life would be a good start to this amend. I knew the hardest, yet most important, amends would be my ex-husband. And so she told me to begin to write a letter of amends and bring it to her. I had amends to my new husband and my children. My amends were not based on running around saying I'm sorry. I had been sorry all my life. I was told to look up these words in the dictionary. Amends means to change, so I began attending the PTA meetings and volunteering at my children's school. I began participating in their lives. I was a scout leader for Anthony's troop, and I coach for Brandon's soccer team. I coached Danielle's cheerleading team. For my amends to my husband I started making nice dinners on time.

Tried not arguing and letting him have the right to be wrong. I had monetary amends to make. My sponsor said, if it was important enough to borrow the money, it would be just as important in my amends to pay it back. So I called creditors and made arrangements to repay them in small increments. It took me three full years to resolve all my monetary amends, but I did it and felt cleansed once again.

My husband was suspicious of my activities and started following me to A.A. meetings to see who I must be having an affair with. The change was very apparent to him, although I could not see it in myself. I was happy and more relaxed, so he began his observation of my A.A. meetings and friends. They welcomed him with open arms and my sponsor's husband befriended him. Joe told me one night he wasn't sure if Tony was an alcoholic, because only Tony could decide that. But he said he sure did ruin any fun Tony thought he would have drinking! My doorbell rang in the middle of the night sporadically for three months. Tony slammed his fist to the table July 2nd, 1982 and said to me, "If I asked you to choose between me and A.A,. you would take A.A. wouldn't you?" And I said to him, "How can you ask me to choose between you and God. It's not the people, it's God talking through the people. Tony!" That night he went to a Big Book meeting with me and announced he was an alcoholic. The whole room cheered and welcome him. And after that night, our doorbell quit ringing in the middle of the night. God came calling both of us to find peace, happiness and joy through A.A., as a family.

The letters to my ex-husband were read by my sponsor and thrown away for nearly nine months. I finally wrote one the way she wanted it. She never would say what was wrong, just pray about it and write another. Oh, how I wanted to kill her! And I would get angry and she would say, "Well, God bless me for getting you angry enough to look at yourself." That was the whole clue. I was to clean off my side of the street and not bring up the wrongdoings of others. It took some time for me to get that part. But after I did, it made it so much easier doing the changing and making the face to face amends. When I finally got to Step Ten, my sponsor gave me permission to think. Hey, it took eighteen months to clean my system of all the drugs and alcohol. Daily I use my Big Book and reread pages eighty-four and eighty-five. I daily watch for selfishness, dishonesty resentment and fear, as it says. I make amends as quickly as possible, and don't let the old me rebuild herself in the new me. I use the prayer on page eighty-five frequently, "How can I better serve Thee—Thy will not mine be done." And that prayer is still a constant, seventeen years later, in my life today.

Step Eleven, I had trouble with. I had so many voices talking and yakking up there I just couldn't get them all quiet at once. So, once again my sponsor suggested I get a small compact mirror and just focus on my left eye. It sounds crazy but I would have stood on my head if that were the suggestion. I was willing to go to any length, thank God. By using that mirror, after a while the voices started to get quieter and I was able to listen and hear God speak to me. The one simple prayer I use for Step Eleven is the St. Francis Prayer in the "12 & 12." It helps me get centered and to focus on God, and what He is trying to show me on a daily basis, as I walk through the storms of life.

My sponsor took me on my first Twelfth Step call when I was three months sober. I was so scared and told her she should have taken someone with more sober time to help her. She assured me it didn't matter and she was right. When we arrived at the women's home she asked how long we were sober. I said three months and Natalie said eight years. Well, the lady wanted to talk to me the whole night. She said she couldn't fathom eight years but she could believe my three months. I don't know if that lady ever did stay sober, but every Twelfth Step call has been a success for me. I never drank through or after any of them! My Twelfth Step is worked daily, as I share in a meeting, help make coffee for my home-group, do my general service work, be it inter-group, or GSR—or just simply chairing a meeting or sponsoring the girls God has blessed me with in helping them work the Steps so they too can find peace and permanent sobriety in their lives.

I have had spiritual experiences throughout my sobriety. From Christ appearing at my door, to my being modified gradually over the years.

I have brought drunks home and given them a roof over their heads for the first few days. But it's never a long-term thing. Just a few days or weeks to get them through the detox.

It's been seventeen years now since I drank or drugged and life hasn't always been wonderful. My stepson, who we raised, had a terrible drug problem throughout his teenage years. He could always see he had a drug problem, but could never get that he may be alcoholic. Dominic got clean at nineteen and stayed clean, best I know. He bought his first bottle of booze on his twenty-first birthday. He called me twenty-seven days before his twenty-second birthday from North Kingston, Rhode Island, where he was living with his friends. His exact words to me were, "You know, Mom, I could never get the alcoholic part in treatment because I never really drank that much back then. It was always drugs in my teenage years. But now I have been sober for three weeks and I need to come home. I can't do A.A. up here, my friends just don't understand." On March 5th, 1991, twenty-five days before his twenty-second birthday, Dominic hung himself in his bedroom in Rhode Island. It was a very hard and sad time in our life.

We had to bring his body back here to Florida to cremate. We all miss him to this day. He is one of the statistics now that didn't make it back to A.A. God did for me through that funeral what I could not have done for myself. His girlfriend was blaming herself and flew in for the service. I was able to be there for her and share about the disease of alcoholism. She left here much calmer and very grateful that I spent so much time with her. Her parents thanked me and were in awe of how we were able to get through this without drinking. Tragedy is not made easier by not feeling through it. Today it is good to feel good and bad. The miracle is that I don't have to drink no matter how I'm feeling. As long as I don't pick up that first drink, I have a choice today. And I choose to live happy, joyous and free with God in my heart and a smile on my face. The true miracle of permanent sobriety that the Big Book promises is being able to live through the storms of life knowing, and being absolutely certain, that God will keep me safe in His arms. I don't have a God that punishes me or keeps a list of the wrongs I do, today. He gave His son to die for my sins and He loves me. Free will is what seems to be the fault in the world. Man's free will. And if we were all able to trust God, keep our own house clean and help others, no one would have the need to ever again choose to kill themselves or others. You, too, can enjoy permanent sobriety just as I have. Just do what I did. First stop drinking and drugging. Clear away the physical aspect of this disease. Next, look deep inside for the God that will show you the one, unlimited person He originally created. Keep turning you thoughts and actions over to Him to create the really *true* you! Know the truth about you and the truth will set you free for life! God keeps His promises, they are on page eighty-three and eighty-four in the Big Book and they have all come to pass in my life. If it can happen to me, I know it can happen to you.

Taking Back My Life

Zane C.—Adirondack foothills, New York

My name is Zane. I have recovered from alcoholism by working the Twelve Steps. I am not in recovery, not suffering, and not sick. I'm not insane, and I'm not dependent on meetings. In short, I worked the Twelve Steps to their original, intended purpose—the complete removal of the drink problem and the beginning of a way of life that the Big Book told me would solve all my problems. Today alcohol holds absolutely no power whatsoever over me.

My first drink was at the age of six. My grandfather, one of the many heavy drinkers and alcoholics in my family, decided a shot of whiskey would ease the toothache in one of my baby teeth. I remember to this day that drink of liquor, and I can still taste the sour mash whiskey in my mouth as I write this. I remember the warmth—the full-body glow that one little drink gave me. It wasn't long before all my teeth started to hurt on cue while I was around my grandfather, and in fact, I tried to convince the other drinkers in the family (and some who did not drink) that whiskey was the best medicine, just like Paw-Paw said it was. I was a crafty little booger.

I didn't start drinking on the sly—seriously that is—until I was of driving age. That brought on a whole new set of complications. From the time I got my learner's permit to drive until I was seventeen years old, I did some serious experimentation with alcohol. Shortly after my eighteenth birthday, our family physician pronounced me "an incurable alcoholic." I informed him I knew more than he did; I was simply having trouble with my blood pressure.

Over the course of the next seventeen years, I spent most of my waking moments trying to conquer booze and trying to prove the doctor wrong. During those years, those ones I call my "genius years," I managed to drink my way into trouble many times. I single-handedly managed to go to jail sixteen times for alcohol-related offenses. I had my driver's license suspended four times. I managed to get married and divorced four times as well. I lost twenty-something jobs, slit my wrists, hung myself, and ended up barricaded in a room with six cases of beer and a gun in my mouth. Still, I had no idea why I drank and could not stop, no matter what I tried. My attempts to prove I was a social drinker failed miserably and damned near cost me my life

I had no clue what had hold of me. None.

Every attempt I made at controlling alcohol—drinking different beer, whiskey, wine, whatever—always resulted in the same consequences: me trying to figure out how to kill myself without getting hurt too badly. I was a godless fake, a total shell of a man. At night I'd lie in bed and cry. Other times, I telephoned everyone I knew, slurring my words, and telling them either what sons-of-bitches they were or how much I loved them before I hung up to go take a leak in the cat box, the yard, or on the neighbors car. Blackout bladders have no conscience, that's for sure.

The three alcohol treatment centers I checked myself into showed me no answer with which I could live. Instead, I told them all how to improve their treatment regimen, walked out of the door, and drank a half case of beer.

All the praying I did was pretty much limited to "Please God, get me out of (you name it) and I'll never drink again." However, as soon as I realized my number wasn't up, I went straight to one of the few bars within a hundred miles where the bartender would still serve me and celebrated by getting blackout, shit-faced drunk and trying to find someone to make bail—again.

What changed all that was so simple it baffled me. I'd attended Alcoholics Anonymous off and on—mostly off—for a number of years. "Meetings, meetings, meetings," they told me. "Don't drink even if your ass falls off, and if it does fall off, put it in a paper sack and bring it to a meeting," was another bit of wisdom I frequently heard. Quite frankly, I didn't own a paper sack that wasn't already full of beer cans. I was told I wasn't "ready for the Steps" and "I'd always be insane" by others in the rooms of A.A., some with decades of so-called serenity. Something wasn't adding up.

There were probably some well-meaning folks in those rooms. I admit that. I also realize today that listening to those who were clueless could have cost me my life. Telling me not to drink was like telling me not to breathe. I didn't drink because I *wanted* to; I drank because I *had* to. I knew nothing else, no other way to exist. Alcoholism owned me and was my master. I was dying, and it was happening fast. I told them that the Big Book, their cutesy name for the book *Alcoholics Anonymous*, was a nice attempt at a book on alcoholism, but "Here's what you guys need to do with it . . ." I left A.A. again, only to end up drinking and getting into still more trouble than before.

After another brush with both death and the law during one of the darkest times of my life, I decided to go back to A.A. and have another look-see. I was suicidal, hopeless and clueless. I was living in a run-down, low-rent motel, stealing and picking up aluminum cans to get money for my next six-pack, living paycheck to paycheck, drinking myself into oblivion every night, and wondering why every son-of-a-bitch in the universe had it better than I did.

Maybe I was ready. Maybe I could hear the original message of A.A. among all the parroted jargon, platitudes and psychobabble being tossed about the rooms. At any rate, I did go back, urged by my aunt, one of the very few folks in my family who didn't run from me. I tried several different meetings, but mostly what I heard were newcomers bitching about how bad their lives were, which I expected. What I did not expect were the other folks I heard—those who were "sober" for decades—also sitting around bitching, whining and complaining about how insane they were. It was baffling, to say the least, and I certainly did not need to be taught insanity; I had that down to an art form on my own, having achieved a master's degree in bullshit before graduating grammar school.

It was at a small meeting at a little white church that I met a man who spoke with a calm easiness, a surety and conviction I'd previously either not heard or had somehow missed. He presented himself as a man who had "recovered from alcoholism," a feat that I had previously been informed was impossible. I asked him to help me. "Can you tell me what this whole A.A. thing is really about?"

"Are you ready to get well?" he asked?

"Get well?"

"Yes . . . forever."

He explained that A.A. has only one program of recovery, that it's called the Twelve Steps, and that everything shy of that is a cheap imitation. He helped me realize that all those folks I thought were crazy and killing me were actually just sick and kept so by what they'd been taught. He told me that the crap they spouted in meetings wasn't their fault, since they'd been taught that way. He did something far more important than that though—he showed me in the Big Book that the whiny, malingering tripe I had heard in meetings about powerlessness-for-life, recovery-for-life, insanity- for-life, and sickness-for-life did not exist in the A.A. program of recovery.

He told me how the Twelve Steps could be worked in a matter of days, and he showed me where it was in writing in the book. I was shown how the early members worked the Steps in mere days—not years—and I pursued the remedy in that book with a passion.

I learned much about alcoholism from him as he took me through the book *Alcoholics Anonymous*, page by page, concept by concept, and Step by Step. What became apparent to me at once after reading our text was that what I'd been hearing in meetings had so little, and in many cases nothing, to do with the original message of A.A. It seemed shameful that some meetings carried the A.A. name. On seeing the truth, I also felt ashamed of myself for briefly taking part in all that misinformation in the meeting rooms, and I saw how some of those people who came to A.A. before me could have and would have been easily confused.

I came in the door pretty much convinced of Step One. Having tried all my best ideas—and they were winners, let me tell you—and having failed in every conceivable way, I think that's where the bottom came for me. Nothing I did relieved me of my obsession to drink. I had admitted to every judge, doctor, family member, therapist, and psychiatrist who'd listen to me that I was powerless over alcohol. Big deal, huh? I did that for years to shut them up.

I found out soon enough what Step One really meant. It was in the darkest time of my life—at 3:00 A.M. barricaded in a dark room with a gun in my mouth—that I was finally able to admit to myself that I was licked. That's when things started to look up. All those confessions to others meant nothing until I admitted to myself—in my heart of hearts—I was defeated. I remember seeing the devil that day. He was in the mirror and he had green eyes, just like me.

Fear is, at times, a great motivator.

My friend explained to me that in order to work Step Two, I would have to believe in a Power greater than myself or at least be willing to believe. He showed me where the Book says there is only "One who has all power" and that "that One is God." Not a doorknob, not a fire hydrant, not a tree or a cocker spaniel, and not Elvis. My mother had forced me into ministerial school at the age of seven and had kept me there for seven years. She beat me when I resisted, so while I had no trouble believing in God, I thought God was a total bastard. My friend helped me understand that I could lose all of my childhood resentments at God and my mother, and that I could have my own conception of that Power the book spoke about. I remember thinking if there was anything that could relieve me of my insanity, it would certainly have to be a Power greater than me. I was completely defeated, and all my best ideas had failed miserably.

Step Three was a simple decision, and a prayer—a conviction and a leap of faith followed by a prayer. I remember that prayer still, and I believe I always will. At that same little white church, I held that same man's hands when I prayed. I asked God, whatever It was, to help me. I offered to do anything It wanted. I had written this wonderfully edited prayer full of big, long words so God would be impressed, but when I opened my mouth to pray, that edited version didn't come out. What did come out were the begging pleas of a frightened man who was willing to surrender his life in order to get it back.

It seemed strange to be talking to what appeared to be thin air, but the results were amazing. I actually felt something very powerful happen that night. The proof of God's existence and Power was made apparent to me at that moment, since the compulsion to drink was removed and has never returned.

My friend told me if I didn't go on with the rest of the program, I'd drink. He impressed on me the absolute necessity of working Step Four immediately after making the Step Three decision, and, in fact, he showed me in the Book where permanent success is unlikely unless this Step is done quickly after Step Three. Since everything else he'd told me had come true, I sat down that night to start writing my Fourth Step, which incidentally took me twenty-one days to complete. I was lazy and so high on God that I thought I could take a break. I sat on my haunches, writing at my leisure, praying every day to this new God-thing, and just enjoying being free of booze for the first time in my adult life. There were times during the writing of this Step that I cried. At others, I felt so ashamed of myself I was frantic. I could not believe all the trash I'd been carrying for all those years. I wanted my life back, and I got hungry with determination.

As it turned out, I did finish writing it but was a little apprehensive about discussing some of that stuff with another person. It was pretty sick and terrible. Actually, I tried to avoid working Step Five with him, slipping into a meeting at noon one day while I knew he'd be at work. When he showed up out of the blue, on his lunch hour, I was busted. Later that night, I sat with him and went through my lengthy list of resentments, fears, dishonest acts, and all the selfish tendencies of my entire life. The spiritual shower bath I took by working this vital Step lifted so much weight off me. I was amazed. All that wicked stuff that had been crammed back into the dark areas of my mind for so many years came out—along with tears—and when it was over, I actually felt God was with me for real.

I asked him, "What's next?"

"What does the book say is next?" he replied, as he always did when asked that question.

Afterwards, my friend took me home so I could have some quiet time to review—that "hour" the Big Book tells us to take between Steps Five and Six—so I did exactly as he and the Book instructed. I read the section where it told me to look back over the first five Steps and to see if I had omitted anything. When I was convinced I had been honest, fearless and thorough with the first five Steps, I turned to page seventy-six and made the decision for Step Six right then and there, having become ready for God to relieve me of the bondage of self. I certainly did not want to keep any of the items we had covered in Step Five. Hell, who would?

Completely humbled—crying and relieved at the tremendous burden of pain, guilt, and shame that had been lifted from me—I bowed at the edge of my tub, and at that makeshift altar, I begged God to take away those years of living in the dark. I asked God to remove those sick ways of thinking from my makeup. I asked that God please restore me to a useful condition, and I offered to do anything required of me. I got off my knees in a state of complete grace, and for once in my life, I felt whole. I believed.

Having completed Step Six and Step Seven, I knew there was more work to do, and by now, I was more than willing. God's spirit was lighting me up more and more. I had made a list of persons to whom I needed to make amends while writing my Fourth Step, just as the book told me I should, and with that list in hand, I took the rest of those papers from the Fourth Step to the river's edge. I struck a match to them, burned them to ashes, kicked them into the river, and walked away a free man.

I did not look back.

Being ready to make amends to all those persons I could and having my list ready, I had completed Step Eight and was ready to work Step Nine. My friend told me to make the most frightening of my amends first. I knew in order to make that particular amends, I'd have to go to prison, and I told him so.

"I'll visit," he replied. He reminded me I had agreed to pay any price for absolute victory.

The next morning, I picked up the telephone, called the government, and turned myself in. I was crying and afraid. I explained I was an alcoholic working the Twelve Steps and that I had to come clean with them, or I'd drink. I told the lady I'd wait there for the authorities to come get me.

"Sir, there might be another way," she said.

"What did you say?" I asked.

"If I can get this action against you put on hold, will you make this right?" she asked.

"I will do anything you ask." I answered.

It was then that the Power shown through, because in her next sentence I heard the words I had heard so many times before in meetings of A.A. . . . . "Sir, before we hang up, there is one other thing I must tell you: We are everywhere."

Out of the thousands of employees working at that particular agency—and on my very first amends, the very first call of Step Nine—I got a member of A.A. on the telephone. Miracle? Coincidence? I am not qualified to ascertain and understand the Divine, but I can say I felt as though I was bulletproof at that moment, and I felt the Hand of God touch me more strongly than ever before.

The remainder of my amends—and there were many—fell like dominoes in a row, and not once did God let me fall. Old friends talked to me as though they thought I'd been reincarnated as a nice person. Some of my family members started to respect me. Old grudges gave way, replaced by renewed friendships. My daily contact with the Power was growing, building on the little inexplicable occurrences in my life, those things I refer to as "miracles."

I took a look at the Promises on pages eighty-three and eighty-four in the Big Book and realized, with my eyes smiling, that while I'd been working the Steps, they were being shown to me in so stark a manner there could be no doubt God was holding me. Only later did I realize how true it was that the Promises come true after the working of the first nine Steps, since that's where they're located in the Book. Everything else I'd seen was mild compared to what was revealed to me after I stood clean before God and man, a channel of enlightened spirituality, absolutely free of the past which had haunted me all my life.

Getting through the first nine Steps—from admitting my alcoholism to myself to making all the amends on my list (eighteen single-spaced typed pages of names)—took fifty-three days and a few hours. My friend taught me the daily process of working Steps Ten, Eleven, and Twelve as maintenance of permanent sobriety and happiness, and I've continued that maintenance program constantly in my life since I recovered. Today when I hear folks being told to do one Step per year, I cringe because I, myself, would have died had I listened to that sort of nonsense.

Each day or thereabouts, I look at my life and see where defects (which I was warned about in the reading on Step Ten) have cropped up. I follow the process on page eighty-four in the Big Book for making those things right, since the exact instructions for doing this are there, plain as day. Life in the world of the Spirit requires work, lots of it; but the rewards are beyond my wildest drunken dreams.

Step Eleven taught me to seek a closer relationship with God and to use prayer and meditation as a means of accomplishing this. I think about God every single day and pray more often than that, and I'm constantly amazed at what has been revealed to me beyond the first nine Steps. It just keeps getting better. I realize now how A.A. was initially only about sobriety but is now also about a way of life that is both wonderful and fearless.

The Power I found through the working of the Steps has never left me. I have strayed from It at times, but I get back to It through the maintenance Steps as quickly as possible. I do not want to revisit the hell my life once was. I detest the irritability that comes to me when I do not pray. When I occasionally revert to being an egotistical genius, I get on my knees to pray. I call to memory those days when I was dying, crying, and begging for my life back, and I believe remembering those times has saved my sanity on several occasions.

I let God discipline me today when I am unable. I work to mold my own will into accordance with what I think the will of God happens to be. The simplicity of God's will for me was once beyond the scope of my knowledge, but nowadays it's so simple: Be happy, joyful, fearless, and free. Help others. Be nice. Trust God. I am thankful to have become less "smart" in return for being more blessed, in spite of my occasional self-induced ignorance.

Today, I am God's kid. Nothing out of the ordinary. Just another human with a Divine birthright I once disregarded. I have earned back my place in the world. The truths of life continue to come to me in inspiration, vision, meditation, and prayer. I am not confused about what is right and what is wrong. Today, I know. At times, it's a struggle to behave myself. I am prone to all sorts of character flaws. I don't think I'll ever master them, but then, that's not my job. It's God's. All my years of trying to do God's job are over. Today, I seek perfection knowing I will not reach it, but believing in my heart that reaching for it is what refines my thinking.

I refuse to carry the watered-down, diluted version of A.A. I hear so often. For this I have been ridiculed and called a Big Book Thumper, a guru, and an egotist. I do not back off the message in that book. When I am asked for help, I do everything in my power to convince the new person of those words on page ninety-eight of the Big Book, "Burn the idea into the consciousness of every man that he can get well regardless of anyone." I did that. I got well.

My life these days is inconceivably beautiful. For the most part, my fears have died. I walk intrepid into the world each day, assured of God's love and protection, knowing that when a defect of character comes back to temporarily haunt me, that I can count on God's power to relieve the fleeting pain. I am whole because of God. My own love has blossomed. Now that I have gotten clean enough to love others, my love has been returned to me tenfold. God has blessed me with a mate, a beautiful, captivating woman who is also a recovered alcoholic and who shares with me the working of God's plan. We are a team, partners in faith. All those years of failed relationships, even in their most seemingly happy moments, are nothing compared to the God-given love I share with her. She shares with me the carrying of this message in meetings, prisons, hospitals, on the Internet, and at local mission houses. Our joint life is spent in service of the alcoholic who still suffers, and she teaches me compassion and tenderness where once I had only hard edges. She has stuck by me through every adversity I have faced. Our life is not a golden cage, but we try to work through our difficulties as best we can, trusting God to right anything that's wrong with us as we walk through life as partners. Together, we do this thing.

I do not worry about ever taking another drink. I am not one drink away from a drunk; but instead, one God away from that drink. That buffer comforts me. I am asked, "Zane, do you think you'll ever drink again?" I always say the same thing, "Not until God dies."

That is the message I carry today, the same one I will carry until death. I too, like those mentioned earlier, am a product of what I was taught: "The Story of How Many Thousands of Men and Women Have Recovered from Alcoholism," just like it says on the title page of my all-time favorite book. Thank God I was given the truth—the Twelve Steps in their purest form—straight from that blue book by a man who cared enough to pass on to me the original message of Alcoholics Anonymous.

I am one of those "Many Thousands" now. I have recovered from alcoholism and its deadly lifestyle.

That Book is *my* story, too.

Section Two

Coincidence

Who Needs God with All This Coincidence?

Dr. John—Vancouver, Washington

Have you ever had heavy thoughts about somebody or something only to have the "somebody" immediately or soon show up, or the "something" mysteriously happen? Most of the time we call these events coincidences because they happened at the same time we were thinking about them and most of the time they are exactly that—coincidences.

Then there are the totally inexplicable events—those that seem only to confuse and intrigue us, that dangle just on the edge of the explainable but go no further. We call them remarkable! Often we even attribute them to forces beyond our understanding. "I had an angel sitting on my shoulder!" Or "God was with me!" and other picturesque banter.

You are about to read of such a chain of events for which there seems to be no explanation—neither for the order and harmony in them nor even for the fact that they exist. I wonder: Are they any less inspirational than those events seen in the Koran, Talmud, Torah or Bible?

That is for you to decide.

I have never been to Manchester, Vermont, but if I were to go there it would be for two reasons. First it would be as a fly fisherman, to visit the world famous Orvis Fly Fishing school, which is associated with the resort of Equinox—an 1,100-acre tract of taverns and lodgings which has existed in various forms since 1769.[1]

But there is a more important reason. For, here is the birthplace of a coincidence that would eventually save my life.

I would check into the Equinox, go to the front porch and settle in a chair, there to dream of days past when four unrelated children wan-

193

dered in and around Equinox Mountain. This was in the summers before our entry into World War I—the early 1900s. At the time, these children would have no idea their lives would blend in such a way as to create the taproot of one of the greatest health organizations ever known to man—Alcoholics Anonymous.[2]

In Manchester, Vermont, was a preparatory school, and down from a town called East Dorset, came a boy named Bill Wilson to go to school there. [3]

Over from Albany, New York, came Ebby Thatcher, the son of a prominent businessman who owned a summer home in Manchester.

Up from New York City through Newport, Rhode Island, came a rich family from the chemical business and their son, Rowland Hazard.

And from Brooklyn, New York, came a physician and his wife named Burnham, who spent every summer in Manchester and brought with them their daughter, Lois.

These children intermingled like young people would and wandered around the country club and took their little trips to Equinox Mountain.[4] But unlike most child groups, their paths in life did not become any less affiliated as history would later show.

When World War I came, they disbursed. Bill W. had graduated from the Manchester Preparatory School and Norwich College (a semi-military school) as well. He held a commission in the Vermont National Guard and was assigned as an officer in an auxiliary unit that went to France, where he served with honors.[5]

When the war was over all four gathered again and, after interacting in a way to bring back their childhood, all went their own way still having no idea the coincidence of their first meeting meant anything more than a chance meeting.

Bill W. went to New York City where he went to law school but then, admitting the law was not his corner, he became involved in the securities business on Wall Street. Lois was seeing Bill. Ebby tried to become a CPA and Rowland went into his father's chemical business.

No more was expected or planned between the four. The chance of their earlier meeting was forgotten. But there seemed to be another purpose for them. The first became evident when Rowland Hazard got into trouble with alcohol. His family was deeply concerned and, because they were very rich sent him to every available facility they could find that dealt with alcoholism but nothing seemed to work. At their wit's end, the family sent him to Europe there to undergo the treatment of Dr. Carl Jung in Switzerland. Rowland stayed with Jung for one year and finally Jung said, "Rowland, I have done all that I can for you. You are going to have to leave."

Rowland left Switzerland for Paris and while there someone asked him the wrong question. "Do you want a drink?" Of course he had a drink which led to a vicious binge, and he woke up broken and alone. He went back to Dr. Jung who had been able to keep him sober for a year. It was then that Dr. Jung gave Rowland his death notice.

"Frankly," said Jung, "I think you are hopeless. I have never seen nor heard of an alcoholic of your type recover."

"Never?" Rowland said. "Is there no hope at all"

"Well, I have heard of people having a religious experience that is so profound that it seems to reform the personality in such a way the person does not drink anymore and all the symptoms of previous conduct melts away."

"Great!" said Rowland, his hope restored. "And how do I find this religious experience?"

"Therein lies the problem, Rowland," Jung replied. "I can't tell you that. It is something you are going to have to find for yourself."

So Rowland, his hope at once aroused and then dashed, left Jung and went to England where he heard of the Oxford Group, a religious gathering of charismatic Christians started by Frank Buchman. It was the theory of this crowd to live like Christians lived in the first one hundred years after Christ, and before the real foundation of an institutional church, and it was with them that Rowland became so involved that he got sober. He took this program back to the States and started a commune near Manchester where the people living there based their lives on the four point rules of the Oxford Group

Ebby Thatcher's story was different. But like Rowland's parents, the Thatchers owned a summer home in Manchester and though Ebby had been ostracized from his parents home in Albany, New York, they did permit him to live in their summer home in Manchester because of his drinking. It was a coincidence that he would be able to go back to the village where an old friend, Rowland Hazard, had settled down.

But Ebby's drinking had not ceased. One day he was driving the outskirts of Manchester when he missed a turn and drove his car into a farmer's kitchen, stepped out and asked the farmer, "Anybody here have a drink?"

He ended up in front of the judge—he had been there many times before—and was warned one more time that if he ever did that again he would—blah, blah . . . you get the picture. He was only given another scolding because the judge knew the Thatchers to be good people in the community, and he had known Ebby since he had been a youngster.

But that courtroom turned out to be a Godsend and one more coincidence that really could not be explained but a coincidence all the same as you will see further along. A couple of weeks later, Ebby decided he would straighten up, at least for that day, and try to get on the good side of his parents by painting the family's summer home.[6]

Having gotten out the ladders, brushes, scrapers, etc. including a lawn chair and bottle of gin, Ebby put a coat of paint on the front of the house and then, stopping to examine his work, sat down in the lawn chair to have a "touch" of gin with ice and lime. One leading to another, Ebby eventually "relaxed" in the chair when a sea gull came by and defecated on his new paint job. Irate, Ebby went into the house, got his father's shotgun and began shooting at the bird—not a smart thing to do in a quiet New England community. Once more he landed in front of the judge.

But this time, for no special reason short of coincidence, in the hallway of the court Ebby, bumped into a public phone and decided to call Rowland Hazard at his rehab. Getting permission to do so, Ebby called Rowland and Rowland told the judge about his rehab and would take the responsibility of Ebby. The judge approved and Ebby Thatcher was reunited with his old friend, Rowland Hazard.

After getting sober, Ebby came to New York City where the Oxford Group became associated with Sam Shoemaker's Calvary Episcopal Church.[7] Attached to the church was a soup kitchen where Ebby worked handing out food to the needy. One day, as he was handing out food, a drunk came through the line that looked a great deal like his old friend and drinking buddy, Bill Wilson. The thought came to him that he should go visit Bill. It had been years since they had "celebrated" and now would be a good time to tell Bill about the marvelous occurrence he had experienced at Rowland Hazard's farm. The experience that caused Ebby to be able to put the bottle away.[8] So he called Bill and Bill invited him over.

Bill was eager for this reunion. He and Lois Burnham had married and on this day, since Lois was at work he figured he could get a bottle of gin and he and Ebby could drink and talk over old times. Bill had often thought of Ebby, and every time he did he remembered the time he and Ebby had chartered a plane and had been the first ones to land at the Manchester airport. But they landed there a day early. The airport was to be opened on Saturday and they landed there on Friday. They were arrested and taken before the judge. One thread of reality that seemed to weave itself through the fabric of their lives was to spend a considerable amount of time before the judge.

While he was reflecting, there was a knock at the door. Bill answered the door and was greeted with a man he hardly knew—Ebby.[9] Ebby stood there looking healthy and glowing. When Bill asked him what had happened he replied, "I got religion," and when he offered Ebby a drink he refused it saying he had stopped drinking.[10]

Bill thought, *First a drunken crackpot and now a religious crackpot!*

But after hours of talk Bill realized Ebby had come to carry the message of the Oxford Group to him and he did this by telling Bill how Rowland Hazard had helped him and others.

"I'm not much for religion," said Bill.

Ebby replied, "Well the way we do it is that everybody forms his own opinion of God." This made sense to Bill. What Ebby seemed to be saying was he had found an answer to the drinking dilemma and had offered it to Bill if Bill was interested.

Bill didn't stop drinking that day. In fact it was not until December of 1934 he once again entered Towns Hospital, for the eighth or last time. The hospital was run by Dr. William D. Silkworth—who actually was a neurologist—but due to the hard times, took the job of running the hospital.[11] The doctor arranged for Bill to have one of the "freebie" beds and it was there that Bill was destined to do combat with alcohol for the final time.

It was there that Bill fell to his knees and asked for help and experienced what was to become known as "Bill's Hot Flash." He went through a spiritual experience that caused his room to light up so brightly he could hardly see the walls. A soft wind blew through the room and Bill seemed to be transported into a fourth dimension.[12] He sat in the presence of a Power he could not explain and it was there he walked away trembling but assured. The coincidence of meeting Ebby seemed to affect his spiritual soul, and he was certain he would never drink again.

So it was that the four children who had met by coincidence years before met again. Bill went with Ebby and Rowland to work in the soup kitchen of an Episcopal church in New York while Lois Wilson—nee Burnham—stayed at her hardware store job. The four were together again, held by the spiritual glue of life's experiences. Or was it due to the higher order of things that this coincidence continued?

As Bill worked on Sam Shoemaker's soup line in his spare time, he tried to help drunks on the street. He even went into bars trying to interest them in stopping drinking. Nothing worked. He went back to Dr. Silkworth and told him he couldn't sober anybody up.

"How are you going about it?" Silkworth asked.

"I am telling them about how, after praying, my room lit up and a wind blew through the room." answered Bill.

"That isn't the way you do it, Bill!" answered Silkworth. "Tell them they are going to die! Tell them that! Tell them about the hopelessness and the fatal nature of the disease.[13]

Shortly after this, Bill went to Akron, Ohio, to close a business deal to buy a small rubber company. But the deal went sour and his colleagues went back to New York, leaving him in the Mayflower Hotel with only $10 in his pocket. Standing in the Mayflower Hotel lobby, Bill was tempted to drink, especially when he saw all the happy people in the bar that led off the lobby. Bill knew he had only two options—getting drunk or making a phone call to find somebody he could help. He chose the phone. But first he needed a number!

At the end of the lobby there was a church directory and a telephone that seemed to be calling out to him. "This is it!" he thought and picked at random the number of the Episcopal church.[14] Rev. Walter Tunks answered the phone and gave Bill a list of ten people. Bill started calling the names but with no results. They were busy or weren't interested but finally, Henrietta Sieberling answered and agreed to help. The angel had landed!

Henrietta Sieberling was the wife of J. Frederick Sieberling whose father, Frank A. Sieberling, was a one of the founders of the Goodyear Tire & Rubber Co. in Akron. Among other things, she was an ardent devotee of the Oxford Group and was one of many who had participated in prayers for Dr. Bob who had previously confessed his sins of gluttony with liquor. As was the custom of that group, anyone confessing their sins would receive daily prayers from the membership for thirty days. So Henrietta prayed daily for help to come to Dr. Bob.

About the tenth day—Mother's Day, 1935—the phone rang where Henrietta and her husband, lived in the guest house of the senior Sieberlings.

"Hello. My name is Bill Wilson and I am here to fix drunks."

"Of course you are. I have been expecting you!" said Henrietta, in a nonchalant way. "Come on over."

Bill had yet another problem. At this point, he had only ten dollars in his pocket, his room rent at the hotel wasn't paid and the hotel management was pressuring him for the money he owed. What to do? Embarrassed, Bill mentioned his plight to Henrietta. "Not to worry," she said. "I will see it is taken care of." And she went to the phone and made arrangements with the hotel. The Sieberling name was very weighty in those days.

Henrietta got on the phone with Anne Smith, Dr. Bob's wife. "There is a man here from New York, Ann and I think he can help Bob. Would it be all right to drop by?"

"Ordinarily I would be happy to do that but Bob brought home a potted plant for Mother's Day and right now he is under the table more potted than the plant!" Ann said. "But I will see to it we get together with him tomorrow."

Henrietta arranged to have Bill put up at the club, and on Sunday, Anne and Dr. Bob met "with this guy from New York, and give him fifteen minutes of [the doctor's] time." They met and they talked for four or five hours. And that was the story of how they met and that is how it all started.[15] The rest of the story can be gleaned from the Big Book of Alcoholics Anonymous and the other books of that organization.

This is a condensed version of what happened and there is considerably more in the history of A.A., but isn't it odd that Bill had a church directory handy when he needed help along with a telephone right by it? Furthermore, that a stranger—Dr. Tunks—would give him ten names, including Henrietta's, and when the previous nine calls showed no interest the last call was to Henrietta Sieberling who, unbeknownst to Bill, had been praying for someone to show up to help her friend, Dr. Bob Smith?

Yes, there is considerably more about the history the reader can find out and it is readily available. We are only striving to point out the COINCIDENCES that have occurred along the way. Does it not seem every bit as providential as Noah's flood and Jonah's whale? Is it pos-

events were something in the order of actions of a power and beyond those of mortal man?

The reader might ask, "So what?" How does this guesswork about some "power" working, or perhaps creating, certain events of the past come into play in the big scheme of things? Four kids from different places gather in the same part of the world; three of the four become alcoholics; one goes to Europe and then England, and with the help of a world-renowned psychiatrist, puts away the drink; another takes advantage of his friend's rehabilitation facility and puts away the liquor; he in turn carries a message to the remaining man who stops drinking; The lady of the group marries the third man and through her labors keeps the home fires burning so the third man can go to Akron, there unknowingly to meet a lady that had been praying for him to come. The third man and a physician meet and the physician eventually puts down the bottle; and all events were surrounded by the idea of God or a Higher Power acting in their lives. That is their cursory history.

It seems to be just that: coincidental. But if it is due to a Higher Power, does it make sense that such a Power, that most call God, would be responsible for the "accidental events," that the final result—Alcoholics Anonymous—would be abandoned by that Power? We think not. And it is through their future experience the men saw certain things to be true—namely that everything is dependent upon God.

The Big Book of Alcoholics Anonymous points out three basic concepts which, over the years, experience has proven to be accurate. Those concepts are: An alcoholic is powerless over the use of alcohol and because of that their lives become unmanageable; that no human power seems capable of arresting this powerlessness; and God, or a personal Higher Power, could relieve that malady if He were sought.[16] These concepts are shown in most meetings of Alcoholics Anonymous. But the importance seems to lie in the total conviction that these three elements be present in the individual who wants to get well. History has shown this to be not only true but essential.

One concept worth examining here is that which says "Probably no human power could have relieved our alcoholism." An analysis of this statement shows it to be more of a symptom than a declaration.

For instance when an alcoholic tries to "quit" on his own, he usually fails and repeated attempts usually result in failure.

"I swear I will never drink again!" is heard over and over, and when loved ones and friends rejoice in this "promise" they are usually soon disappointed as the individual, staying sober for a time, falls once again to demon rum. Though there may be some who succeed in quitting drinking for good and all, for the vast majority this human power proves to be futile.

Many have opted for the "geographic cure" where the alcoholic just *knows* if his environment were changed he could eliminate alcohol from his life. There is even one example of a person in Ireland, who did everything he could to stop drinking without success, so he joined a missionary group and went with them to the darkest reaches of Africa. *It took him one day to find the local liquor!*

The alcoholic soon learns the hard way there are only two ways to run. One is *away* which always fails and the other is *toward*, which if it is toward God, *never* fails.

Hobbies have been suggested to fill the alkie's time. One man, who having been urged to get a hobby, went down in his basement and built a bar!

Physicians have prescribed certain drugs such as Antabuse, a substance that causes the person to become ill if drinks after using it to "cure" the problem. But the cunning alcoholic—affectionately referred to here as an "alkie"—will, if supportive means are not taken, often stop using the drug long enough to safely drink alcohol. Some have tried drinking with the drug in their body and suffered extreme malaise. There have even been recorded cases of deaths.

Further, the medical profession will threaten with such warnings as "If you don't quit drinking, you are going to die!" And, to make death a bit more palatable, they take another drink.

In the field of psychology and psychiatry, long sessions of mental probing seem, in most cases, fruitless. Finally the practitioner resorts to threats with "If you don't stop drinking you are going to go insane." Again, because his actions of the past bear out insane behavior, the alkie takes another drink. One very honest psychiatrist—Dr. Jung—was even partly responsible for the genesis of Alcoholics Anonymous.

The religious professionals also are concerned about the alcoholic and warn, "If you don't quit drinking, you are going to go to hell!" a place he swears he has gone on more than one occasion—the thought of which requires another drink.

So here are various professionals trained in helping people, wanting to help people, but failing in the case of alcoholism because they use fear to help a person full of fear.

Along with the above, many methods have been tried and failed. Hypnosis, mystical meditation, nonalcoholic drinks, religion, hobbies, karate, Gestalt, Eastern philosophy, exercise, diet, anger management, group therapy—the list of human powers is endless.

So it seems that no power on earth is capable of arresting the disease, logically leading to the conclusion that if there is an answer to the dilemma—which experience has shown there is—and no power on earth will help them, the alcoholic must pursue a power not on earth . . . or as Alcoholics Anonymous states, *"God could and would if He were sought."*

In the true accounts of the concepts of God of the writers of this book that follow, the reader will see how several alcoholics coming from various environments, were able to arrive at a concept of God or, as many state, a power greater than themselves that has led them to a life without alcohol, and without fighting the desire to drink. Though, as you will see, the concepts of a Higher Power vary, they all ultimately reach the decision as to the necessity of a spiritual entity in their lives that results in an alcohol-free existence bathed for the most part in a calm and serene sea.

Read these stories carefully, and whether you be alcoholic or not, perhaps take advantage of one that parallels your life or the life of a friend or loved one.

Endnotes

1. Http://www.AskJeeves.com (Manchester Vermont/Equinox)
2. Tape: "History of A.A."; Ray O'Keefe; Attorneys Retreat; Matucha Retreat House; Portland, Oregon; 1991
3. Ibid.
4. Ibid.
5. *Alcoholics Anonymous*, third edition; page 1-16; A.A. World Service Inc., New York City, 1976.
6. Dick B.; *The Oxford Group of Alcoholics Anonymous*; Glenn Abbey Books, Seattle. Wash., 1992; Page 81-84
   It was here that Rowland learned of the four absolutes of the Oxford Group. Absolute honesty; Absolute unselfishness; Absolute love; and Absolute truth.
7. Tape, op. cit.
8. A trip to the Calvary Church in New York City will permit you to see the main window in the church donated by the Hazard family. Reverend Sam Shoemaker was the pastor.
9. *Alcoholics Anonymous*; op. cit. page 9
10. Ebby really never got sober although he had periods of sobriety and some say he died sober. Others say he died drunk, which according to research is true. But the moral is: "It is not the messenger but the message," which is of value.
11. Tape: "History of A.A."
12. *Alcoholics Anonymous*
13. Tape: "History of A.A."
14. *Alcoholics Anonymous Comes of Age*; 1957 A.A. Publishing, Inc. page 66
15. Op. Cit.
16. *Alcoholics Anonymous*, third edition, page 60, A.A. World Services Inc., New York City, 1976

Section Three

Alcoholics and Their Ideas of God

In the section that follows you'll read about the concepts of God of the alcoholics who wrote the previous stories. Leading this section is a thought-provoking essay that examines a chain of events that occurred at the onset of the A.A. movement. Please examine these pieces with an open mind, and to look for similarities between your thinking, and that of these alcoholic authors. Perhaps you'll find something that intrigues you.

It is our hope that, as you read these essays, you'll find something interesting or familiar to you, whether it be the understanding of God eventually arrived at by the writer, or perhaps his or her childhood conception which may have changed over the years. At any rate, one thing is apparent: Most concepts of God changed along the path of recovery. They grew. Those who had dubious or nonexistent notions of God saw great changes occur in their lives once their willingness to believe became strong enough to outweigh the destructive forces of self-will. Even those who had a believable concept of God from their youth came to know God better, and learned how to utilize that Power to great successes.

The common thread that runs through all the pieces that follow is that every single person found something greater than him or herself to rely on while fighting the malady of alcoholism. Each of them found that Power they sought—and which healed them not only of their alcoholism, but also from a host of other problems associated with the human condition.

Take what you can use and we wish you well.

Love is Our Soul Purpose

Jennifer Page—Upstate New York

My concept of God is simple: God just is.

Looking back over my childhood, I never once remember hating God or blaming God. To me, God was good. God was just. God was an elderly man, in His rocking chair, up in the heavens, watching over us. But how could He see what we were doing at all times? As a child, I remember walking up our road with my socks over my new sneakers so they wouldn't get dirty and wondering if God was watching me. I remember picking up baby birds from their nest, when I wasn't supposed to, and wondering if He was watching me then. Could He really see everything I did, or everything that happened to me? He'd have to have real big eyes for that, I thought.

When I was a young girl, my parents instilled in me a decent concept of God. My father was raised Presbyterian and married my mother, an Episcopalian. My brothers and I were raised in her faith. Our Sunday worship was set up so that the children would leave halfway through the service and attend religious education in another part of the church. It is my recollection that, although my father did not join us in church, he was there every Sunday for the second half—to teach Sunday school to the sixth graders. For several years, Dad taught Sunday school in our home, and in the winter months, he held skating parties afterward on our ice rink. I remember being proud of my father, because he was a "teacher." I was in awe of this. After all, Dad wasn't a member of our church, and yet he was teaching these children about God and Jesus.

I believe that my mother, being an outdoorsy woman, finds solace and peace in God's divine world of nature. From her I inherited my love of natural things from the wilderness to the sea, from wild mushrooms to ocean coral. She spoke of a pristine world without cars, gasoline, or any other spoiling effect of man, a world all to itself. Today, even in her mid-seventies, she continues to teach us.

When I was young, I recited children's prayers, and as I grew older, I continued to pray in a childlike manner. I went from "Now I lay me down to sleep . . ." to "Bless my family, and can I get the newest Barbie doll?" to "Oh God, please let my son live, and I promise I won't snort cocaine anymore" and finally to "Please get me out of this DWI."

When I decided it was time to quit drinking for good, my old way of thinking had to go. It was time to pray to a new God and in a new way. It was time to start praying for God's will for me, instead of my will for the world.

The concept of God that I have today came gradually as I worked the Twelve Steps of A.A.—a concept much different from the rocking-chair God. This one works, and my life changed as a result of true faith. It is a powerful Spirit that flows through the collective soul of the universe. It's everywhere: in the sweet air I breathe when the trees begin to bud in the spring; in the gentle flight of seagulls over the lake at sunset and the endless calming roll of the ocean's tide in the summer; in the crisp, wood-smoke air in Autumn; in the glittering of a new layer of snow when the moonlight casts its glow upon it, and in the honking of the Canada geese in perfect formation in the sky, signaling a change of seasons.

This powerful and loving Spirit of God is in us all. At momentous times, I can see It in another person's eyes and feel God's Love exude from their very soul as it connects with mine. At such times, I feel the presence of the Holy Spirit. If I were to put a concise description on this feeling, it would be simply one word: rapture. Spiritual and emotional ecstasy. The most comforting feeling of all is that I have the Power within me to reach out and become enraptured by God. In times of joy, I am thankful. In times of darkness, I can step into the grace of God's light and still be thankful. All will be right, no matter what.

I can witness God in the smiles and laughter of a child; in the forlorn despair of a destitute soul; in an embrace from another human being, and in tears of bittersweet sadness. The Power is within to reach out to help one another. It is visible in simple acts bestowed out of kindness and concern. "Seek to understand rather than be understood." God's true message is one of love, and it is my absolute belief that love is our soul purpose.

A Return To the Plum Tree

Bill R.—Brandon, Florida

As a child, I experienced the presence of God in all of nature. Sitting in the top of the plum tree in my backyard, I lived in another world, free from all cares, worries and other misconceptions of life. I was six years old.

When I was eleven, my mother and father and I started attending church. My parents became active in this religious organization and, of course, I was forced to go along with this change in their lives.

Through the teachings of this organization, and my misunderstanding of some of those teachings, a concept of God was being formed in my mind—one that was to remain with me until I was forty years old. I came to believe, at that time, that God was an old, angry man sitting on some throne in some place outside of this realm, watching and listing every "wrong thought or deed" that I or anyone else had or did—a resentful, punishing, vindictive being, playing out some sadistic game with humans.

I walked away from this religion and thought I had walked away from God. At times through the years, I suffered from guilt concerning my relationship with God.

Stepping into the rooms of A.A. for the first time, I saw the Twelve Steps on the wall, listened to the Serenity Prayer, heard "How It Works" read from chapter five of the Big Book, and said to myself, "I am in the wrong place."

By the end of that meeting this idea began to change. Those attending said they had their own understanding of God, individually, and that I could have my own as well. Little did they know, I already had an understanding, and that God wanted nothing to do with me. I heard from their experience that my understanding had to change, but what about all I had been taught as a child? Could I have missed it that far? Is it possible that I was wrong? I had hope.

Then, during the meeting, I heard someone say that we shouldn't talk so much about God since it might scare away the newcomers. I was ignorant about many things, including spiritual matters, but I was not stupid. As I have already said, I, myself, could see the Steps on the wall, I had listened to the Serenity Prayer, and heard reading from the Big Book, which mentioned God, all within the first minutes of the meeting. And now here they are, trying to hide the fact that *this is about God*. Interestingly enough, the meeting closed with the Lord's Prayer!

My lifelong understanding of God, the one I'd held since childhood, changed drastically over the next few days as I worked the Steps; however, it did not change totally. The total change came after experiencing God in my life for a while.

My understanding, through experience, is that God is all-loving and all-powerful. God has always loved me but needs my permission to work in my life. I can claim God's power any time I choose, as long as I have not blocked myself from Him. The channel to God is open— if I am not self-seeking, selfish, dishonest or afraid. These defects are taken care of through Step Ten, all throughout the day.

As I stay free of self, I have God's power in abundance. Through prayer and meditation, my understanding of God increases, my experience of God increases, and my faith grows. As suggested in the Big Book's description of Step Eleven, I read other spiritual materials and incorporate spiritual practices into my daily life as my conscious contact with God grows.

My path of spiritual growth lies directly through one-on-one work with others, especially alcoholics. Every time I take someone through the Steps as outlined in the Big Book, I grow spiritually. This is a fact for me and for many others I know. Every day as I am practicing the spiritual principles in all my affairs, I grow spiritually. Why can I do this? Because I had a deep and effective spiritual experience as I worked the Steps.

My spirit woke up!

Now I know that God doesn't test me, life tests me. I test myself and other people's free will tests me. God gives me the courage and strength to walk through these events. Every day my understanding of God changes a little and I hope this will continue throughout my life.

In the beginning, I was told to spend an hour every day in prayer and meditation, even if it only lasted five minutes. In other words: Make an effort.

My concept did change. God is not sitting on some throne outside of this realm. He lives within YOU, and me. Yes, YOU whose lovely eyes are looking down upon this page. Surrender yourself totally to God as you understand Him, then what's left but to soar with the eagles, swim with the dolphins, run with the lions, and uproot trees with the elephants?

Cold words cannot express the experience of God.

No Need to Struggle

Gail L.—Minnesota

During my adolescent years, I thought of the almighty powerful God as the master of discipline. I thought of Him as a long-haired man in robe attire—the commander, making sure I would go to hell if I did anything inappropriate. I, on the other hand, was a small person who was terribly frightened He would get me. He could and would make my life unhappy, I thought, by not letting good things happen or go my way. I thought He would pay me back for my indiscretions, for not being a good example.

Trying to save my own rear, I tried to acquire God's love. I had my own meditation area decorated with bibles, crosses, a baptismal, and candles. I created this little house of prayer to please and impress God, to show Him I was trying to get religious. But that area did not transform my mind or heart, and it certainly didn't make me religious.

So I had a limited experience with God. I figured He somehow created this world and everything in it. But I didn't buy the notion that He was a loving, guiding, and protecting Being. I tried prayer but believed God didn't listen to me. I even prayed for Him to come into my life but still felt unchanged. Why should I rely on Him then? We could coexist, I thought, without having a relationship—He in His world and me in mine. That didn't work either. I couldn't manage my life; I couldn't make things happen; I couldn't "fix" things. The distance I created between me and God nagged at me. I needed some answers but came up empty-handed.

When I quit trying to understand what God was all about, I slowly began to sense His presence. I had to relax and believe God would help me if I only allowed Him to. It was a matter of opening up my mind and heart, letting Him in and acknowledging His presence. It called for a total change of attitude and the belief that God loved me . . . unconditionally. I faced myself in the mirror and repeated a certain prayer until I could come to see this truth. It did take some practice but I did it every morning, eventually coming to believe He created me just the way He wanted and I was beautiful in His eyes.

I began to see God working in my life during the working of the Twelve Steps of Alcoholics Anonymous. I can honestly say, it was God who kept me sober and removed my obsession. I believe He saw my suffering and planned to free me from this addiction. I know I had nothing to do with it; my own will power had failed me numerous times. When my first cries for help were answered, I seized the moment as a true gift. It was the origin of immense serenity.

Once I admitted I was defeated by my addiction and that there was something much more powerful than myself, it was not difficult to trust God to rescue me. Just as the Big Book says, I had to rely on the fact that "either God is everything or else He is nothing." As I connected with God, my understanding of Him became more and more clear. As I depended on Him, I gained independence.

Surrendering to God came rather easily as I was more than ready to seek His help. As I progressed through the Steps, God provided me with the necessary power and courage. Each Step brought me closer to Him.

I now know God truly does answer my prayers and works miracles in my life. Although His answers may not be exactly as I wish to hear, they are always answered. It gets easier and easier to accept His will for my life.

Listen, and He will guide you. Relax, understand, and know He is all around. There is no need to struggle. Continue to maintain a relationship with Him, and always remember who is in charge. Know He is everywhere, guiding us—one day at a time.

Like the Pieces of a Puzzle

Dan B.—Pennsylvania

While I was growing up, every aspect of life was influenced and directed by the Catholic faith of my parents and extended family. My maternal grandfather's family was Lutheran, but that just seemed to be a different version of Catholic. It all seemed the same to me. Everyone I had ever come across in life seemed to have some kind of religious connection, and those connections seemed to influence how they lived and thought. I expected it from people. As a matter of fact, it was one of the things that defined people for me.

I found this to be a comfortable and secure way of life. Everything made sense. There was order and purpose to all things. I had no feelings of uncertainty. God was in heaven, and all was right. It made no difference who was president or what the stock market was doing. My first concern was to do the will of God, for He had given me all things.

I don't remember when I began to lose sight of this way of life, and I never ceased to believe the truth of any of it. But as I grew into my teenage years, the awareness of the world and its possibilities began to crowd out the teachings of my parents and church. What I know today is that I was marching into the adult world with a child's understanding of God and His ways. It all seemed just a little too hokey for me. I began to view my parents as naive hicks—ignorant and unsophisticated. I concluded I was just a little smarter and worldlier than they were. All the stuff they had taught me just seemed irrelevant. Not having seen any burning bushes or miraculous cures of lepers, I decided that even if God did exist, He was doing His thing, and I would just go ahead and do mine.

I started on a slow but steady course toward drunkenness and despair. I stopped living by any sort of ethics or morals. Lying for the

215

sake of convenience was standard practice. I believed laws and rules were for other folks, not me. The odds of "getting caught" determined whether I would or would not engage in any activity. My motto was: "Do unto others before they did it to you." This would have been fine, except that I was not very good at it. Twelve years of Catholic schools leaves one with a finely tuned conscience. Even under the influence of booze, I was unable to completely suppress the idea that certain things were just wrong. Since I did not view life on spiritual terms, I couldn't explain why they were wrong; I just knew that they were. I was not very good at being "bad," and I was even worse at being "good."

At the age of twenty-four, my drinking landed me at an Alcoholics Anonymous meeting. I was unable to stop drinking on my own, and I knew that A.A. could help. I was somewhat disillusioned, when I discovered that A.A. was a "God Thing." I immediately thought of the bible-thumping, self-righteous hypocrites who had become my excuse to stay away from all things religious. I was looking for a way to live without drinking, not religion. But I was desperate, and I figured if religion was the answer, I would just go back to the one with which I was familiar; no sense complicating the whole deal. And so I started to go back to church . . . and prayer meetings . . . and Bible studies . . . and I drank even more. Now I was really screwed up. I was missing something and unable to stay away from booze.

Eventually, things started to fall into place for me. It didn't happen all at once; it was like the pieces of a puzzle suddenly beginning to make a picture. There were a number of turning points for me. One was the statement "God either is, or He isn't. What was our choice to be?" I never realized that it was actually this easy. I came to believe that the purpose of my "free will" was to allow me to make this one life-changing decision. I didn't need long, windy arguments proving or disproving the existence of God. All I needed to do was make a decision. Another was the A.A. tradition that instructs us to consider "principles before personalities." I realized that my distaste for religion was caused by my uncanny ability to spot the phonies (it takes one to know one). I was confusing the message with the messengers. And the turning point for me was the day when I became "willing to go to any lengths." I came to fear the prospect of turning my life over to God less than I feared booze.

I had been waiting for God to show me a burning bush or something. But once I honestly made the decision to seek God's will, I began to see signs of His existence and like-minded people everywhere I went. The A.A. Big Book talks about being rocketed into the "Fourth Dimension: the Realm of the Spirit." I don't think I have been rocketed, but I feel as though I stumble there on a pretty regular basis. Seeking and doing God's will has become the primary motivating force of my life. I know, to the depths of my being, that that is where true peace and joy can be found.

I am now married, and my wife and I have a son. I have laid aside my prejudice against organized religion and have reconnected myself with the church of my childhood. Initially, I made this decision in the hope that my son would be able to connect with the message in a way that I had been unable to do, and it has been successful thus far. I continue to maintain this contact as a sign to the community that the change in my life, from drunk to sober, has much to do with God. I try not to get too involved in the maneuvering of the various factions of the church, and I actually find the antics quite entertaining. I have learned to see the good that each is trying to do.

I have always maintained a commitment to the Fellowship of Alcoholics Anonymous. It saved my life. The Fellowship gave me the chance to stay sober long enough to grasp the actual program of recovery contained in the Big Book. It provided a place to meet and seek guidance from people who had been in my same predicament, and to learn how the A.A. Program had helped them. I believe this commitment is the best way I may be of service to God and my fellow man.

The Farther I Went

Edy G.—California

I was never opposed to the "God idea." I was raised in a staunch, fundamentalist religion, and I was infused with much dogma as a child. I didn't agree with all the "thou shalts" and "thou shalt nots," but then again, I was a kid. What did I know? I was told that in order to get to heaven, you needed to be a member of our religion, and we were encouraged to "witness" to our friends and neighbors. I was very frustrated because I liked the next door lady (who was my mom's age). I wanted her to go to heaven, but I knew she wouldn't change her religion because of me. I asked the preacher what happens to the people who never hear of our religion. Would it be fair of God to keep them out of heaven if they didn't even know our religion existed? He told me something that stuck with me for the rest of my life: he said as long as people lived their lives to the best of their ability, God in His fairness would make sure they got to heaven. That was about the time I started distrusting the dogma, which governed my religion. From then on, I stopped fearing religion and did just about anything I wanted, rationalizing that I was doing the best that I could.

After a series of events that brought me to my knees, I realized I was powerless over alcohol and that my life had become unmanageable. I needed to get some sort of power into my life. I was told I could use whatever concept of God I wanted as long as my conceived power was greater and more powerful than I was and had the ability to restore my sanity. (In other words, it couldn't be a doorknob.)

I initially believed this power was a God individual to me. He couldn't be yours—only mine. This God never left me, never set me in motion and forgot me, and never played tricks on me. My conception served me and only me. I believed we all had our own gods, and they all got together and planned out our lives for us. This way, we would all intersect at just the right time and place doing just the right thing.

As I have continued to follow A.A.'s spiritual path, my conception has become simpler and simpler. I have found that everything in this material world has inherent positive and negative forces. Sometimes I can see, hear, taste, smell, or feel the results of these forces, but I can not see the force itself. I have also noted there is nothing of this world that is one hundred percent positive or negative. However, my Higher Power, which is deep down inside me, is purely positive. My goal today is to become one with that force—that is, to become entirely positive.

I am eternally grateful for my present conception of God. Had I not come to know I am an alcoholic, there is a good chance that I would have never found the solution by which I live. I may have never found God. Today, the consciousness and presence of God in my life is beyond words and comprehension. That presence is, for me, the path to a truly happy, joyous, and free life.

As They Say

Doug B.—Southlands

As they say, a man is known by his work. For a primitive such as myself, so is God. I grew up in the Bible Belt and never could grasp the concept of God that organized religion promulgated. Too foreign, too alien, too mean to fit the image I had of Him in His works all about us.

The delicate wings of a butterfly; the precisely engineered single wing of a maple seed; the intricate veins of a leaf; the iridescent colors of many birds; the unmatchable hues of flowers; and the very design of life on Earth tells me of the fine eye and sensitivity of God. Every creature has a job that makes it useful to the ecosystem and contributes to the workings of the whole that sustain life for all of us. Trees come in all kinds of wood, the properties of each suited for a wide variety of tasks. People often wonder at the purpose of the mosquito. Easy to discern through the eye of the primitive. It guards the wetlands—a major nursery for so many creatures! Why do bugs attack artificial light at night? To try and restore the gift of night to the Earth. The entire Earth is bursting with life in too many astonishing varieties to dismiss the hand of God in all this wonder.

It took me many years to come to this simple appreciation of God. One could say religion drove Him out of my heart, and then alcoholism and the need to recover brought Him back in. It seems I had to be brought low, thoroughly humiliated and disgraced before I sobered enough to wonder at myself and realize that I had lost my place in the world. Rejecting the world and its values, I turned to the Earth I had loved as a boy. Responsibilities of adulthood had taken me so far away from the Earth into the world that I almost lost touch with in life itself.

Sensing that the land has been ruined by the world, I took up ultralight seaplane flying within a few months of getting out of jail. Long flights along the beaches and over shallows teeming with sea life and birds; the wind blowing in my hair; skimming the waves as well as the bottoms of low clouds; and going inland to ride thermals rising off plowed fields—all of which brought me to a better understanding of the relationship between Earth and the world.

I came to believe that God created the Earth, and it gives us life. Man made the world, and it demands how we live. The Earth is a sweet mother; the world a bitch. This simple understanding finally brought me back to God and to a full and complete recovery.

I See God in Everything

Laurie S.—New Hampshire

I was raised in an Irish Catholic family, and we attended mass every Sunday after Bible School. For as long as I can remember, I wore lacy dresses, black leather-strap shoes, and a camel hair coat on the Sabbath. I had to look my best while I pretended to listen to the old man at the altar as he dictated what I should think about God and how I should lead a moral Christian life. I was in God's house, and anything less than my Sunday best just would not suffice.

The whole Catholic philosophy of God was somewhat baffling to me. I did not want to fear this Being, but I was told that if I did not practice what the church taught, I would be a sinner—a bad person—destined to float around in purgatory, never reaching the gates of heaven. If the threat of purgatory was not frightful enough, there was always the notion of burning in hell, an idea which seemed more like an April fool's gag than the truth. After years of forced attendance at mass every week, every holy day, every time my parents told me I had to enter the doors of Holy Cross Church, I decided the idea of organized religion—and the notion of God in general—was not for me. I was tired of people telling me how to live my life, what I must believe, and where my soul would or would not go. I did not want their God.

A few years after leaving the Catholic Church—and all other forms of religion—I became sober for the first time. I struggled with sobriety for more than nine years. I could not follow the Twelve Steps because I did not have a Higher Power with whom to connect. I thought there might be a God, but I had no idea if He would even dare work for me. All I know is that I was living a miserable existence, doing things my way, and bouncing in and out of the halls of Alcoholics Anonymous. Sometimes I thought I was more fulfilled when I was drunk or high.

Eventually, I came to realize I needed a Higher Power because I could find no happiness on life's course doing things my way. There was no Band-Aid big enough to cover my wounds. In order to start healing, I knew that I needed to turn to something or someone bigger and more powerful than me. I did not want my Higher Power to remotely resemble the Catholic God I was raised to know. This seemed like an obstacle to me, one which I did not have the ability to hurdle on my own, for I did not know any other notion of a God. A friend of mine, a sober fellow, told me that I could choose my own idea of God. This was the best news I had heard in years! I would no longer be forced to believe what other people were telling me to believe, for I could create a Higher Power of my own understanding. That is exactly what I did. It all seemed so simple, and really it was.

Once I created my Higher Power, my confidence in Him was no longer an issue. Establishing contact with my God had become as easy as resting my mind and talking to Him. Today, I can drive along the interstate and simply say aloud, "God, let me continue to do your will throughout the rest of this day." I don't find it necessary to stop everything I am doing to have contact with my Higher Power. Having humility and remaining small and willing are the only requirements for this alcoholic. I only say this because I know it to be true. I have seen it in action. As soon as I establish contact with my Higher Power, I can literally feel a sudden calm overcome my body. The effect is amazing. I pray daily, sometimes five or six times each day, depending on how often I feel my will returning. Once I feel that my Higher Power has touched me and charged me with His will, I continue on my daily path.

Today, my Higher Power is everywhere, in everyone and in all things. My God will not send me to hell for any sins I have committed. I can see Him at night when I gaze across a pond watching the brook trout rise at a caddis fly hatch. I can feel His presence in the blustery wind on the coldest of winter days when I am high atop a mountain, trying to ski my way to the bottom. I can see His beauty in a rainbow I recently witnessed in northern New Hampshire, stretching across a valley between the mountains. I can see my Higher Power's presence in the children with whom I work. Most of all, I am able to feel Him deep within my soul, even during some of my darker moments when I momentarily return to my selfish state of being.

I recently asked my Higher Power to help me to find my birth mother so that I could satisfy a seemingly unfillable void in my life.

This miracle has happened—I have found her—the void is slowly being filled as my relationship with her grows. This is proof to me that my Higher Power is real.

My God is beautiful, something akin to Mother Nature. This Higher Power has not let me down—not once, not ever—as the Catholic God of my youth did so many times. God's essence is spiritual; my essence is spiritual. Today, my Higher Power and I walk on the same path. Together.

Good Orderly Direction

Louise L.—Southern Oregon

My concept of God has been an ever-evolving one. As a child, I was taught about a Christian God, one of hellfire and brimstone. From there to a more forgiving God, yet still very judgmental. I started looking elsewhere in my late teens for answers to my questions. I felt that there had to be some kind of source of power that created all this world that I know and keep it all going. I didn't think it was some great puppet master in the sky, though. Not some big old man with long flowing robes and beard. I read some about different religions of the world. I was very untrusting of religions and the leaders representing them. I saw them as wanna-be gods—human failures. They didn't practice what they preached. I wanted no part of organized religion. Some of the ceremonies were fun to watch and some fun to participate in. But they didn't have a direct connection for me to the God they represented.

When I first read the book Alcoholics Anonymous, I was most intrigued by two things. First, they presented a solution to a dilemma that worked. Second, the concept of a Higher Power.

What I learned by reading more and talking with recovered members of Alcoholics Anonymous was that the source for the solution was a power greater than myself. Most everyone I spoke with chose to call that power God. At first, I was taken aback, fearful that "here we go again with this God crap." Then it was explained to me that I could choose whatever I wanted my higher power to be. I didn't need to use their conception or some other prefabricated one. I could custom tailor mine to a perfect fit.

At first, I used something that was outside of myself. I wanted something tangible to acknowledge a source of power greater than myself. I found a rock. It was smooth from being pounded by the surf of the Pacific Ocean. It fit perfectly in my hand, grasped between my thumb and forefinger. It was small enough I could carry it in my pocket and in any time of need I could hold onto it and tap into my power source. I needed to take this physical action of connecting into my Higher Power to feel that strength. I carried that rock with me daily for a few years. Then one day, it just vanished. I couldn't find it anywhere. To this day, I still have no idea what happened to my rock. I was terrified to be left without my Higher Power—or so I thought. Instead, what happened was I allowed my Higher Power to grow. To grow within me. My rock became a place within me that I could tap into. I had enough belief in this power that I no longer needed to have it be tangible. I could tap into it by just asking. I always got my answer as a gut feeling kind of thing. My intuition was awakening and I was learning how to use it. I believe that intuitive thought is, in its purest form, what is the right thing to do. Purest of motive. If I can take my intuitive thought and turn it into direct action, then I can change. I could sit here all day long, thinking about what actions would be the right and good thing to do, but until I take the action, nothing changes. All this internal struggle going on.

What happened next to my evolutionary conception happened on the beach. I used to love to walk on the beach, listen to the surf slap the sand. Watch the gulls do their scavenger thing. And most importantly, I learned on the beach to be a part of something. I was one of those grains of sand on the beach. One grain alone doesn't make a beach. I learned that no matter what my idea of a power greater than myself was, I was a part of the greater group. That was a first for me. To actually feel like I was a part of something, that I belonged. My beliefs didn't set me apart from, they included me. No one but me needed to understand what my Higher Power was and how I used it.

Today, I choose to call my Higher Power God. Not because I see it as a religious thing. God is just the name. It is the outward distinction between the power source and me. What matters most is what is in the inside of the power and how I use the power to guide me through my day: **Good Orderly Direction.**

To Have Him Be My Center

Michael B.—Philadelphia

When it comes to God, would you say you are ice-cold, lukewarm, or on fire? After looking back on my own relationship with God as it grew over the years, these are the stages I, myself, went through, and I see them clearly now.

For most of my life, I have been ice-cold. Despite what I learned in three years of Catholic school, I didn't really believe in the power of God. He may or may not exist, I thought. In either case, it didn't matter to me; it had no bearing on my life. God's existence didn't make me feel wanted, loved, adequate, strong, or whole. It didn't stop my step-brother and uncle from beating me; it didn't make my mother pay attention to me; it didn't bring my brother and me closer; it didn't stop me from self-destructing.

As a way of coping with my life, I started to experiment with drugs and alcohol, hoping they would numb me and help me forget my pain. I felt alone, shut off from everything and everyone. I didn't know how to connect. Before I knew it, I was constantly drunk and out of control. I hid my depression and anger deep inside me. Alcohol and drugs brought those feelings to the surface. When they were unleashed, I was violent and arrogant like an erupting volcano.

God, my father said, would punish me. He would break my arm, cover my face with pimples, or involve me in a bad accident, depending on what I did. So I said, "Screw this God, my father's God who wanted only bad things for me." I encouraged this God to act, challenged His power. "Bring it on," I'd say. "Show me what you got." My underlying hope was that He would punish me—end my life and misery. He did not. I was ice-cold and had no intention of making contact or forming a relationship.

God, however, had other ideas. After drinking and drugging for nearly nine years, I went to rehab to escape the accusations that I was alcoholic. I expected the counselors to agree with me—to say I didn't belong there and should go home. But no one did. In fact, I began to question my drinking when I listened to others share.

One man in particular caught my attention. He often shared of his experiences with prayer, claiming that he knew God was listening. *How did he know this*, I wondered. *God had never listened to me. This man must have known something I did not—the secret to prayer.* So I asked, "What do you say when you pray? How do you get God to listen to you?"

He smiled and said, "I just talk to Him like He's my friend. Before I go to bed, I thank Him for letting me live."

I laughed, because my prayers had always been for death. I was skeptical but willing.

"You should try it," he said. "What can it hurt?"

He was right. If I approached God in a different way, it might work. My first prayer was awkward but sincere. I asked God to help me with my alcohol and anger problems. I asked God to be my friend. I talked, and as my friend predicted, God listened. For the first time ever, I felt a connection; I felt I was beginning to understand something about God. Unfortunately, this did not last. As my fears and loneliness relaxed, so did my prayers. I thought I no longer needed God.

Soon after, I started to feel depressed again, and I reverted to the "why-are-you-doing-this-to-me" prayers. At last, I was convinced that God did not work for me. I was hopeless and tried to commit suicide several times.

During one of my attempts, a friend called to offer good news—that he had found a way up and out of his alcoholic torture. He was going to share it with me, whether I wanted it or not. It was then that I was introduced to the *Big Book of Alcoholics Anonymous* and the program of action. This program demanded my willingness to believe in a Higher Power. I couldn't say for sure whether I believed in God, but I was willing. Thankfully, that was all that was required of me to start.

As I worked the Twelve Steps, I made contact with God again. I even felt as if I had entered another realm. I could feel a new Presence flowing through me and directing my eyes and thoughts. I was amazed. But "it is easy," the Big Book says, "to let up on the spiritual program of action and rest on our laurels." I know exactly how easy that is.

Once again, I mistook God's grace. My comfort led to inaction. I was lukewarm, meaning I knew of God's power and mercy but . . . "faith without works is dead."

Knowing that my inaction was causing me pain, my brother invited me to the Harvest Crusade—a gathering of thousands meant to bring people closer to Jesus Christ. The pastor stirred something in me that hadn't been stirred in quite some time: a willingness to give my life to God. He invited us to come forward to receive Christ, and I went. I accepted Jesus as my Lord and Savior. Immediately, I felt at one with my Creator, and the desire to further develop this contact followed. I was on fire for God, and that demanded action. I dove back into the program of Alcoholics Anonymous.

Steps Ten, Eleven, and Twelve strengthen my relationship with God. When I fall short of His ideals—and I do—I inventory and right my wrongs. I ask for forgiveness and guidance. I ask Him to show me the way of patience, tolerance, kindliness, and love. I ask for direction and intuition. Then, I sit quietly and meditate. I write my thoughts and test them to determine which are mine and which are God's. If my thoughts are selfish, dishonest, resentful, or fearful, they are obviously mine. If not, they belong to God. Then, it is my job, as His child, to obey the guidance He has given me. When I do this, I feel His Power blazing inside of me.

This fire inspired me to go beyond A.A. I began to read the Bible to uncover more of the truth. What I found was that God had been a part of me my entire life and that He had given me the ultimate sacrifice: His Son, Christ Jesus. When I find it difficult to set aside my selfishness and work for God, I am reminded of His love for me, of His grace and mercy, of my new life, and I get right to work by carrying this message of hope and forgiveness to others. I know and trust that God will reveal more to me everyday, as long as I remain willing to have Him be my Center.

A Faith That Has Sustained Me

Amy C.—Philadelphia

Coming home from school that day, I was about thirty-four days sober and quite irritable. I had been living in a world of rationalization: My drinking wasn't that bad; I was just a normal teenager who went a little too far; things would be different this time. Now, how to convince my mother? I'd just tell her, whether she liked it or not. Hey, I'd say, I decided to quit A.A. That was enough of an explanation. I breathed deeply, attempting to push my discontent through my nose.

The slob next to me on the bus was taking up entirely too much room. I could feel his sweaty skin rubbing against my arm as he breathed. He made me itch. I had what they call "meth bugs," the delusion that bugs are crawling across your skin, falling into your pores on their backs then flipping right-side-up. I elbowed him repeatedly.

As we neared my stop, I saw my ex-something-or-other through the scratched window, leaning against the traffic light and smoking a "funny" cigarette. At twenty-three, Joe was eight years older than me and balding. He waved me toward him. I knew what he wanted: that he had a pile of speed waiting to be devoured. He hadn't seen me since I got out of rehab.

For the first time in a long time, I was afraid—of what, I wasn't sure. This was my chance to surrender my sobriety, to feel snug again in my own skin. This was my chance, and I couldn't do it. Everything but my lips was frozen. Cynically, I mouthed: *If there is a God, there will be somebody waiting for me when I get off this bus, somebody I've known for a long time who will walk me all the way home, somebody Joe wouldn't talk to, somebody not involved in my insanity.* I pushed the signaling button and prepared to exit. When the back doors opened, Steve, a lifelong friend and neighbor appeared. He stood in that tense distance between Joe and I and said, "Come here, Aim. I'll walk you home."

Joe nodded his round head at me, pushed himself off the pole with his back, and walked in the opposite direction, taking the promise of an awful high with him. That was the last time I saw him close-up.

Seeing Steve in the flesh at just the right moment astonished me. I said that hasty prayer expecting to be disappointed, ignored, neglected. The truth of the matter was that I did believe in God; I just didn't believe He wanted anything to do with me. I thought my actions had closed me off to Him forever. Steve must have had no idea that he was my "proof," that God had used him to make a point.

Later, I discovered that God had been poking at me my entire life, nudging me to come closer and accept Him. These pokes were constant and usually accompanied by incidents which left me on my knees with clasped hands and teary eyes: for example, my cousin's suicide or being battered by a lover. I could feel this prodding finger in the center of my stomach—the echo of which rang in my ears. As my addiction progressed, the pokes increased in impact and frequency. Steve's presence that day was like a loud clap in front of my wayward eyes.

Unfortunately, this "revelation" about God did not last, as it was not followed up by action. I still demanded control of my behaviors and thoughts, allowing my will to run wild and harm others. I continued to lie, steal, manipulate, and resent. At meetings, I would profess my belief in a Power greater than myself; outside the rooms, however, I didn't pray or do anything else to enhance a relationship with that Power. To believe, I thought, was enough, but it wasn't. I lived in this lonely darkness for five years in Alcoholics Anonymous, feeling the point of His finger against my spirit.

In sobriety, I reached a spiritual and emotional bottom, a point at which I had to decide whether I would accept God in my life or drink again. Despite its simplicity, this was not an easy choice. I was licked by my defects. I talked with other A.A.'s, members who could match calamity with serenity, who claimed to be recovered from alcoholism, who worked diligently for their daily reprieve. They embraced me and promised a return to sanity, if I was willing and honest.

"I thought there were no promises in A.A., " I said. I had heard this a thousand times in the rooms.

"The Big Book guarantees them," they said, while thumbing through my book.

Together, we reviewed those promises: perfect peace and ease; fearlessness; freedom and happiness; and an amazing relationship with my Creator—surely, attractive promises for a desperate alcoholic! I rode their coattails, assured and calmed by their faith in the program of Alcoholics Anonymous and in God. They worked with me daily, instructing and encouraging me through the Steps.

My understanding of God was transformed by incorporating the program of action into my life. I could feel His Presence in my life and my heart. "You will love God and call Him by name," my sponsors said. I enjoyed this new feeling of worthiness and love—so much that I began to pray for more faith. This was the defining point at which my sketchy idea of God would become specific and lucid.

After expressing my desire for a deeper faith, I was presented with the news that my ex-boyfriend, John, was infected with AIDS and that he most likely contracted the disease during the span of our relationship. I was resentful, fearful, and full of the desire to retaliate. Again, my sponsors worked with me daily, instructing me to trust God, clean house, and help others. Again, I rode their coattails. As I was repeatedly tested for HIV for the next year and a half, my sponsors and I prayed together, asking God for guidance and strength, for the removal of self-will, and for willingness. This was the hardest and most important time of my life, but I was not alone.

At first, my prayers were insincere, drowned out by my will which screamed, "Please don't let me have AIDS." As time and life rolled on, my prayers became more focused and less selfish. I continued to work with other alcoholics, and that promised peace began to flow through me again. I understood the Steps.

Being compelled by desire, I began to read the New Testament. I was sure it was there that I would find relief. I stumbled across a parable which I had read a thousand times before. As I read the lesson, I was overcome with a sense of peace as I had never known. I repeated the parable over and over to myself, tightly hugging its promise. The story comes from Mark 5:25-76 and follows:

There was a woman who suffered greatly from a hemorrhage for twelve years. She visited many doctors, but her condition continued to get worse. She heard of Jesus's power, so she came from behind Him and touched the fringe on His robe. By touching Him, she thought she would be cured. Immediately, her bleeding stopped. Jesus felt the power escape Him and asked, "Who touched me?" The frightened woman came, fell at His feet and told Him what she had done. And He said to her, "Daughter, your faith has made you well. Go in peace. You have been healed."

I emerged the following year disease-free and with a faith that has since sustained me through many trials. It was then that I gave my life to Christ. My loneliness and depression have vanished. Life is now filled with direction and purpose, joy and opportunity. I am indebted to God, for He has done for me what I could not do for myself. My faith and His Grace have made me well. Amen!

A Mouse in a Maze

Robin K.—Illinois

When I was a child, I was taught that God would punish me for everything I did wrong and every wrong thing I thought of doing. There wasn't much of a difference between doing and thinking in the eyes of my church and my father. So by the time I reached thirteen, I was convinced I would never be able to find favor in God's eyes, and I literally put down the Bible and stopped trying to be good. Instead, I turned to drugs and alcohol and fell into a cycle of guilt and depression almost immediately. I drank and drugged more often to escape those feelings.

At age twenty-one, I found myself in the Fellowship of Alcoholics Anonymous. They talked of God at my first meeting, and I thought I was doomed. I honestly thought God was mad at me and wanted nothing to do with me. After all I had done, I feared His punishment and could not pray. But I wanted to get better, and I decided the Twelve Steps would help me get positive attention from Him. I did what I was told to do: I applied the "fake it until you make it" philosophy. I had faked my whole life, so faking this program would be no problem at all. . . . I relapsed.

Even though this relapse lasted for only one day, I hated the way I felt. I went straight to my sponsor's house, and she took me to a meeting. It was time to get real, she said. In other words, I could not fake my way through the program and that meant I had to find a Higher Power and form a relationship with Him. There, I began. I got on my knees that night and I thanked God for all that was good in my life. I asked Him to help me with the Steps and to help me to be honest. But something was still missing. I didn't feel the closeness that others talked about. I couldn't understand it. Somewhere deep inside, I still believed

He was mad at me. He knew me like no one else did, I thought, so how could He even look at me.

My life still wasn't easy, and I wondered why it was so hard to turn it around. I blamed God and exploded, yelling and screaming at Him with full force. I don't remember what I said, but I know it was ugly. I must have gone on for twenty minutes or more before I exhausted myself. When I was finally quiet, I heard a small still whisper in my spirit that said, "Now that that's out of the way, we can get on with a real relationship!" An unexplainable peace came over me, and I felt Him comfort me. I began to understand what people had been saying about God being their friend. That day, I found a friend: one who would never let me down; one who would always be there for me; one who wanted to know me personally; and one who would laugh with me and sometimes even *at* me (as a mother laughs at her toddler child). That day, I realized I am His child.

The A.A. program brought me to the truth about God: He is a lovely grace who wants to have a relationship with me, who created me and loves His creation—good and bad, warts and all. He wants all of me. I initially had a hard time with God because I saw Him as a punisher. But after I realized it was God who sent His Son to save us, I was able to reconcile with Him. I felt safe with Jesus because He walked on the Earth and felt my pain. Today, I have a relationship with both of Them. I can talk to God and tell Him everything. It is a comfort to know God knows my every thought; it is no longer a fear.

When I experience disappointments, God wants to comfort me, and sometimes, I don't let Him. I may get angry and plan on staying that way for a while. I may want things to go my way. But I have come to learn that God's plans are always better than mine. I trust Him and bring Him close to me. It comforts me to walk side by side with Him.

In order that I might better understand God, I was once told to picture a mouse in a maze, sniffing for a piece of cheese. I know the path he should take and watch as he frantically runs into dead ends. I cheer him on and tell him which way to go because I really want to see him get there. Then, I was told to imagine that God looks at my life the same way. He knows where it is heading and how to get there. He will give me guidance, but it is up to me to take it. He is happy when I make progress, and He cheers me on. Oh, if I would only listen better, I would have all the cheese I wanted!

Learning to Walk

Joyce W.—Missouri

Coming to believe: not merely believing that there is a God but truly accepting that He has the ability to bring about miraculous changes for me personally. This process of coming to believe was a most difficult leap from my previous thoughts of God—as an untouchable and invisible being who was much too busy with more important matters to consider my sorry predicament.

I can't deny there were times in my life when I experienced moments of awe and gratitude for some of His works . . . when I held my newborn babies for instance. I was deeply moved at the miracle of the event and sensed that surely some divine, awesome, and intelligent Power had brought this about. On occasion, I was also moved to acknowledge the hand of God in the world, especially when witnessing a particularly moving scene: looking at a beautiful sunset, a magnificent ocean, or an expanse of stars; watching puppies being born; or listening to an especially emotional sermon. These feelings of God-consciousness were triggered briefly, but they were fleeting and never very personal. They weren't substantial enough to hold on to or use to build a relationship with God.

I think I was feeling completely responsible for controlling my life. I never allowed myself to think for a moment that I couldn't handle realistic issues. Besides, God seemed better suited to things of grandeur, things of import, things that involved righteous people—those who were perhaps better acquainted with Him than I was. I never considered needing or using Him as a source. I looked to more realistic sources of stability. God never signed my paycheck, baby-sat my children, fixed my car, or knocked on my door with a sweepstakes award check; and I had no idea that He could provide things like courage, comfort, strength, love, and forgiveness. I didn't know those things were missing from my life.

I muddled through life from childhood, and into alcoholism much like a toddler just learning to walk. I held onto stable objects for security, stability, and safety as I moved from place to place. Like a child, I did not let go of one thing until I had a firm grasp on the next. Eventually, the day arrives when the parent should encourage the child to let go. Even though the child has not experienced this unknown avenue of motivation, he is not afraid. Because all things have been provided by the parent, because the parent has demonstrated love, and because the child desires to please the parent, the child lets go and flings himself into the unknown with faith and trust, believing that he will not be allowed to fall. When the child succeeds, there is joy all around.

I was much like that child, feeling secure only when holding onto a job, a family, money, or health. However, several things compelled me to let go: the absence of a chemical in my body, the mental anguish and fear of the unknown, the rage at not being able to resolve my inner conflicts, the lack of peace or security, and the uncertainty about how to trust a Power greater than myself. Desperate and in pain, I tried to kill myself by overdosing on chemicals and ended up in the hospital. After recovering from a comatose state, I started to hear voices—actually just one voice that repeated my name. At first, I stayed in my bed and prayed, but the voice continued. So I got out of bed, walked to the door of the room, and looked up and down the corridor, but I saw no one. Suddenly, I knew Who was calling my name. I knew He had thwarted my plan to escape my miserable life and must surely be listening to my prayers. It was as though He was right in the room with me, and relief came at once. I believe this was my introduction to faith.

I found myself in the arms of the God that other people talked about. I discovered I had hope and a desire to learn faith. And guess what? He did not let me fall! I was caught and safe, and faith began to grow.

In the beginning, this relationship with God was very fragile but extremely intimate and personal. And it worked. I was protective of it and held it close—careful not to share it with anyone for fear they might tell me I wasn't doing it right. It was too precious and too valuable to expose to criticism. It felt so good, so warm and safe. When I had difficulty sleeping, anxiety attacks, guilt over past deeds, or fear of what was to become of me, I'd pretend to crawl into the lap of God at night—in the dark, in the quiet of my room—and in my mind, I was there. I said prayers of gratitude for all the things He'd always provided even though I didn't have the sense to ask for them. I realized that real prayers do not ask for things; instead, they are praises and thanks to God for providing what is needed.

Gradually, I became more like that child, wanting to please my new Father and bask in His presence. I was no longer alone, and a great relief washed over me. My life from that moment changed— completely. Today, I remain humbly aware of the miracle of healing—spiritual, physical, and mental—which was granted to me, not by my own merit, but by the grace of God. It was that humility that enabled me to walk with confidence into recovery and a new way of life.

As Though by Magic

Zane C.—Adirondack foothills, New York

I cannot explain God, and that's not my aim here. What I can do is this: I'll tell you, as best I can, how the Power of God came into my life. I hear some speak of "finding God." I didn't find God. God wasn't lost— I was.

Growing up in a home where my father was a drunk and my mother a very sick and twisted woman, there wasn't much favorable talk of God. The most common reference to God, the one I heard screamed at the top of lungs with alarming regularity, was "God damn it!" Sure, there were those in my family who revered the Almighty when it suited them; but for the most part, they were religious hypocrites, living a life at home much different from the one they exhibited for the congregation at their place of worship. From the age of seven, when my mother enrolled me in ministerial school, until the age of fourteen, when I rebelled and got the hell away from home, I watched those "more religious" members of my family contradict everything I'd learned about God. At home, they smoked, drank, cursed, and raised hell; yet at the halls where they met for worship, they were the most laughable examples of piety imaginable—a true farce.

So, in short, I grew up knowing several things for certain: God was an object of convenience; my family were all fakes; and as long as they weren't scaring me shitless by telling me God would destroy me for masturbating and stealing candy, I was pretty much OK with the God idea. I could stay close enough to God, as close as I dared, with automatic prayers in bed ("God, bless everyone, and please help me get away from my mother."), and the token "grace" forced on us at the dinner table. That covers my initial conception of God; after that, all hell broke loose.

I walked out of the ministry, out of that cultish religion with one thing in mind: escape, at any cost. Next mission: run. I had listened to enough of how God was going to kill me, how my family would walk on my bones at Armageddon, and how God saw everything I did, including my looking and leering at the girls in the catalogs, the lingerie section in particular. If all this were true, I needed to run, because God would surely send me straight to hell for all those times I'd sat in beer joints with my father, playing pool when I was so young I had to stand on a stool to make my shots. I was a goner for sure; so I hit the road.

No matter where I ran during the next seventeen years, I could not escape the possibility of God, the inkling of some divine, spiritual seed planted deep inside of me. I saw churches everywhere and heard people of faith speaking on television and radio of the great miracles in their own lives. It seems, looking back, that I was always running, always headed somewhere, anywhere but where I happened to be at the moment. I must admit, trying to outrun God was truly a full-time job. It stressed me out so badly that I was forced to take up alcohol as an equalizer.

Yes, I had thoughts of God during those years, but honesty prevails upon me and compels me to admit that most, if not all, of my contact was during times of personal crisis brought about by my own actions. Constantly, I asked God to get me out of scrapes and precarious situations with the law, with my family, and with anyone else who got in the path of my escape route. I even remember asking God to help me not pee in the cat box at my friends' house, because it would be too embarrassing to wake up in the morning and admit I had a problem with my drinking. Evidently God was absent that night, and the cat wasn't pleased at all either. God was convenient, and prayer was simple. But the jailers still locked me up. My friends wisely avoided me. My family wanted nothing to do with me, and even my best prayers went "unanswered." I was lost out there—having a helluva time, but lost.

There came a point in my life, during my college years, that I sought to go back to find what I'd lost, to seek God in all the religious tenets of the most ancient of religions. I dabbled in Catholicism, voodoo, Primitive Baptism, Methodism, and Zen Buddhism. You name it, and I have probably "read up on it." Still, the peace I inherently knew I should possess eluded me. Considering the fact that I personally decided I was a genius of epic proportion (that and the fact I had only been jailed twelve times for alcohol-related offenses in the last ten years), I felt as though I should have had an answer by this time. The sum of my intellectual "book-learnin'" about God had failed to produce the desired results: a way out of the dark.

So, I did the usual. I drank.

When God was finally revealed to me, I was at my lowest point. Perhaps it took a trip out to the edge of nothingness to clarify my vision enough that I could see the root of all my problems. I damned near had to die to gain what I have today, so I value it greatly. I was sitting in a locked room, barricaded in with six cases of beer and a loaded gun, and I was truly tired. I remember being so weary I wished I could go to sleep and never wake up. More than seventeen years of drinking had taken their toll. I could not drink enough to pass out or drink enough to escape. Alcohol stopped working that day, just plain stopped. Running from God had not worked. All the books, the preachers, the psychologists and psychiatrists, the religionists, and the professors had not worked to show me the answer. My very best ideas put a gun in my hand. What removed that gun still remains a little bit sketchy, but I am here telling this tale, so it must have happened.

I'd seen something very scary earlier that day. A soul-dead man, looking back at me from my own mirror.

What had amazed me about the man's appearance was his resemblance to me, down to his having my green eyes and drinking beer as though it were water—that and the fact that he always appeared in the mirror, of all places. He was one tricky bastard; that's for sure. It was in that mirror that I saw the truth, and it was that moment of truth that unlocked all things wonderful in my life since.

After that last night of torment, I must have been licked. I did not pull the trigger, nor did I ever manage to drink enough to escape what I now refer to as "the end." In fact, it was then that I knew, with amazing conviction, that I would soon beat the drinking game. As it turned out, a window to my soul had been opened that night. It was as though the edge of death had revealed to me the door to life, and in that moment of clarity, God appeared as a light of wondrous warmth. For the first time, I knew I could be OK. I had no idea what would be required, but at least I had hope.

During the days that followed, I sought out the help of persons who understood alcoholism better than any other group of folks in the world: Alcoholics Anonymous. It was there that a man showed me that God is not so scary after all, and that God is available to those who are honestly seeking Him. I hesitate to place a label, a gender, a solid concept or moniker on the Power that is God.

Since working the Twelve Steps, I have seen things beyond the scope of my previous human experience. It was in the practice of the maintenance Steps—those last three of the twelve—that I came to know more and more and, at the same time, realized I would never know it all, nor would I need to. Earlier, in the first three Steps, I'd made contact, but that was just the tip of the proverbial iceberg. What followed has grown beyond explanation: the ability to think and reason sanely and the desire to walk with that Power daily, knowing It is always there, always available to guide, to comfort, to inspire. What a magnificent Presence God has proved to be, once I got honest enough to uncover myself, to make myself naked and ready, defeated and humble. The Power of God manifests Itself repeatedly and in direct proportion to how willing I am to stay free of those defects of character I addressed during the first nine Steps of A.A.

I am comfortable today with God. I do not have any photographs of this Power, and I don't have a definition. The reason for this is simple: God is unlimited, and any attempts on my part to quantify or explain God pale in comparison to what I feel the true infinity of the God Idea represents. This I know: the will of God is so simple it baffled me in the beginning of my new relationship with Its Power. These days I know that the will of the God, as I understand Him, is simply to treat others as I would like to be treated and to seek the beauty and happiness of life. It is through prayer, through periodic searches through meditation, and through the actual practice of faith (meaning the actions of trying to do the right thing for all concerned in any given situation), that I find God filling me up where once I was empty and dead.

For me, it is in the "not knowing" all the secrets of God that the mystery, which makes God a Power greater than I am, can exist. Both the mystery and the simplicity of this Power contribute to Its makeup. I believe more is being revealed to me daily. I work through prayer and meditation to keep my conception of God open-minded. When I cannot reasonably or logically explain the awesome miracle of healing I underwent during the Steps, or when I cannot justify scientifically why certain events are taking place around me as though by magic, I can easily smile and say "Thank you, God."

My Saving Grace

Jackie A.—California

As a child, I believed God could not be counted on. I prayed often that He would save me from the physical and sexual abuse I suffered at the hands of my father. But God didn't seem to be listening to me. If He did hear me, He didn't seem interested in helping me escape that terrible situation. I felt as though He had abandoned me.

When I came to Alcoholics Anonymous, I was told I had to believe that something could keep me sober. They said it could be a doorknob, a tree, or a light bulb. I could take my pick. It didn't matter as long as it was stronger than I was. But I didn't understand. How would a light bulb keep me sober? And what if that tree burnt down?

I turned back to God. I wasn't sure whether He would forgive me for all the wrong I had done in my lifetime. I was scared. I wondered how and why He would do anything for me, and I had a difficult time praying. I was sure that if God ever caught up with me I was going to be in trouble.

I started listening to old timers share about their loving God and the miracles He had performed for them. They said He was partial to drunks and that we were blessed and lucky to be alive. Soon, I began to accept the good things people were saying about God. I, too, began to feel as though God had chosen me—to live and work for Him in Alcoholics Anonymous. There were certain things I had to do to stay sober, and seeking God was one of them.

I started to feel a little peace and serenity. My days were getting better and better, and I began to like sobriety. After beginning to work the Twelve Steps, I apologized to God for my actions and asked Him to help keep me clean and sober. Prayer and meditation has been my saving grace.

I would get up an hour before anyone else in my home to have quiet time with God. That is how my belief and trust in God developed. I am able to just get quiet and listen for the voice (down in my soul) that guides me. Sometimes, the voice of God just reassures me—telling me I will be OK or to continue on my path. It takes time to get to the point where we can listen to God, but we must get there. We need to hear Him because we are not building a one-way relationship. If I ask God for help, I must listen for the answers. I am now ready to receive whatever God has in store for me.

Today, I know God wanted me to work on myself so I could help others. That is the whole premise of Alcoholics Anonymous—to be of service. I have always had a twenty-four telephone and a twenty-four-hour house. I open my home the way others did for me. I attend church regularly and channel my energy into helping others in and out of Alcoholics Anonymous. Today, I continue to seek God's will for me.

The Process of Finding God

Bill R.—Apollo Beach, Florida

Near as I can recall, my spiritual awakening started when I was about two or three months sober. And God knows that I didn't come to A.A. looking for a spiritual experience. I was just kind of hoping to use it as a way to get my wife off of my back for a little while, as a place to slow down on my drinking for a little while and kind of regroup so that I could go back to drinking heavy just on the weekends, and maybe some social maintenance drinking during the week.

Anyway, I had been going to a lot of A.A. meetings regularly, at least two, and sometimes three, per day. So I had become friendly with a few of the A.A. members.

For most of the first two to three months, I was pretty scared that I would probably drink again and wind up in big trouble. I was fighting the urge to drink just about every day and whenever I had to walk past the liquor section in the supermarket I would hear the bottles singing or talking to me "We're on sale this week. Bacardi rum $12.95 per 1.5 gal.—Jim Beam bourbon $13.49 per 1.75 liter."

I tried very hard to avoid that section of the store since I wasn't quite sure that someday I might not just say "Oh, hell, what's the point in hanging on any longer?" and just grab a couple of half-gallons and get good and loaded.

One day an A.A. old-timer, Al F., stopped me after the 7:00 A.M. morning meeting and asked me if I was still obsessed with drinking or not drinking, if it was still a constant preoccupation, an hour-by-hour battle to resist the temptation. I told him that surprisingly something had changed, and I really wasn't always walking around wondering *when* I was going to get struck drunk and that lately even the bottles in the market had stopped calling to me with their siren song.

Al said he thought that was wonderful news and then he told me, point blank, that another miracle had happened for me—that God had removed from me the obsession to drink, my preoccupation with booze.

He explained to me that if I define an obsession as something so strong that I alone cannot successfully resist it through my mental efforts or exertion of will power, then it is something that can only be removed from me by the action or grace of God or a Power greater than myself.

As I think back on it, I don't know that he was one hundred percent right in his explanation, but as a relative newcomer to A.A., I wasn't much in a position to argue with a guy who had ten-plus years sober, and maybe more importantly the idea that God had done me another favor made me feel pretty special inside.

I wasn't a low-bottom, gutter drunk so I didn't need a major miracle to straighten me out, maybe just a minor one, but the idea of being part of a miracle, even a small one, felt pretty good.

By the way, Al F. was also the guy who first put in my mind the idea that me even getting to A.A. was a gift of God's grace. He told me it was called a "moment of clarity." It was called that because somehow some way in the midst of my drunken insanity, a light had gone on and I had been able to see that I could not keep drinking the way I had been without some very major negative things happening in my life— an idea or perception that I had never had in all of my previous drinking years.

He told me to hang onto that moment, 'cause I could not be guaranteed that the grace would be granted again if I chose to go back to drinking, thinking I could get back to A.A. whenever I got tired of getting into trouble from being drunk again.

By the time I got through the drinking obsession phase and my education by old Al and other longtime A.A. members, I guess you would say I was pretty well done with Step Two, and on my way to finding a God that I could turn my will and life over to in Step Three.

Much like I had done the Second Step—kind of backwards—and having to first define the word "sanity" (peace of mind) before I could admit that I *had* none and then seeing that I needed an H.P. to restore me to a condition I honestly thought would return just as soon as I had gotten physically sober.

So working backwards on Step Three, while sitting in continual A.A. meetings, I came to see I had a few problems to work out on my old God. He was distant, punishing, mean-spirited, and relentlessly demanding.

While at this point I could see what I had didn't work, and I had heard people share in meetings about a loving, caring God, I don't think I had a very good idea of what kind of God I wanted. And maybe I wasn't supposed to have it. My A.A. friends kept telling me it was an individual journey to God and that my God concept would change as I progressed in my spiritual growth.

I particularly remember a longtime A.A. lady, Jennifer, who one day made the statement that if you ever got to the point where you could totally understand the God that you had, then you would have to get rid of Him, because if you understood all about Him, then He was no bigger than you.

I had a couple of things happen to me during early sobriety that I would call episodes of spiritual awakening, times when I felt that God had actually talked directly to me.

The first happened one day when I was cleaning the leaves out of my swimming pool. There were quite a few trees surrounding the pool, and even after I had cleaned up the leaves on the deck to keep them from blowing into the pool, it seemed that no matter how hard and fast I worked to get them out of the pool, a few new ones would blow down from somewhere and prevent me from getting the pool "one hundred percent" clean. I am an engineer and tend to be a perfectionist, so one hundred percent was the only acceptable result for me. Even as a kid in school, I was dogged by the pressure that anything below an "A" grade was a type of failure. During one particularly frustrating cleanup job, I was fed up and screamed out in my mind, "God, WHY can't I get this pool one hundred percent clean?" To this day, I swear that God spoke back to me and said, "Bill, you can never get it one hundred percent clean because if you did, you would be 'perfect' like Me, and there can only be ONE of Me." My fight for perfection pretty much ended in that moment. Later, I learned that while perfection is an impossibly aggravating goal, it would be good if I would strive for "excellence," and that there were times when I could settle for just a C, a passing grade.

Another time, again when I was cleaning the pool, I wound up thinking of how I envied people who could play music by ear. I'd been a trumpet player in high school, and was actually good enough to wind up as the lead trumpet player in the school band. Despite how good I was, I always needed the sheet music to play the songs, even the school song and the national anthem, which we played many times throughout the year. If I worked real hard, I could memorize parts of the songs, but I could never just pick up my horn and play. What I came to realize that day was that regardless of how good I was, I was *only* a technician. I could execute the notes on the page very well, but I could *not* play by ear. I had *not* been given the gift of being able to play by ear. Thinking along those lines, I came to understood that in spite of my years of religious training in Catholic School, that when it came to a relationship with God, all I had was intellectual book knowledge. I had no feeling for God in my heart. Whether I had that feeling once and subsequently lost it as a result of my misbehaviors and drinking, or whether I'd never received it, really made no difference. It was a sad realization. But amazingly, at about the same instant that I realized that I'd been getting by on my empty, intellectual knowledge of God, I then realized that I was empty. I believe God entered my heart at that moment. It was so beautiful and simple. All I had to do was realize my emptiness and ask God to fill it. I might add here that while the process of having my heart filled by God was simple, the process of going far enough downhill to acknowledge the emptiness and uselessness of my solely intellectual relationship with God took a lot of years and a lot of pain.

Another thing which happened for me in A.A. during my search to understand my God, was to be taught about a loving and caring God. My old God was very mean, punishing and vindictive about all of my sins. I was in a Step meeting one day, when a guy pointed out the single word "care" in the middle of the Third Step. A single word, but so important. In it I came to have a God who was no longer punishing, but who cared, who lovingly held my hand as if I were a small child, and was there to hold me close to His heart and help me feel better when I got hurt on the playground of life.

Besides attending A.A. meetings and having the opportunity to hear from other members about the kind of God they had in their life, being a hopeless intellectual, I also did some research in the library on kinds of gods that were incorporated in different religions. One belief system that made a lot of sense and was comfortable to me and compatible with what I then understood of the A.A. program's spiritual way of life, was that of the North American Indians. From my studies, it seemed to me they had a God, or Great Spirit, who was present on a hour-to-hour, minute-to-minute basis in every area of their existence.

They saw God in the animals, plants, flowers and trees, the lakes, rivers and seas, the storms and the changes of seasons. All these earthly elements were seen as being integrated, compatible, and complementary in God's earth. Everything, in spite of whatever its dangerous outside appearance might be, served a purpose in the worldly plan of the Great Spirit. It was man's responsibility to learn about the things that caused him fear in this world and to accept and understand their purpose in nature, rather than to criticize or eliminate such things from the earth. Kind of like what we are told in the Eleventh Step Prayer of St. Francis "that it is better to understand, than to be understood."

About Ducks

Joe N.—Texas

After a few months without a daily drink (for the first time in more than thirty years), I'd gained a little self-esteem and the notion that I might be an eligible member of the "family of man" after all, and, as such, might also have always been a "child of God." After leaving the treatment center, I met representatives of Alcoholics Anonymous who told me that if I could come to some understanding of just who God is, I might finally become a part of you—of the family of man. But to do that, I'd have to become connected to a personal God—probably unlike the one I'd left behind all those years ago. If I could establish this connection, they told me that my desire to sustain this contact would overcome my desire to change the way I feel and that I might choose to stay plugged into this connection instead of taking my next drink.

OK, I heard it—the reason for the God thing—and I understood it. Getting it from my head to my heart was not going to be easy. I began the search for the God of your understanding by reading everything: The Old and New Testaments, Koran, Bagavadgita, Upanishads, Confucianism, Taoism and more. The results were nil.

I did come across something that finally helped me to understand your—humanity's—ideas of a Higher Power active in even the most mundane things in our world, down to the level of the atoms that comprise it. To quote Albert Einstein, "Something's moving." I had to admit that there were common laws of organization and forces at work everywhere and in everything. These laws were imbedded in the heart of all beliefs and religions and at the centers of everything in the natural world whether rocks or whales, sundials or spaceships. This simple notion marked the beginning of my own journey toward a personal God of my understanding.

I felt as though I moved sideways through a dark and narrow corridor, blindly feeling my way along the damp and mossy sides. After a while I noticed pin dots of light through the old mortar. In time, as I moved along, there were cracks large enough to place my eye to them and see only the pale blue light of what I thought to be a cloudless daytime sky. I was looking for the window in this wall.

I came to a larger break. I could see the horizon. It was the sky after all. There was a river and white capped rocks. Wild flowers and low grass added color and grew down to the river's edge. The river ran with a calm, constant and unhurried power. It had been there before me; it would be there when man was extinct, silently running through time—simple, yet dynamic—limited by its banks but with no real limits at all. The river represented the works of a God I could understand, and it allowed me to be willing to accept that God maintained an active role in our world, leaving a part of Himself in each and every thing generated by and through His design so that He becomes the ultimate "succession planner." He duplicates Himself throughout time and with each succeeding change or creature, assuring me, if I view it simply, that He always has been, is now, and always will be here without and within me.

At some point farther down the causeway, a larger opening revealed a quiet marsh sustained by the river and there, in the bog, was this duck, doing what a duck does: Preening, eating, nibbling under its wings. A flock of them flew in formation overhead. It was morning. The duck took off in a splash and trailed in behind them.

Here I wondered if I could make connection between my search for a God of my understanding. My thoughts rested on its wings and I flew with the flock. It's important to comment here that this was not an "out of the body" or "mystical" experience. I was trying to think as simply as the animals that certainly fit in the natural order of this world better than I had. I wondered if I could, by considering the life of one simple creature, see something I had overlooked in my own.

Searching for food and guided by air currents created by the ducks ahead and around me, I was a part of a whole. I was also the whole and it was part of me. These were the feelings missing in me all those years: I could complete me by responsibly completing you.

I considered the life of the duck: Waking each day, stirred by hunger, or merely sensing the changes that are part of the gray light of morning just before sunrise. I imagined its daily routine, hunting for food, eating and occasionally mating, creating a nest—the unthinking commitments to an intuitive law. How simple to follow the natural rhythms of this life. How easy to appreciate and accept the achievements from beginning to the end of each day. The essence of its being was being what it was, a duck. He contributed to the flock by living routinely through each day, in return, the flock provided a measure of safety, improved the odds of survival, and together they moved in a single direction.

These new thoughts of maintaining constant and diligent action on behalf of the family of man were a long way off from that fourteen-year-old who culled himself from you and measured his true worth by the increasing distance he could maintain from others. The river, as powerful as it was, was defined by a paradox: It was powerful due to its confinement. The duck, as dedicated to the preservation of itself and its species, as perfectly as it fulfilled its role in nature, was not, however, free to explore his own natural world. It couldn't *choose* to undertake spectacular aerobatics or stray from the rigid and required simplicity of its existence. Neither could the river.

I have heard many coming into A.A. say early on, "I cannot give up my Will. My Will is me. I cannot give up my life to the care of God, my life is directed by my Will. Surrendering everything there is about me, as you are asking me to do, would be consenting to *brainwashing*. I will no longer be my own person. I will lose my *self*."

We are not ducks. We're human beings. We have a "free will." I reentered the causeway and the darkness again and again. I believed that if I didn't figure this whole God thing out, I'd get drunk and die. If I turned over what separates me from a duck, I'd be as mindless as that dumb animal. This just wouldn't do. I simply didn't get it. Hadn't I already put my will and my life into the hands of professionals in a nut ward? It was temporary. I could leave. I could recapture my freedom whenever they said they were through with me—when I was cured. Why should I have to turn my free will and my life over to a God of any kind, vengeful or loving? There is a God. He's in heaven. We're on Earth. We exist separately in two different and opposed dimensions and He will pay attention to us when we leave this one for the other. Then He'll judge us; cast people like me into their deserved eternal rewards and gather all of you for Himself. Besides, things were starting to get better. Soon, I'd gain my life and my freedom back, put the treatment center and A.A. behind me and not look back.

But just how free had I been? The duck had shown me that the use of my free will was valid if I exercised my right to choose those things that benefited the flock and behaved in a way that preserved the good for us all. It was not valid if I used my free will to destroy myself and place the rest of you in jeopardy. Free will, in my care, had been like handing a loaded revolver to a chimpanzee. It became mine only because it was in my possession and it glistened in the sun so I dragged it around as a trophy. Now and then, it would make a loud noise and I'd stare into the muzzle with one finger on the trigger. I'd wave it around so others could see that I had it. I didn't respect it. I didn't understand it. I didn't know how to use it. I didn't see it as desirable in you, since you didn't use it the way I wanted you to. I certainly never appreciated its value in me. Now, as the keepers reached to take it away, I brought it closer to me. It wasn't that I didn't want to let it go, in my case, I wanted it back.

As I healed, I faced opportunities to make choices: I could go to a restaurant for what they served, not what they poured. I could get into my car and only check my rearview mirror to change lanes or back up. I could invite non-drinking people over to dinner and accept dinner invitations from people who didn't drink like I did. When I amended my view of myself using the eyes of a duck, the simplicity of the business of living my own life became clearer. I could choose to take care of my own business, relieved of the responsibility of being all things to all people. I could therefore choose to *mind my own business*. I could do that and define my business as being of service to others within the flock. No, I was not surrendering my right to make choices. I simply had to admit that I had misused my will and that, if I maintained a connection with, and allowed myself to be guided by, a common Law or Order, that my will and my life would merely take on **G**ood **O**rderly **D**irection, like that of a duck. I was surrendering the exhaustive responsibilities of fixing you to a caretaker far more powerful than myself. I was admitted that, not only was God part of me and you, but that I was a part of you, too. That, my desire to measure up to who I thought you wanted me to be had compounded a normal compliment of simple fears into endless terror and an inescapable maze of horrors I thought of as living. I realized that I had to surrendered my desire to create you in my own image. My childhood resolve and determination to manipulate and control you while resenting your thanklessness reduced all my choices to one: A drink.

So I cut a deal with the "FEELING OF BELONGING," whom I choose to call God, today. I became willing to turn over the care of my will, which comprises my thoughts about the Family of Man, as well as the care of my life —the sum of my actions in which I choose to consider your welfare, as well as my own, over to a God, whom I understand that I shall never understand, but who is law and love. In exchange for remaining connected to It, Him, Her or You, I am granted the gifts of life, self-esteem, of choice, my freedom from alcohol, and a duck.

Being Convinced

Bill G.—Southern Oregon

Many times I've been asked how I found my higher power, and the thought that comes first to mind is "Not easily," though I usually answer like this: When I was ready, I found Him, or He found me.

I was raised in a faithful, loving, caring home. My folks neither drank nor smoked. They had strong religious convictions, and straight morals. So what happened? Somewhere along the way I lost my faith. Maybe 'Nam had something to do with that, maybe not. I had started drinkin' about age ten or eleven and had realized I was on my own to live my life as I saw fit.

When or if I prayed it was a bargain hunt from the git-go. "God if you'll just help me out of this jam, I'll never mess again." Today I believe my H.P. had infinite patience for putting up with my antics for so long.

When I finally got to the point of opting out with a .357 and it failed to function as designed, there was a voice that said, "There is a way to live without alcohol. Call that phone number now!" I was so dispirited and miserable, I would have tried anything. And not really believing it, I did try it. That was the start of my lifelong experience from that point of "coming to believe."

I've heard several different views on Higher Powers—all had a common theme—that He could restore us to sanity. I little believed that was possible. People told me to "act as if" or "fake it 'til you make it" or even "use the group as your Higher Power 'til you find your own "God as you understand Him." Many times folks would say they believed they had a Higher Power, but could not describe Him. When I heard that I thought, that's why that comment is in the Big Book— "God as you understand Him." I also heard folks say "God as you don't understand Him . . . just try it." I was even challenged once to believe that someone else believed—"Could I believe that she believed?"

I had no problem with that. I just didn't have a "God" period. I also heard people say they had found a Higher Power out of their own experiences. As dingy as I was when I first got sober, that didn't make sense to me. A wise woman told me I would find a God as I understood Him in His time not mine. Even while working the Steps I had a hard time with the concept of God and many times would leave a meeting before the Lord's Prayer, as it made me very uncomfortable. My sponsor told me I was uncomfortable because I was lying to myself about not believing. He reminded me of that old saw, "There are no atheists in foxholes or cockpits" and challenged me about that, too. He really understood my struggles to accept a Higher Power, as he had had similar experiences. He explained to me his concept of Higher Power, not the one of his parents' faith he was taught in Sunday school, but one he had a close relationship with. That helped me a lot, but I still didn't have a H.P. of my own.

One day, after I had done my Fifth, Sixth, Seventh and Eighth Steps, I was talking to several other guys who also had been pilots. We were talking of old planes we'd flown, and how we had advanced in our profession. We got to talking of World War II planes and how they had not had intercom systems, but instead the crew relied on hand signals and loud voices for communications. Now, because of my fire-drop experiences, I'm rated in several types of aircraft requiring copilots, and knew of this type of communication. One thing of particular importance is that both pilots are *not* on the controls at the same time. There is a protocol for this to insure that it doesn't happen, and its like this: the pilot coming on will shake the wheel indicating he will take over the controls, the other pilot will hold out his hands above the wheel indicating he has relinquished control. These actions are accompanied by the words "OK, you've got it" and since it was usually the captain regaining control of the aircraft, the copilot would say, "OK, Captain, you've got it." Having been a copilot and done that, it struck me that *that* was my answer. WOW! How simple it all was; all I had to do was let go, and today I still say "OK, Captain, you've got it" for whatever situation I find myself in. From that it was easy to progress to say my "H.P." or "GOD." It just had to be something I understood. Maybe those old farts in the B.B. knew what they were talking about when they wrote "God as you understand Him." That's what worked for me.

Today I do believe in a Higher Power, as I understand Him. Mainly I think that was because I was willing to listen to folks who had some sobriety. I find they didn't lie to me about this. It just took time for me to become convinced.

It Was God Calling

Jill D.— *Atlantic Coast, Florida*

With a glass of B&B in front of me and a joint in my hand, I sat at the dining room table writing a poem entitled "The God of My Under-standing." Just then, at 2:00 A.M., the doorbell rang. I couldn't imagine who it could be. I walked to the front door and peeked through the sheers of the front door window. My lips froze, and my body shook in fear. I thought my eyes were going to pop right out of my head. Stand-ing at my front door was Jesus Christ in the flesh, and His face shone through the window. He looked as though He had been crying; His facial expression was solemn and sad. He must have been trying to tell me something. But I didn't open the door for Him.

Eventually, I was able to move my body, run to the kitchen, and drape myself over the counter. I was breathless and in a state of com-plete consternation. Perhaps this was a hallucination from the drugs I had been taking. Whatever it was, it caught my attention—so much that I had to take another peek. Was He still there? I wondered what He wanted from me. After all, I didn't go to mass anymore (except on Christmas). I had stopped going during in my teenage years—when living according to Catholic rules became too difficult. Instead, I chose to serve many gods: my husband, my children, alcohol and drugs, and money. So I didn't understand why He came to me. By the time I mus-tered enough courage to go back, the vision of Christ was gone.

However, this sighting prompted me to ask my Al-Anon friend, Alice, for help with my drinking problem. I thought daylight would never come. When it did, I called Alice but didn't share the experience of Jesus with her. I didn't want her to think I was completely out of control. It was bad enough that I was starting to shake and have signs of withdrawal. I had to resist the urge to pick up a drink— one minute at a time. That was my main quest. I was willing to do whatever she said, including going to her house that night for an A.A. meeting.

On my third night sober—with a Big Book in my hand—I sat in my family room and cried the Third Step prayer over and over again. I must have been trying to convince God that I wanted to be sober, that I wanted more from my life! Later, I would come to see how those prayers were answered by God, how He changed my life. God has brought me through the depths of despair and depression and into the Light. As I drew near to him, He disclosed Himself to me. I found He was deep down inside me, that He always had been. This began my journey toward permanent recovery, my journey into the Twelve Steps.

My God is all powerful and loving. He has lead me gently into the truth about myself. As I found this truth, the role of God in my life has gotten bigger and bigger. Today, I must have that power or I suffer— emotionally and spiritually. When I do not have that power, I slip back into my self-created hell. I am not a religious person. Religion, I believe, is for people who believe in going to hell. I am spiritual; I have already lived in the hell of addiction.

Happily, I tell you that God can and has led me out of that hell, into a paradise right here on Earth. God has shown me that in order to nourish my relationship with Him, I must be convinced that I am the problem. I have learned that prayer is talking to God, and meditation is listening. The more I turn my actions over to Him, the better my life. I am happy, joyous, and free. The God of my understanding will change anything about me that He cannot use to His highest good. My job is not to change the world or blame my problems on others; it is to stay open to God's changes and allow my life to mirror the miracle of Love. God continues to give me free will, and on a daily basis, I choose not to put an artificial spirit into my being. Instead, I allow the Infinite Spirit to come out.

In Conclusion

We hope you've gotten something worthwhile out of our experiences. We ourselves certainly grew from the time and effort spent putting this text together. We are eternally grateful to the first one hundred alcoholics who gave of themselves and shared their experience in the *Big Book of Alcoholics Anonymous*. We will be forever in their debt. What amazes us still is that those same Steps founded six decades ago still work to the same desired end now as they did then. The timelessness of the A.A. program in its pure form is inspiring, and it goes to show that some things simply cannot be improved upon.

The sharing of our own victories over alcoholism is a big part of our lives these days. We're thankful to you who read this book, those of you who may as yet have found your way out of the darkness alcohol once brought to so many of us, as well as to those who already understand exactly what this book is about.

If we have at least provoked you to thought, we have done what we set out to do. Perhaps now, when you hear someone tell you that we never recover, you'll be able to say you know some folks who did just that. We do not claim to have all the answers to all your questions. Some you will have to answer from within. Others may be answered along the journey. What we do have is the absolute certainty that we ourselves have recovered from alcoholism, the knowledge that we have been freed by a Power the likes of which no human can truly comprehend. It is with wholehearted sincerity that we wish you well as you continue your journey, your search.

Where do we go from here? In our day-to-day lives, we seek to spread the message that recovery from alcoholism is not only possible, but likely if one follows the path we have followed. We believe this path, the Twelve Steps, is responsible for lighting our way in an otherwise dark existence we once endured. We took seriously the admonition in chapter seven of the Big Book that tells us that if we are to help others, we should be presented as persons who have recovered. We encourage you to seek out those persons who have found what we have, and to ask them how they got it, what they did, what is required. You will know them by the light in their eyes, their serene smiles, and their absolute fearlessness when it comes to talking about God, The Steps, and the Big Book. Look around you. Pray for God to bring you the person who can help you. The age of miracles has not passed.

It never will, you see, because God endures forever regardless of the fleeting fancies of mortal mankind.

May the God of your understanding bless you and keep you as you seek your divine birthright and your rightful place in our universe as one of God's kids.

To order this book, send $15.95 per copy, plus $4 shipping and handling to:

Ursa Publishing Company
P.O. Box 864
Palm Harbor, FL 34682
(Florida residents must include 7 percent sales tax.)

Or use your credit card on our Website http://www.recoveredalcoholics.com

Ursa Publishing Company and all the recovered alcoholics who contributed to the writing of this book welcome your comments and suggestions by mail at the address above. We may also be reached by E-mail at: Ursa2000@aol.com. We invite and encourage you to visit our Recovered Alcoholics Worldwide Network on the World Wide Web: http://www.recoveredalcoholics.com